CHINA TURNED ON

The years following the Cultural Revolution have seen the arrival of television as part of China's effort to 'modernize' and open up to the West. Endorsed by the Deng Xiaoping regime as a 'bridge' between government and the people, television became at once the official mouthpiece of the Communist Party and the most popular form of entertainment for Chinese people living in the cities. But the authorities failed to realize the unmatched cultural power of television to inspire resistance to official ideologies, expectations, and lifestyles.

The coming of television has intensified the fundamental contradictions of China's socialist society. Its presence in the homes of the urban Chinese has strikingly broadened the cultural and political awareness of its audience and has provoked the people, long treated as compliant recipients of state ideology, to imagine better ways of living as individuals, families, and as a nation. In China after Tiananmen Square, television remains crucially important in the continuing struggle for freedom and democracy.

Set within the framework of China's political and economic environment in the modernization period, James Lull's insightful analysis is based on ethnographic data collected in China before and after the Tiananmen Square disaster. He has interviewed leading Chinese television executives and nearly one hundred families in Beijing, Shanghai, Guangzhou, and Xian. Lull shows how Chinese television fosters opposition to the government through the work routines of media professionals, the polysemy of television imagery, and the roles of critical, active audience members.

James Lull is a writer and broadcaster based in San Francisco, California. He is author of *Inside Family Viewing* (1990), and editor of *World Families Watch Television* (1988) and *Popular Music and Communication* (1991).

CHINA TURNED ON

Television, reform, and resistance

James Lull

London and New York

For Kate Schmalhorst and
the memory of
Randolph 'Pony' Schmalhorst

First published 1991
by Routledge
11 New Fetter Lane, London EC4P 4EE

Simultaneously published in the USA and Canada
by Routledge
a division of Routledge, Chapman and Hall, Inc.
29 West 35th Street, New York, NY 10001

Set in 10/12 Baskerville by Intype, London
Printed and bound in Great Britain by Biddles Ltd, Guildford

British Library Cataloguing in Publication Data
Lull, James
China turned on: television, reform and resistance.
1. China. Society. Effects of television
I. Title
302.23450951

Library of Congress Cataloging in Publication Data
Lull, James.
China turned on: television, reform, and resistance/James Lull.
p. cm.
Includes bibliographical references and index.
1. Television and family—China. 2. Television broadcasting—
Social aspects—China. I. Title.
HQ520.L848 1991
302.23'45—dc20 91–2439

ISBN 0–415–05215–7
0–415–05216–5 pbk

CONTENTS

ILLUSTRATIONS

PREFACE

Standing at the top of Tiananmen Gate on a Sunday afternoon in the fall of 1989, looking out over vast and desolate Tiananmen Square that was still under martial law at the time, I realized once again why I am so enamored with China. Thrilling, frustrating, fascinating, disappointing – China *is* a mystery, even to the Chinese. The public outcry for freedom and democracy and the violent military repression of 1989, in some odd and terrible sense, characterize the extreme ups and downs of China's history since the founding of the People's Republic more than 40 years ago.

The massacre on the streets of Beijing was the government's brutal way to reclaim a country that it had lost. The sharp political confrontation that led to the crackdown in the capital came on the heels of a disastrous downward turn in the economy in the late 1980s. But what has torn China apart goes a long way beyond problems of politics and economics. At the heart of China's unrest is a profound change in the way Chinese people think about themselves, a transformation of cultural consciousness that is the byproduct of the nation's attempt to modernize technologically. What I set out to show in this book is that an unsurpassed contributing cause of resistance to the government in China stems from the unforseen impact of the very showpiece of technological modernization and national reform – television.

This book is an ethnography of culture and communication in contemporary urban China. I place the role of television within the nation's cultural, economic, and political development in the communist era and emphasize what has taken place during the modernization period, beginning roughly at the start of the last decade, when television entered the everyday lives of Chinese families. Rather than just describe how China has changed since then, I offer an explanation. The arguments I construct do not rely on surface impressions or on the insights of 'experts.' The story of China's dramatic cultural and political upheaval told here draws directly from the thoughts and words of Chinese people themselves.

The terrible military crackdown of 1989, of course, has sobered the romanticism that many Westerners, including myself, tend to develop about China. The country that for many years appeared to be the most progressive and promising of communist nations had become in two bloody days among the most repressive and dispirited. Nonetheless, I believe strongly that the world should not, and ultimately cannot, turn its back on China completely. As the influence of world communism erodes in nations as different and distant as Romania and Nicaragua, democratic change will come in its own culturally-specific way to China too. In the meantime, it does not make sense to abandon the Chinese people. Nor should the continuing plea for freedom and democracy there be interpreted primarily in terms of the economic interests of foreign countries. I worry that in the excitement surrounding the fall of repressive communist governments, we may lose sight of what the humanitarian principles of socialism mean to the world community.

No one writes a book alone. I want to acknowledge those who have helped me with this project. Unfortunately, given the political climate that exists at the time of this writing, I am unable to thank many individuals in the People's Republic of China who have made enormous contributions to this work. Institutional support in China was given by the People's University, China Central Television, the Shanghai Television station, and the Guangdong Province Television station. Se-Wen Sun's role in the development of this project, described in Chapter 3, was crucial. Ien Ang was, as always, my best critic and discussant. Collette Cowan gave me tremendous emotional support during the hectic last stages of writing. Tommy Kwok's help in Hong Kong and San Francisco is deeply appreciated. My colleagues Phil Wander, Dave Elliott, and Serena Stanford all helped create an atmosphere in which I was able to write. Wen-shu Lee's and Gao Ge's translations and insights were very useful. Alan Howard, Dick Rapson, and especially Stacy Waymire, colleagues and friends on Semester At Sea, greatly enhanced my introduction to China in 1982. Klaus Bruhn Jensen, Jostein Gripsrud, and Kjell Novak made it possible to share some of this work with faculty and students in Denmark, Norway, and Sweden. Thanks to the Volkswagen Foundation for sponsoring a trip to Germany where I had an opportunity to discuss this material with conferees at the 'Rethinking the Audience' meeting in Blaubeuren in 1987. Finally, special thanks to Routledge editors Jane Armstrong and Rebecca Barden for their encouragement in getting this book into print.

James Lull
San Francisco

1

MODERNIZING CHINA
The predicament of reform

Television viewers all over the world watched the incredible drama of the 1989 student and worker uprising in Beijing, the intense ideological standoff between the people and the government at Tiananmen Square, and the horror of the June 4th military repression that – for the moment, at least – has stymied both the country's official reformation effort and its grassroots 'freedom and democracy' movement. Ironically, television had just peaked as a communications medium in China during the troubled 1980s and had become a symbol of the success of the national modernization. By the middle of the decade nearly every urban family had bought a television receiver, many had color models, and some owned more than one set. Journalistic practices and cultural developments in general were more liberal and exciting than ever before. But when push came to shove, the last scenes from troubled Beijing were not telecast in China. While the rest of the world tuned in to pictures of courageous students, intellectuals, and workers standing up to the brute force of tanks and the political power of aging bureaucrats, Chinese television viewers saw very different pictures and accounts of the tragic events in the capital city, and even those images came late. Television had been forcibly restored to its original place as a blatant propaganda device.

By managing television coverage of the brutal crackdown and subsequently constructing a massive propaganda onslaught, Chinese government officials hoped to re-establish social stability, reassert the place of the Communist Party as the nation's legitimate political authority, and minimize ideological damage brought by the economic, political, cultural, and social stresses that China experienced in the late 1980s. But, as we shall see, it's too late for that now. Television does not just serve the government in China and the manipulation of program content certainly does not guarantee that the people will interpret messages as they are intended to be understood. This was clear long before the conflict in 1989.

Although the Chinese government has attempted to use television to unify the people, preserve the authority of the party, and fulfill the promises of the reformation, the medium has also become a central agent of popular

1

resistance against a political and economic system that many loyal Chinese feel has become hopelessly inefficient and out of touch with the people. Television demarcates the current period of Chinese history – an era of technological growth and cultural adaptation that includes the rapid spread of telecommunications technology and the formation of the world's largest television audience. In the process, Chinese citizens have changed.

Television is the star of the story I will tell about China, a perspective on contemporary Chinese society that is grounded in the beliefs, feelings, and articulations of Chinese people themselves. The analysis presented here has been developed from systematic, lengthy discussions that my research partner, Se-Wen Sun, and I had with nearly 100 urban Chinese families and with television executives in 1986 and from similar encounters I had with scholars, students, citizens, and broadcasters in October and November 1989, four months after the Tiananmen tragedy. *China Turned On* is an in-depth study of how television has dramatically influenced the cultural and political consciousness of the people who live in China's cities.

World attention was focused on China long before the poignant images from Tiananmen Square appeared. China has always fascinated outsiders who typically consider the Asian nation to be an exotic and impenetrable place. But during the past few years many popularly-written accounts of life in contemporary China have appeared. Volumes such as Fox Butterfield's *China Alive in the Bitter Sea* (1982), Orville Schell's *To Get Rich Is Glorious* (1984) and *Discos and Democracy* (1988), and Lynn Pan's *The New Chinese Revolution* (1987) among others have all documented and evaluated the remarkable changes in China during the past decade. Many foreign television networks have sent reporters and camera crews to document progress in the 'new China' too.

Behind the changes in China, according to most media accounts, is the economic and cultural impact of the much-publicized achievements of the early years of the Deng Xiaoping era. The common explanation for China's rapid economic development in the 1980s is that the country became successful after Deng opened it up to the West and began to institute capitalistic reforms. This exposure to capitalism is also reported to have provoked civil unrest in recent years. We have frequently heard, for example, that since the people have 'tasted capitalism' they 'can never go back to communism' and that the recent turmoil is symptomatic of Chinese yearning to get what Westerners already have. Typical interpretations made by foreign observers have Chinese people discarding socialism for capitalism and trading in traditional culture for a Western style of life that ranges from democratic politics to sexy entertainment.

China also attracts the international business community that not only views the huge country as a source of cheap labor and a market of more than one billion consumers, but following the proven example of Japan, Hong Kong, Singapore, Taiwan, and South Korea, as a potential major

2

player in the world economy. Sensing China's impending role in the world market, one Chinese-American author has even warned of what he considers to be the nation's plan for international business. In a book designed to teach American businessmen how to deal with their peers in the People's Republic (*The Chinese Mind Game* by Chin-ning Chu, 1988), the author claims that the 'ugly Chinese' can never be trusted and will use dishonest 'war strategies' to earn profits at the expense of helpless American companies!

But the sources of conflict in Chinese society today are far more complex than can be revealed through any 'communism v. capitalism' debate or by any simple evaluation of the necessity for 'freedom and democracy.' Modern technology has decisively entered everyday life in China during the past decade and has played a crucial role. In particular, the intervention of television into the social, cultural, political, and economic lifeworlds of the people is central to understanding the dynamics of change in China. The nation's social stresses have resulted from implacable contradictions existing in the popular consciousness, many of which predate the introduction of television in China but have been accelerated to dramatic proportions because of the rapid spread and influence of the medium in the cities during the past decade. Television's democratizing and agitating mediations interact in the public mind with the harsh realities imposed by a declining economy, the desire for more personal freedom, and with the collective depression that has descended over the country as the people confront a mean and sluggish bureaucratism that punishes them concretely as they negotiate the most basic routines of everyday life. Before discussing the specific roles of television in all this, however, I would like to establish the context for my analysis by exploring the key economic and political developments of the modernization period.

THE OPEN DOOR POLICY

China's famed 'Open Door policy' is, above all else, a strategy for development of relations with other countries that is designed to benefit the national reformation (*gai ge*) – a plan that begins with economic restructuring. Agreements reached with the United States and other Western nations in the mid 1970s and the rush of tourism that followed were but the first steps. By early 1989 the openness had led to the unthinkable – talk of normalization of economic and political relations with Taiwan and an undertaking of far-reaching interactions with all other Asian nations. Even today, despite the gloomy predictions of world economists, China's resolve to keep economic reform on track is at least claimed to be stronger than ever and officials in the People's Republic are still trying to improve relations with their rich, soon-to-be inherited, and understandably paranoid stepchild – Hong Kong.

Reform in the Soviet Union – the nation upon which China depended so greatly for many years after 1949 – came on the heels of change in China. Progressive officials in Beijing must have felt quite gratified when the details of *perestroika* were announced in Moscow, though the Chinese government has greatly downplayed the similarity of reform between the two countries especially in the wake of the staggering political developments in the Soviet Union and Eastern Europe. Nonetheless, after years of bitter disagreement, friendly relations between China and the Soviet Union resumed in the midst of reform in both countries. The first Sino–Soviet summit in 30 years took place when Deng received Mikhail Gorbachev in Beijing in 1989. Gorbachev called for 'complete normalization' of Sino–Soviet relations. Chinese and Soviet foreign ministers exchanged visits.

CHINA'S RICE BOWL

'In the United States or Japan, if you don't have ability you can't survive. But here, everybody eats from the big iron rice bowl. You don't have to have ability here. You just hold your job and your iron bowl. Everybody is the same . . . nobody better, nobody worse.' (40-year-old female buyer for a rubber products company, Shanghai)

'Some people think, "Okay, I'll just hold the iron bowl." Workers get the same salary whether they give good service or not. This causes a service problem, especially for old people.' (61-year-old male retired factory worker, Shanghai)

'Clerks in the stores won't move to help you or pay attention to you. If they let you look at something, and you don't buy it, they will be angry with you. And you can't exchange anything you buy.' (46-year-old female accountant for printing company, Shanghai)

'Eating from the big iron rice bowl and the principle of equality is unworkable. The new socialist plan is to pay you according to your work.' (66-year-old male retired carpenter, Beijing)

'Our society is developing now. This is the great goal of the Communist Party.' (55-year-old male manager of tire factory, Shanghai)

'You say that because you are a member of the Communist Party.' (22-year-old male mechanic in textile factory, Shanghai, youngest son of previous speaker)

By the 1980s the mass media in China were no longer 'tools of class struggle,' a role they first played within the Soviet-style socialism that the country adopted in 1949. They had become instead tools in service of the

4

modernization – symbolic and functional contributors to the economic and ideological dimensions of reformation, the ambitious restructuring that until the late 1980s appeared to be dramatically leading the country away from the debilitating iron rice bowl.

But casting aside the iron rice bowl is not something China can easily do. Nor is it simply an economic transformation. The iron bowl symbolizes the fundamental stability and security Chinese people have felt with their state enterprise jobs and the related guarantees of inexpensive housing and food, free medical services, and public education. At the same time, however, the iron bowl also represents the unchanging, heavy hopelessness that most Chinese people feel about improving their living and working conditions. And while the iron rice bowl stands for equality within Chinese society, it has become more and more apparent to the people that this really means an 'equality of poverty' (Goodman *et al.*, 1986: 19).

The more adaptable 'clay rice bowl' became a symbol of hope for China after the Cultural Revolution as the country embarked on its promise to usher in widesweeping changes in all aspects of life. As Chinese political leaders struggled for positions of power within the party and government during the recovery from the Cultural Revolution, the most compelling issue during the early phases of reconstruction in the mid and late 1970s was economic development – how to forge a modern consumer-oriented economy that would enhance industrial production and raise the standard of living for all Chinese people. The ideological puritanism of the late Maoist period apparently was over. The new arrangement would have to be progressive and risky. The clay bowl could break.

Emerging from party infighting to lead the country toward greatness was the consummate pragmatist, Deng Xiaoping. Three times knocked down by party politics since 1949, Deng's return to power and ascension as national reformer in the late 1970s was nothing less than heroic. His history of personal and political suffering matched what many ordinary people had experienced. Deng became a human symbol of escape from the pain of the late Maoist period – the Cultural Revolution and the reign of the Gang of Four – toward what appeared to be China's new day. The people embraced Deng as a hero at the very time they were trying to forget the cultish fanaticism and disastrous last years of Mao Zedong's life.

Concrete plans for radical economic development in China were issued after the historic Third Plenum of the Eleventh Central Committee meeting of the Chinese Communist Party (CCP) in December 1978. Deng's role as chief architect of reform and elder statesman (he was already 73 years old at the time) was irrefutably cast during this period. The 'spiritual development' that had been Mao's priority was de-emphasized in favor of 'material development,' ushering in an era that, in effect, downplayed many of the romantic, if unworkable, ideals of state socialism – a turn of events that proved to be as much ideological and political as it was material in its consequences.

The national goals were to modernize four areas: agriculture, industry, science and technology, and national defense. This way the country would be able to feed itself well, develop a sophisticated consumer society, and protect itself from outsiders, a sensitive matter for China with its history of foreign occupation. Although the nation's economy had been growing slowly and steadily before 1978 (even during the chaotic Cultural Revolution), major reforms were necessary. The people's living standard was not keeping pace with national growth and enormous mistakes had been made in the 1960s and 1970s in production priorities for heavy industry and the development of energy sources (Perkins, 1986).

Theory into practice: reform on the farm and in the city

The first major alteration in policy after 1978 was development of the 'responsibility system' on Chinese farms, a concept that was later adapted for use in other economic sectors. Essentially, Chinese peasant families in the countryside could enter into contracts with the state for the production and delivery of specific crops that would be sold for profit, money that could be kept by the farmers. And while land could not be owned outright, progressive land-use transfer rights were established, thereby making peasants far more responsible for their own land. Many families made decisions about what to grow, when, and where. Others decided not to farm the land at all, using their space for development of various cottage industries, many of which proved at first to be very profitable.

The underlying premise of the changes in agriculture is that of material incentive – an unfamiliar concept in China's economy before 1978. At the same time that communal agriculture was being converted to small collectives and individual management, China also moved away from heavy industry and expanded its production of consumer goods, including the manufacture of electronic media. An economic system that permits the ascension of talented and hardworking individuals while it also meets their growing consumer demands seemed to be in place.

Along with the material incentives that (some) workers were given, including bonuses and variable-scale wages, people began to think about the possibility of changing jobs and many of them did something about it. Central economic planning gave way in some areas to market-oriented decision-making and local autonomy. Many big state-owned companies were privatized. The selling of stocks and bonds was introduced. Marketing, advertising, and public relations – areas that are invariably underplayed in socialist economies – gradually became parts of industry and commerce.

Laws, regulations, and formal procedures were developed for putting economic reform into practice, thereby challenging some of the traditions with which China had conducted its business before 1978. Especially targeted for change was the reliance on unofficial channels – personal connections – which are the way things get done in every sphere of life in China. Government action was to be taken against corruption. Special privileges enjoyed by party officials and other cadre were to be eliminated as was the arbitrary authority that middle-level bosses exercise over their subordinates (Harding, 1986). Older cadre and workers were given incentives to retire early in order to make room for better educated, more progressive, and more ambitious young people. Reports of enforcement of the new policies appeared on television and in the newspapers.

The 1978 reforms were reinforced and extended with additional policy changes resulting from the Third Plenum of the Twelfth Central Committee held in 1984. Greatly encouraged by the success of the reformation during the preceding five years, success that was largely attributable to a quick and illusionary economic boost coming from the agricultural sector, the party began to concentrate more on urban reform. Strangely enough, some of China's peasants were getting rich while city dwellers, who long had considered their status to be superior to the farmers, feared they were falling behind. Deng proclaimed that 'to get rich is glorious,' a phrase that really meant that the Chinese economy as a whole would be stimulated by the innovative ideas and hard work of individuals who will 'get rich first so as to lead all people to wealth.' Successful examples of China's *nouveaux riches* were publicized by the media. China was to develop fully a 'socialist commodity economy with Chinese characteristics,' according to the party, a promise that would improve the living standard of city people too. In the short term, some urban residents did benefit from the policy decisions of the 1984 meeting. In particular, some of them were allowed to enter into private business such as small retail outlets, restaurants, repair shops, and pedicabs – opportunities that produced income greatly surpassing most government jobs (Perkins, 1986).

Many of the citizens who got permission to develop private businesses were unemployed urban men who had been sent to the countryside during the Cultural Revolution and had not been assigned government jobs upon their return to the city years later. In order to help solve the unemployment problem and give these unfortunate victims of the Cultural Revolution a better chance in life, the government conferred 'private unit' (*ge ti hu*) status on many of them. They pay little or no taxes and their financial records are not carefully scrutinized. But beyond the material perks, this new class of Chinese citizens is able to *feel* free and independent – an enviable emotional state in such a controlled environment.

China's economic development led to rapid export of domestically-produced goods which was matched by importation of foreign goods, especially high technology items. Joint economic ventures were established

1 A 'private unit' street vendor sells tea eggs on the streets of Shanghai under a sign that claims China is governed by law and the constitution.
(Unless otherwise noted, all photographs are by James Lull.)

with foreign countries. 'Special Economic Zones' (SEZs) were developed in the south and along the coast where Chinese workers could be hired for pay that exceeded government compensation. Scientific, cultural, and educational exchange programs were set up with many foreign countries. Tourism flourished as upwardly-mobile China became an 'in' place to go.

THE REFORMATION PEAKS: 1985–86

'Year by year our life is better now.' (41-year-old female bank clerk, Beijing)

'Since 1979 things are much better. We keep walking in this direction, improving the living standard. Now we don't just invest in heavy industry and war equipment. We take care of our lives better. We like the direction of the reformation.' (32-year-old male cadre in electric company, Guangzhou)

'The living standard is much better since 1979. We have good food now, even fashion.' (29-year-old male cartographer, Guangzhou)

'In my generation everybody should try to be a specialist, to have knowledge and belong to himself.' (18-year-old male student, Shanghai)

'We have a very good rate of production in my department. Some factories have excellent production systems now. Our factory does well because we have a small number of workers.' (48-year-old female telephone operator for steel factory, Shanghai)

'My husband has private unit status. He sells fish and makes more than 600 yuan (six times the average wage) a month. The only reason I keep my government job is for medical insurance for our baby.' (26-year-old female worker in a battery factory, Guangzhou)

The Chinese economy performed so spectacularly from 1979 to 1986 that even the most outspoken skeptics could not reasonably deny the progress. Most people inside China agreed that their living standard was truly on the rise. They dared to dream of political changes too. The world's oldest and largest civilization seemed to have buried the backwardness of its feudalist past and the misguided politics and human atrocities of the Cultural Revolution. Suddenly, China had apparently become a model socialist nation embracing egalitarianism with a progressive economy and an increasingly liberalized cultural atmosphere.

The United States celebrated China's success. Deng Xiaoping was honored as *Time* magazine's 'Man of the Year' for 1985, praising the 'Comeback Comrade' for his 'attempt to combine communism and capitalism' while improving China's agricultural production and opening up opportunities for joint business ventures with other countries. Deng was also hailed as a hero by *National Geographic* in a cover article titled, 'China Changes Course,' featuring a picture of a broad-smiling farm family from Sichuan Province.

In fact there was good reason to praise Deng and the reformation at the time. Agricultural reform was an unqualified success. The responsibility system led to an 'immediate and dramatic' increase in the standard of living for Chinese families, achieving more in the five years after 1978 than in the previous 21 years (Perkins, 1986: 50). By 1985 China produced more wheat, rice, cotton, and tobacco than any other nation on earth. Wages increased across the board. Earnings for urban workers in 1985 increased nearly 11 percent from the previous year, and they were up again 8.4 percent in 1986. And while less than 5 percent of China's non-farm labor pool in 1985 was employed in private unit status, the government promised that the proportion of persons engaged in private enterprise would increase year by year. Even as late as 1987, former General Secretary of the Communist Party, Zhao Ziyang, a partner with Deng in the original formation of the revised economic policy and a man widely respected for the successful reforms he enacted in Sichuan Province, predicted that by

9

1990 only 20 to 30 percent of China's economy would remain within the old, centrally-controlled system. In essence, two very different economic systems had been put into place and were expected to function side-by-side.

China did indeed start to become a consumer-oriented society, especially in the cities. By 1986 everyone could own a bicycle and nearly every family in the urban areas had a full complement of electronic media and was looking to upgrade their equipment. Where there was space, more and more families bought refrigerators and washing machines. They hoped to put modern furniture in their living rooms and sleeping areas. People wanted new clothes for fashion, not just serviceability.

Economic reform not only had a temporal origin (1978), but also a geographical origin. The SEZs of the southern and eastern coastal areas of China have been like a mecca to some Chinese. One young photographic technician in Shanghai told us during a family interview that he had seen a television program about Senzhen – the bustling SEZ near Hong Kong – that stimulated him to go see it for himself. He came home raving about the 'modern houses and roads' there. His case is not unusual. The myth of economic prosperity in the SEZs led to an ever-increasing, and often illegal, migration of many young Chinese workers to the southern provinces.

Much of the economic success was the product of joint ventures that China struck with foreign countries. The United States alone had developed more than 2,300 joint ventures with China by the end of 1985. Japan began to invest heavily in China and trade relations with Hong Kong improved to the point where it appeared that the British colony's transition to Chinese rule in 1997 might not be so traumatic after all. For the first time, China was producing large quantities of goods that other countries wanted, causing the trade balance to begin shifting in favor of the People's Republic. Inside China, the country was on the way to modernizing its military, having developed a rapid deployment force by the mid 1980s.

It's not surprising that by 1985 and early 1986, many Chinese people were confident that the remarkable changes the society had experienced in the preceding few years were just the early fruits of reform. Though many people were cynical about the system, or held reservations about the true intentions of the nation's leaders, it seemed clear that China was developing impressively as a leader among Third World nations. Life expectancy was steadily increasing, illiteracy decreasing, relationships with foreign powers were improving, production and trade were booming, and nearly everyone enjoyed greater income and exposure to the creature comforts that money can buy. The whole mood of the country was changing. With progressives Hu Yaobang and Zhao Ziyang at Deng's side, the political future of the country looked bright too.

THE CLAY BOWL CRACKS

'China's golden past is difficult to keep in perspective now. The country is working hard to modernize and to take its proper place in the world. But even though people are talented, their jobs demand so little.' (24-year-old male mail sorter in city post office, Shanghai)

'The students have many interests but the system does not let them achieve anything. There's no choice for children unless their parents have a very good background. The government will not help kids achieve what they want.' (42-year-old male representative for battery factory, Beijing)

'The private unit concept may work against the motivation of most of the students. The government jobs they will get even as college graduates don't pay as well as private unit positions.' (41-year-old female accountant, Shanghai)

'Study hard or not, in the future we will still hold the iron bowl.' (19-year-old female student, Xian)

'What can really be done except to wait for the next generation? We need people who are better trained – more efficient, well-prepared, and determined to make fast decisions. What we need is serious and strict control in management with a system of rewards and punishments.' (63-year-old male president of a continuing education college, Shanghai)

'We must correct the problems within the Communist Party. For example, we must continue to promote the "responsibility system." But we should also eliminate everything that is not appropriate to our nation and to our culture.' (33-year-old female agricultural researcher, Communist Party member, Beijing)

'Workers and leaders now are singing impractical tunes. These songs have notes that their voices cannot reach.' (22-year-old male mechanic in textile factory, Shanghai)

The reforms set in motion by the Third Plenum have deliberately raised popular expectations . . . if the party fails to deliver on its promises, its ability to sustain the momentum of reform will be seriously jeopardized.

(Goodman et al., 1986: 33)

By 1989 everything had changed. The June 4th military repression and subsequent persecution of 'counterrevolutionaries' was the government's desperate attempt to regain control of a country that seemed to be in chaos. People were massively disappointed and frustrated with the severe economic setbacks they suffered and with the constant reports of corruption among party officials even in the highest ranks of government. Student demands for 'freedom and democracy' were but the most visible sign that China's reform movement had gone almost completely astray. The country was mired in a deep economic recession. Increases in production during the previous years had stimulated unparalleled consumer demand, causing prices to rise faster than wages. Unbearable inflation hit the cities. By summer 1988, China was in an economic crisis so severe that Deng, with the support of fiscally conservative premier Li Peng, announced that the pace of reform would have to be drastically slowed down.

Agricultural production, the cornerstone to economic success during the early stages of reform, dropped off greatly from 1986 onwards, a problem that retarded development of the entire economy from that point forward. Farmers faced higher operating costs and began to receive far lower prices for wheat, rice, and corn. Some families gave up farming entirely and tried to develop rural industries that seemed to promise greater income. The dropoff in agricultural production sent shockwaves through the country as shortages of key staples including grain, pork, sugar, salt, and cotton were felt in the cities. Production of steel was also down by 1989, and electrical power, which has never been in sufficient supply, became even less reliable.

China's rate of inflation ballooned to 18.5 percent in 1988 and the inflationary spiral increased month by month to 27 percent by March of 1989 (Reynolds, 1989). City dwellers in Beijing and Shanghai were hardest hit. The social effects of inflation were exacerbated by development of a 'double track' pricing system; public and private markets had been established so that commodities were priced at different levels, permitting easier access to some goods by those who had benefitted from the economic reform. As a result, families who must exist on fixed incomes – still the vast majority in China – felt themselves falling hopelessly behind. Though Deng had assured the people that reform would not lead to a stratified society, great disparities in income, owing fundamentally to the failed 'one nation, two economic systems' experiment, became a reality. Those who lost out include some of the country's best educated and most dedicated workers. They were quick to interpret their losses in political terms.

Both the people and the government panicked. Some families withdrew their savings and bought consumer durables, including additional television sets, as hedges against the rising prices. The government stopped selling stocks and shares of new industries and cut back on economic growth generally. Construction projects were halted. New taxes were levied. Loans were curtailed. New restrictions were imposed to cool down what the government called the 'overheated' growth of various collective and private businesses. By the fall of 1989, more than three million industrial collectives and private companies had been shut down. Great unemployment resulted from these closings as many farmers refused to go back to farming. After living nearly four decades with the fundamental security that was provided by the old system (the upside of the infamous 'iron rice bowl'), many farmers suffer even today from such great psychological shock caused by the economic collapse that they roam around the villages and countryside with no destination or purpose in what the Chinese call 'black movement.' The most popular and controversial novel in China in 1989 was Jia Ping-ao's *Anxious (Fu zao)*, a gripping story of the mental torment of China's newly-disenfranchised peasants.

It's important to realize that despite the reform's success from 1979 to 1985, China had not become rich. Per capita yearly income as late as 1988 was but $349 US, higher only than Laos, Cambodia, Vietnam, and Burma in the Pacific Rim. The literacy rate in 1988 was only 69 percent, and according to the United Nations, nearly 10 percent of China's population in 1986 was still unable to feed and clothe itself at a subsistence level. Population growth became a problem again too as economic incentives for rural families to have more than one child became far more influential than the negative sanctions that were imposed by the government's 'one child policy.' The supreme family sacrifice of limiting the number of children had become mainly an urban requirement, further contributing to the hated realization that China was becoming more and more a nation divided in its privileges. Tourism began to slump in 1986 too as foreigners had become irritated by bad service and a lack of entertainment venues.

Reports of corrupt business practices grew day by day during the economic crisis. It wasn't only the new private businesses that were to blame. Competition spurred by the mixed economy unexpectedly increased the unethical dependence on personal relationships for negotiating transactions within state sector enterprises too.[1] Deng's own son was implicated in a business scam that led to closing down the company where he worked. Zhao Ziyang's son was reported to have been given advantages in his highly successful business. Unscrupulous capitalistic ploys such as artificially inflating prices, hoarding key commodities, extorting, and profiteering were common. Stories of willful abuse – such as the famous account of the 'King of the Foolish Seeds,' a millionaire Chinese businessman who knowingly poisoned thousands of people with bad sunflower seeds in order to turn a quick profit, circulated. Troubling accounts were commonly heard about corruption in the SEZs, areas that seemed to live by a set of rules so different from the rest of China that they were thought to be more like Hong Kong, Macau, or Taiwan than the mainland. By early 1989 there was an unmanageable mass migration of young workers to the Guangzhou area in search of more money and a better future. The government announced in the spring of 1989 that the centrally-assigned job location method would be strengthened once again.

The clearest indication of disorder in the reform, however, was the decision in late 1988 to control prices. Endorsed and announced by Deng himself, the government intervened to slow down the economy by establishing price controls on many commodities and by reducing growth in the private sector. Central planning, not the market, was to drive the economy for the forseeable future. Government-regulated pricing would last, according to the officials, into the early 1990s. The alternative – to let the economy run its own course – threatened to destabilize further the society, according to Deng. As the news worsened, people rapidly lost confidence in the Communist Party. Within the party, Zhao's viability as CCP chief was being questioned, at the same time support was being mustered for his conservative fiscal opponent, Li Peng.

Through it all two other difficulties kept nagging at the authorities in Beijing. The 'democracy issue,' the most basic political question in China for decades (Nathan, 1985), was rekindled by student uprisings beginning in late 1986 and early 1987 and continuing off and on in China's major cities. The resistance movement had not been extinguished despite a general tightening of security, the removal of the tolerant and popular Hu Yaobang – Zhao's predecessor as General Secretary of the CCP – from his post, and the firing of a national public security minister who had been criticized for his lenient treatment of the protestors. The other public embarrassment for China was the seemingly unsolvable struggle for independence in Tibet. Chinese troops were flown into Tibet to quell anti-Chinese rioting in 1987, 1988, and again in 1989. The Chinese government continued to blame the exiled Buddhist leader, the Dalai Lama, for the violence while the rest of the world honored him with the Nobel Peace Prize.

China's deep infrastructural problems

As I have already outlined, the reasons for the economic crisis of the late 1980s are many. One of the causes, however, is central to the very foundation of Chinese socialist society. China's human and technological infrastructure – particularly its styles of decision-making and its systems for the transfer of information – is woefully inadequate to sustain a stable and rapid transformation of the economy. The severe shortcomings of China's infrastructure became all the more clear within the requirements of reform. The challenge to develop a more market-oriented domestic economy that can operate within a socialist framework, and at the same time participate in the unfamiliar and fastmoving terrain of international business, was a difficult adaptation for the huge, heavily-bureaucratized country to make.

Veteran bureaucrats often have not only been unable to handle new assignments, many of them are unwilling to do so as it frequently means giving up personal power – status which has been accumulated over many years of doing things the old way. Equally problematic is the inability of China to move information around efficiently. There are few telephones and

14

computers, unstable and insufficient sources of energy, and poor systems for sharing data (in part because information is a commodity which, in a system with few formal regulations and sanctions, becomes property which is easily abused by those in managerial positions). Managing capital proved to be a major problem for the Chinese too, as monetary transfers and the supervision of loans were poorly coordinated, resulting in unreliable transactions for Chinese and for foreigners. In fact, many foreign investors have been reluctant to do business in China all along for these very reasons.

The politics of Zhao Ziyang and Li Peng

'Reform has become the tide in the socialist countries. Without reform, there is no way out.' (Zhao Ziyang, former Premier and General Secretary of the Chinese Communist Party, in *Beijing Review*, 1987)

'The order of China's development must be changed. It is essential to control societal demand and curb inflation.' (Li Peng, China's Premier, October 1988; quoted from Reynolds, 1989)

Zhao Ziyang, who was unceremoniously removed from his position as General Secretary of China's Communist Party in the middle of the struggle in Beijing in 1989, and Li Peng, who as of this writing in 1990 was still China's Premier, were the key players during the crisis. Their positions represented the basic choices China had. Zhao was forever the optimistic reformer. Together with Deng, he had invented the plan for reform. Zhao's election as party chief in fact was considered a victory for Deng who had declared himself a 'setting sun' and was apparently satisfied with the succession of his partner in reform as China's senior statesman. The economic problems, however, eventually vaulted Li into power.

Zhao desperately tried to weather the storm even in the midst of the economic crisis. He continued to appoint reform-minded officials to key posts and played down differences in the party. In late 1988 he announced plans to expand China's exports and engage in more joint ventures. Zhao never stopped promoting the importance of rapid modernization and argued for reliance on the market as the best economic strategy. During the turmoil in Beijing, the former party leader was a symbol of hope for progressive forces in China. He was no hero – Zhao was considered by many people to be a businessman above all else and he could never live down a widely-publicized picture of himself playing golf – but he certainly appeared to be the best alternative available.

Li Peng had taken the conservative road long before the 1989 uprising. Far more a pragmatist than a visionary, Li mimicked Deng's call for austerity and retrenchment when the economy faltered. He swiftly advocated returning economic decision-making to the central government. Li and his conservative colleagues in the politburo feared the consequences of an economy and polity that were no longer firmly under the control of the party. According to Li, drastic steps were necessary for China to repair the sagging economy and defuse the mounting social unrest. When the government invoked price controls and cut back growth in the private sector economy in 1988, Li's position within the party decision-making apparatus was greatly enhanced at the very time Zhao's influence was declining. And later, in the face of mounting political dissent, the man who was still ultimately in charge, Deng, proved himself once again to be the model pragmatist. Zhao was dismissed. It was Li who was at Deng's side when the tanks rolled into Tiananmen Square.

We will revisit Tiananmen Square in detail in Chapter 9. There is much ground to cover before going there, however. Exploring the significance of television in reform and resistance in China is the focus of this book, a task that I embark upon by examining a considerable amount of historical and ethnographic evidence. To further set the stage for analyzing television's decisive impact on contemporary developments, I present in the next chapter a brief political history of the development of the mass media in socialist China and introduce the structure and status of the Chinese television system.

2

IN THE NAME OF CIVILIZATION
Development of the mass media in China

Modernization in thinking . . . implies that the people abandon out-
dated concepts and ideas and the influence of the small-scale peasant
mentality, cultivate a strong sense of democracy and initiative, and
pursue efficiency and discipline at work. The cultivation of these
qualities depends on education and the media.'

(*China Daily*, 1986)

'Even as recently as 1979 we couldn't believe that ordinary people
would have television sets in their homes, but in just a few years
everybody got a TV. Television developed fast in China because of
the Open Door policy.' (48-year-old male telecommunications engineer, Communist Party member, Guangzhou)

'Once the family has television it cannot be rid of it. Television
cannot be taken away from old people or young people, from workers
or from intellectuals. Television has a huge influence on Chinese
society.' (Wang Chuanyu, Director of Production, Central China
Television, the national network, Beijing)

China's 'material civilization' corresponds to economic development, of
course, and in the 1980s there was no material device that symbolized
prosperity more than television. Even the most disaffected Chinese people
admit that their ability to buy new television sets is real testimony to the
improved living standard that took place during the modernization period.
The maturation of China's material civilization is not only symbolized by
television, it depends on it. Commercial TV advertising is used by the
government to provide information about products and to provoke consumer interest and activity. But the official functions of television are not
limited to its economic representations and capabilities.

Television is also expected to help cultivate a 'spiritual civilization' fit
for the times by providing mass recreational activity, supplying entertainment that is in 'good taste,' and reinforcing state ideology and morality
(Ming, 1987). Any attempt to promote education, art, literature, language

17

instruction, even practical training in areas such as home and child care is designed to advance the spiritual civilization. In general, the concept refers to whatever the government thinks the people should know in order to evolve satisfactorily along the ideological and cultural planes of the socialist trajectory. Consequently, a steady stream of suggestions, directives, and announcements is issued not only from television and the other modern mass media, but from neighborhood posters, billboards, even public blackboards. There may be no more blatantly prescriptive society in the world than China.

The government's plan for development of a new material and spiritual civilization has led to reform in the mass media too, although the economic decline and political turmoil of the late 1980s drastically set progress back. Overall, however, more information has been made available to the public and the number of 'internal' (confidential) channels was reduced during the 1980s (Wang, 1988b). Chinese people believed by the end of the last decade that their mass media were becoming more diverse, artistically intriguing, and open. And they were. Several trends were evident. The number of operating media of all types increased. Content became less politically direct. Journalists, broadcasters, and filmmakers developed more sophisticated and professional work styles, enjoyed more autonomy and critical freedom, and created far more intriguing and relevant products than ever before. All in all, China appeared to be evolving toward a 'multi-culture structure' stimulated by diversification of the mass media and the formation of specific audiences (Ming, 1987).

DEVELOPMENT OF THE MASS MEDIA IN SOCIALIST CHINA

In 1949, the revolutionary Chinese government inherited less than 400 functioning newspapers and only 49 radio stations throughout the country (Womack, 1986). Television did not yet exist in China. Since then, the mass media have been central to the implementation of socialism under the direction of the Chinese Communist Party. Electronic media have been particularly effective tools of communication especially because the literacy rate in rural China, although greatly increased since 1949, remains low. This, taken together with problems of distribution of newspapers in rural areas, makes the electronic media attractive to the government for their ability to reach people directly.

Newspapers

The number of newspapers and their circulation have fluctuated greatly since 1949. The ups and downs of newspaper publication can be charted in accord with variation in China's political and economic climate. The

Anti-Rightist movement of 1957, the economic depression of the early 1960s, and especially the Cultural Revolution were periods when the fewest newspapers were published. The Communist Party also asserts its authority much more forcefully during stressful times. The party controlled 84 percent of China's newspapers during the Cultural Revolution, for instance, an increase of 23 percent from the years just prior to the disruption (Ming, 1987). Newspaper offices were occupied by the military during the martial law period in 1989 too.

The greatest surge in the number of newspaper titles, circulation, and readership took place in the few years that followed the onset of the modernization period. By 1986 nearly 2,200 newspapers were being published in China. Circulation of the national and provincial press now is more than 200 million, meaning that there is a copy of a newspaper for about every five Chinese citizens, more than a three-fold increase from 1978. More diverse types of newspapers are published now too, including the popular television program guides.

Radio

China's introduction to radio (and seemingly to everything from the West, good and bad) came from foreigners living in Shanghai. The Radio Corporation of China was formed in Shanghai in 1922 under the supervision of an American engineer as a ploy to sell radio receivers to the world's biggest potential market (Guo, 1986). Until 1949, nearly every radio station in Shanghai was privately-owned and transmitted light entertainment programming. Shanghai's economy was far more able than the rest of the country to support commercial radio. The city's leadership in economic and cultural matters is a longstanding Chinese tradition.

But the Shanghai case is not typical of what happened with radio in China. In his analysis of the growth of Chinese media industries, Brantly Womack (1986) describes 'three waves of development' in the broadcast media since 1949. The first two waves involve radio, originally considered by the founders of the new government to be the most viable means for reaching the rural areas where the vast majority of the Chinese population lives. A national radio network was established after the communist revolution composed of the existing Guomindang stations and, within a few years, of the commercial stations in Shanghai too. But because most peasants did not have radios in their homes, the government's broadcast authority – the Central People's Broadcasting Station (CPBS) – constructed a national rebroadcast system. Radio signals from Beijing were transmitted to people throughout China via a series of repeater stations that fed the signals to loudspeakers that were hung in central locations of villages so that everyone could hear the new government's voice. The years 1949–57 represent by far the most growthful period in the development of the radio broadcast system with an increase in the number of 'wired' installations at the county level expanding from 11 in 1949 to nearly 1,700 by 1957. Communication by radio, however, was inhibited not only by the lack of receivers in people's homes, but also by language problems. The language of the national radio network, Mandarin with a distinct Beijing accent, was not understood in many parts of the country. The ability of national radio to serve a unifying ideological purpose, therefore, was limited in part by language – a difficulty that would later confront television programmers as well.

The 'second wave' of electronic media development took place in the 1970s with the distribution of personal radios to be used in homes. Still, by 1978 less than 8 percent of Chinese homes had a radio, and even by 1982 the figure was but 18.2 percent (although penetration in the cities was 32.3 percent, revealing a discrepancy in media experience between the rural and urban areas that later became true of television too: see Womack, 1986, for detailed statistics). Today, virtually every urban home has a radio. There are more than 800 FM and AM radio broadcasting stations in China now, and more than 624 shortwave stations, including three channels that cover the entire country (Wang, 1988b). The number of hours of daily radio programming is steadily increasing and citizens listen regularly. Beijing residents in the early 1980s reported that radio was the mass medium with which they were most likely to have daily contact (97 percent of the respondents to a Chinese survey summarized by Rogers *et. al.*, 1985).

Television

Experimentation with television in China began in 1956 and by 1960 stations in a dozen cities were sporadically transmitting programs that they traded among themselves. In these early years, however, almost no one had a television set with which to view the shows. Progress in the development of television hardware and software was slow. There was, first of all, a devastating break in relations with the Soviet Union, the supplier of parts and expertise, in 1960. China's economic crisis in the following years and the Cultural Revolution after that further curtailed development of the country's television system, although a few thousand sets were produced domestically and sold from 1967 to 1970. By 1978 roughly half a million sets were sold per year – a tiny figure in such a large country.

The most dramatic jump in sale of TV sets took place in 1979 when nearly two million sets were sold. The 1980s represent what Womack calls the 'third wave' of electronic media development in China – a period when nearly every family bought a TV set – a phenomenon that is similar to what happened in the United States in the 1950s. The growth curve

20

2 Domestic TV sets have been produced in abundance during the last decade.

reflecting sales of domestically-produced and imported television sets has increased steadily in China since 1979. The price of TV sets had been out of the reach of most Chinese families until the economic breakthrough of the modernization period. Until then even poor-quality, domestically-produced, small screen, black-and-white models were very expensive. The price of one of these sets could equal a year's wage for workers.[1] And, at first, televisions were not readily available outside the big cities even for families who could afford them. For example, families we talked to in Xian, a city that is relatively small and out of the way, complained that TV sets were in short supply there for years after people in Beijing and Shanghai could easily buy one. And when sets were available, persons with 'connections' were more likely to get them than families without special privileges. Even today television sets are used for barter and political influence. *China Daily* reported that as late as 1987 more than a million sets, half of them color, are used this way each year.

China's major cities developed their own regional stations in the early days of television. Beijing Television and Shanghai Television went on the air in 1958 and Guangzhou Television followed the next year. From the very beginning, the regional stations developed programming specific to their geographic areas. Videotaped presentations of Chinese operas featuring traditional local stories that are spoken and sung in the regional dialects, for instance, were main staples of programming.

21

Beijing Television began color telecasting in 1973 and went fully color four years later. Province stations also transmitted in color by the late 1970s, just in time for the explosion in sale of television sets in the 1980s (though nearly all families first bought the less expensive black-and-white sets). During the period of economic growth since 1978, more and more programming has been produced and transmitted as China has made a major commitment to the development of its television system on the road to becoming an 'information-intensive society' (Sun, 1987: 22).

A major step in this direction was taken in the mid 1970s with the gradual formation of the national network, Central China Television (CCTV), which was designed to unify the country through presentation of official news and information, culturally-appropriate entertainment, and use of the official dialect – puonyantin Mandarin – which is promoted as the national language. CCTV was formed as an administrative outgrowth of the original Beijing television station.

Major television stations throughout China, whose operations had been severely disrupted during the Cultural Revolution, resumed regular programming in the late 1970s. Many more stations signed on the air. The most popular early programs were news, dramas, and movies, many of them imported from Eastern Europe, Britain, and the United States.

Beginning in 1984 a sizeable jump in the purchase of television sets by farm families took place, reflecting profits from incentives paid within the economic reform of the nation's agricultural system. At the same time urban families were trading in their black-and-white sets for color models. Just before the Spring Festival of 1986, Hu Yaobang, then chairman of the CCP, publicly encouraged people to buy color sets, a policy recommendation that was criticized in some quarters for pushing people beyond their living standard.

The price of domestic TV sets was decreasing at the time because of improvements that had been made in the manufacture of integrated circuits. But despite the advances in Chinese television technology, the more expensive imported Japanese sets were clearly preferred to the domestic models. Chinese families are no different from people anywhere else in the world when it comes to television. They want to own good television sets. So, while most families originally bought Chinese-made black-and-white television sets, they were anxious to trade them in for a Japanese color model. Many of our narrators told us that Chinese sets are of far lesser quality. The importation of Japanese television sets was permitted by the Chinese government as a way to boost the image of the modernization. But it was an economic decision that backfired in several ways. Consumer demand for television sets – generally considered to be an indication of economic growth – in this case led to dissatisfaction on the part of many people with Chinese television set manufacturing, and, by implication, with China's ability to produce sophisticated consumer products generally. The

3 Transporting a new TV set home.

economic potential of the Chinese electronics industry was undercut in the process too. Furthermore, many families were frustrated by their inability to afford a Japanese TV set. When I visited China in 1989, a 28-inch, Toshiba color model was being sold for 8,200 yuan, roughly $2,500 US, in a country where most workers make about $350 US a year. Smaller sets are cheaper but are still priced out of the range of most families. Many Chinese families have relied on their overseas relatives to bring them a Japanese TV.

The number of TV stations, their coverage areas, and the amount and quality of programs transmitted by the network and the regional stations have all increased simultaneously with the production and consumption of television receivers. By 1990 Chinese families owned some 150 million television sets – about one set for every eight people nationwide and one set for every three or four people in the cities. There is a home viewership now of more than 600 million in China. With the introduction of telecommunications satellites, more than three-fourths of China's total population can see at least CCTV's first channel which is transmitted via repeater/booster stations to many remote areas. The cities are saturated with television. Ninety-five percent of all urban families owned at least one television set as early as 1986, according to Xinhua, the New China News Agency. More than two-thirds of the sets now being produced are color

23

models and the yearly domestic production of TV receivers is about 20 million sets (Sun, 1987). More than 400 television stations broadcast throughout the country, of which about 100 produce original programming, and there are an additional 3,500 telecommunications relay installations that are used mainly for military purposes and for communication with the outlying regions.[2]

A tremendous improvement was made at CCTV in 1987 when a massive new building that houses 20 studios and hundreds of offices, editing booths, and technical gear was opened, replacing what had been an antiquated facility. More than $10 million US was spent on equipment alone, nearly all of which bears labels such as Toshiba, Canon, Ampex, and Wang. In February of the same year, the network initiated a second channel of national service which is now carried by nearly 300 stations throughout the country and in all the cities. A third CCTV channel serves Beijing only.

Structure of the Chinese television system

Three basic types of television stations operate in China. The national network channels can be seen throughout the country on hundreds of stations that receive signals from Beijing via satellite links and retransmission facilities. The majority of the repeater stations do not originate their own programming. Others do. Among these are 30 province-level (regional) stations, and more than 200 city-level stations (though some, like the station in Shanghai, have province-level authority). Stations in these categories produce programs locally and/or receive programming from other sources. To make it even more complex, some of the stations transmit on more than one channel (Shanghai and Guangzhou, for example) while in other cities (such as Nanking) two separate stations – one at the province level, the other at the city level – each produce and air programs.

Since 1982, television stations fall under the administrative umbrella of the Ministry of Radio and Television in Beijing with CCTV assuming practical authority for much decision-making related to the development of the system. The creation of this ministry was part of a bureaucratic reorganization that signalled the rising importance of telecommunications in the 1980s. Prior to that time, administrative authority for television was spread out over several agencies, making effective coordination nearly impossible. Of course the Chinese Communist Party Central Committee, Secretariat, and Propaganda Bureau ultimately determine policy and play the role of censor for all Chinese mass media (Womack, 1986). Local media, including the television stations, are also responsible to local party and government authorities. But CCTV is, in practice, the first-line administrator of television in China.

24

4 The new China Central TV facility completed in 1987 (photo courtesy of CCTV).

Broadcasting officials told me in 1986 and again in 1989 that under normal circumstances the regional stations exercise a great degree of autonomy from the Ministry of Radio and Television and from CCTV in their day-to-day operations. This arrangement has not been destroyed by the alarming events in 1989. Stations still regularly develop programs without having to clear the ideas or the finished products with the authorities in Beijing. Regional stations also routinely sign contracts to import foreign shows and need not observe the more strict standards that CCTV uses to evaluate imported programming. When I returned to Beijing in 1989, for instance, the American action series, *Hunter*, was being aired by the Beijing regional television station. CCTV officials said this program would not have been acceptable at the network level. Much of the more adventuresome domestic and foreign programming is transmitted by the regional stations and is sometimes picked up by CCTV later.

This does not mean that the regional stations operate independent from the central system. In fact, there are firm national guidelines regarding the purposes and standards of telecasting that are well understood by the regional and local leaders and, as we have recently seen, allegiance to the political authority is absolute during peak periods of a national crisis. Officials at the regional stations are quick to point out that under normal circumstances, however, Beijing issues only *informal* directives and that a kind of implicit understanding determines what is appropriate and what is not. One regional television executive said that the relationship between his station and CCTV is like that of brothers. Another said that the relationship is more competitive than it is subservient (a 'little competition, not big competition' according to him). Province stations often compete with CCTV in news programming by presenting more newscasts than the network and by featuring local stories. Regional stations also adjust their program schedules after CCTV announces its lineup in order to compete effectively for viewers – a tactic known as 'counterprogramming' in American commercial television. In cases where the regional station also controls retransmission of CCTV, there may even be some shifting of network program schedules (by taping the shows and playing them back at less desirable times, for instance). A longstanding competition exists between CCTV and the local Beijing television station, a problem that is exacerbated by the fact that CCTV's formation superseded the operation and facilities of the Beijing Station, creating some professional jealousies and in-fighting among the staffs (Howkins, 1982).

Television programming

The trend is for all television outlets to increase the number of hours they transmit programs. Most stations sign on late in the morning and broadcast (sometimes with an hour or two of 'dead air' in the afternoon) until late at night, totalling an average of at least 12 hours daily. The content of Chinese television is a topic that is treated in detail throughout this book. With some important exceptions to be taken up later, programming reflects the emphasis on propaganda, instruction, education, and national culture. Among the programs being transmitted on CCTV in late 1989, for instance, were *Lecture on Computers, Beautiful China, Science Film: Windsurfing, A Variety Show: Ode to the Motherland, Learning Japanese, Economic Events, Beijing Opera, TV Serial: China's Older Generation of Revolutionaries, People's Army and the Motherland*, and *TV Drama: Happiness and Bitterness of a Woman Bureau Leader*. You get the idea. While these are not the only kinds of programs on the air in China, they set the tone for how shows are perceived by viewers. As we shall see later, many of the more popular offerings are foreign series and films, a category of programs that cannot exceed 8 percent of the total airtime.

Telecommunications satellites

China launched its first telecommunications satellite in 1970, developed its first land station in 1972, and joined the International Telecommunication Satellite consortium (INTELSAT) in 1977. Television broadcasting was not the first priority in the development of the system. The main purposes were point-to-point communication, telex, facsimile, and related high-tech information capabilities. The efficiency of satellite communication is well-aligned with China's plan for technological modernization.

But modernizing telecommunications in China is no easy task. Like most developing nations, China does not have a good telephone system. The situation in China is, in fact, much worse than many other poor countries. Only about 1 percent of the residential dwellings has a telephone. Most existing phones are used by government officials in their offices. Even by the year 2000, China expects to equip but 3 percent of its residences with telephones, although the rate in the cities will be considerably higher at 25–30 percent (Sun, 1987). The technical development of television has advanced more rapidly than that of the telephone.

According to Chinese information systems specialist Lin Sun, the current idea is to transform television broadcasting from the 'present combination of microwave and satellites to one based entirely on satellites' (Sun, 1987: 20). Satellites have proven to be especially effective for transmitting CCTV programming throughout the country. The network programs are sent from production headquarters in Beijing directly to INTELSAT's geostationary Indian Ocean Satellite, and then beamed earthward to even the most remote parts of the country – Tibet, Xinjiang, Qinghai, Gansu, Ningxia, Guizhou, and Shaanxi – where they are retransmitted. The land stations are also used to pick up satellite transmissions of international news from various sources, which are then recorded and replayed as part of the newscasts with Chinese language narration added.

China is trying to even further expand its involvement with satellite-based telecommunications in the 1990s. The country now offers satellite launching services and has entered into various international high-tech business relationships, including a joint venture with Brazil – the China–Brazil Earth Resources Satellite – which uses remote-sensing devices to gather information about the planet that is sold to other nations. China's plans along these lines hit a serious snag following Tiananmen Square, however, as export of necessary satellite equipment from American aerospace companies was temporarily banned as part of the United States' congressional trade sanctions against the Chinese government.

Videocassette recorders

VCRs and videotapes are very expensive in China so few families have them, though, following the example of countries throughout the world, the machines are likely to be in wide demand when economic conditions permit. Ownership of a VCR has become a status symbol even more impressive than owning a Japanese color television set. Like the expensive TVs, families who own VCRs often have been given the machines by overseas relatives. In other cases, families who have private businesses have been able to purchase a VCR – another material indication of the difference in earning power between state and private employment.

Families that own VCRs seldom use them to tape programs off-the-air in order to 'time shift' or to create video libraries, with the rare exception of some sports and movies. Instead, families that can afford VCRs exchange copies of films, many of them imported from Hong Kong and the West. Video 'pirates' are at work in China now too, making illicit copies of videos for profit. Although the vast majority of these trades and sales involve general entertainment movies, a highly-publicized police action in Beijing was brought against an exchange ring that dealt in pornographic videotapes, and similar cases have been reported in other cities. One of our young narrators in Beijing (the son of a high-ranking Communist Party official) admitted that this practice continues among people he knows.

The use of TV sets by adolescents for viewing pornographic videos surely was not part of the government's plan to develop a new spiritual civilization in China, but it reflects one theme that permeates this book – the inability of the government to predict the consequences of the medium. Television is user friendly. Although the government has always considered the medium to be, above all else, technology that efficiently disseminates information from official sources to a mass audience, the implications of television's widespread presence in Chinese homes are far more complex and subversive than could have possibly been imagined in 1978.

3

KNOWING CHINA
From inside and out

The rapid development of television in China during the last decade provokes a wide range of fascinating and important research questions. Unfortunately, however, empirical and critical research in the Chinese social sciences, especially in communication, remains underdeveloped. The political atmosphere, of course, also limits the range of questions that can be asked. Still, many Chinese scholars are fighting to find support for research projects and foreign scholars continue to be attracted to the intriguing country. In this chapter I will discuss China's social and cultural research traditions and practices, including investigations of the television audience, work that is undertaken mainly by personnel inside the television institutions. I will also describe how I researched China in order to write this book.

SOCIAL AND CULTURAL RESEARCH IN CHINA

Two basic types of social and cultural research are done in China: that which is undertaken by Chinese about their own society, and work that is done by foreigners designed primarily to inform agencies and publics outside the People's Republic. China has never mounted research efforts on social, cultural, and communication issues the way Western nations have. But China has been, and surely always will be, an intoxicating subject for analysis by foreigners. The Chinese government, therefore, has had to deal with an unending flow of non-Chinese-speaking foreign researchers over the years (including me) who stand to advance their own causes while the payoff for the Chinese is not always clear. Imagine what this would be like in reverse: scores of Chinese researchers tramping through America's or England's cities and villages asking questions and taking pictures.

China's social and cultural research history

Foreign researchers headed East long before the birth of socialist China and it was mainly from this infusion of Western ideas that Chinese social and cultural research developed. The very concept of sociology was introduced to China shortly after the turn of the century, and beginning in the 1930s many European and American sociologists and anthropologists conducted research there. This contact promoted the adoption by Chinese scholars of new Western philosophies of (social) science, theories, and research methodologies that were brought to the country by their foreign mentors (Guldin, 1987: 761; see also Pasternak, 1983).

But Western-influenced social science did not have much time to develop after its introduction in China as the Japanese invasion and the communist revolution ensued shortly thereafter. After 1949, Marxist–Leninist–Maoist social theory and Soviet-style socialist intellectualism replaced the more scientific perspective that had been encouraged in China by American, British, and most European scholars. The 'bourgeois thought' that was said to permeate Western research had to be expunged. The social sciences, including the fields of sociology, anthropology, and linguistics, were declared 'useless' (Guldin, 1987: 763). The Chinese believed that there was no need to study social and cultural processes in a system where the political, economic, and ideological agenda is fully managed. This was the Chinese version of Marxist–Leninist determinism: ways of thinking and characteristic modes of everyday life should be thoroughly predictable since the state, acting through the unchallengeable authority of the Communist Party, and in the name of the people, decides what citizens should know and do. Social behavior, then, was thought to be produced by and reflective of state ideology. Beyond this, government leaders believed that the people would cooperate with the policy dictates anyway since it would be in their collective best interest to do so. After all, the communists had won the civil war with popular support and the people were anxious to shed the vestiges of feudalism that many of them believed had been preserved in the nationalist era.

Consistent with emerging ideological visions and national priorities after 1949, colleges and universities were reorganized to exclude departments of sociology, anthropology, and political science. Except for a brief moment during the Hundred Flowers campaign of the mid 1950s, social scientists were not heard from during the early years of socialist China's history. The Cultural Revolution (1965–75) threw intellectual life in China into total disarray. Many universities and research institutes were closed, professors were harassed and frequently sent to work in the countryside, policies for admitting students to higher education reflected political and personal favoritism over academic achievement, research stopped, subscriptions to foreign publications were cancelled, teachers and intellectual life in general were scorned. All academic disciplines suffered immeasurably during this time.[1]

A gradual reconstruction of scholarship in China took place after the Cultural Revolution. An atmosphere developed in which scholarly work, including the eventual redevelopment of social science education and research, could take place. The first new department of sociology opened at Fudan University in Shanghai in 1979. Other departments within the social sciences began to operate throughout China in the following few years.

Social and cultural research in China today

In their edited volume *The Social Sciences and Fieldwork in China*, Anne F. Thurston and Burton Pasternak (1983) explain in careful detail the most important thing to know about research undertaken by the Chinese during the current period: it must promote the objectives of the four modernizations with a clear emphasis on the practical. Above all else scholarship must serve the requirements of the state. Researchers must adhere to the familiar four cardinal principles: Marxist–Leninist–Mao Zedong thought; a commitment to socialism; acceptance of the dictatorship of the proletariat; and acceptance of leadership of the Communist Party. Furthermore, research in China is part of the national planning process. Social research of all types must be relevant to policy matters.

Just as China looks outside its borders for technological expertise to help fulfill the plan for national modernization, it now again relies on foreign models for development of research in the social sciences. This reliance has produced certain problems. For example, the use of Western sociological theory sometimes has led to the formation of culturally-inappropriate concepts and categories in family, marriage, and fertility research (Hareven, 1987) and in recent collaborative mass communication research as well. Some Chinese scholars now are trying to adapt foreign theories and research methodologies to better fit Chinese culture. In much the same way that the country promotes 'Chinese style socialism,' there is a desire to develop 'Chinese style social research.'

Within the demands of the prescribed pragmatism in the era of technological modernization, social research has become more 'objective' – scientific and empirical. This development contrasts sharply with traditional Chinese intellectualism and 'ways of knowing' that, before the birth of the socialist nation, were mainly intuitive, philosophical, literary, poetic, and metaphorical in nature, and after 1949 were in strict accord with the political mandates of state socialism.

In principle at least, the new attitude toward social research is still consistent with state policy. A famous contemporary slogan in China, 'seek the truth from facts,' puts to a test the blind following of Marxist–

Leninist–Maoist approaches to research, though the spirit of socialist dogma still guides the basic purposes research is to serve. For example, while public opinion polls and other social research influence policymaking now for the first time in China, some issues and findings cannot be considered or made public. As a Chinese professor told me: 'The authorities don't like to hear that there is more than one voice in China. We are supposed to be unified.' Public opinion polls, of course, presume a multiplicity of voices. So, some recent studies of mass media habits and opinions, which do not reflect favorably on the media system or on political leaders, cannot be published outside the internal channels. A proposal to study perceptions held by television viewers of the media images of China's top political leaders was nixed, according to the would-be investigator, because the government feared what the results might reveal. The 1989 turmoil will also dampen the Chinese research agenda for years, further limiting insights that could be produced by systematic social analysis. Still, the fact that any empirical research that problematizes social behavior is undertaken now in China is important.

The new enthusiasm by Chinese scholars for doing research on social and cultural issues is also tempered by lack of access to foreign-language books and journals for 'catching up' theoretically and methodologically.[2] Not enough researchers are being trained. China's severe economic situation affects the academic community greatly. There simply is not enough money available for educational purposes. Nonetheless, some new publications are emerging in the country for reporting scholarly research and graduate training in the social sciences continues to expand, albeit slowly.

A quantitative bias

Thoroughly consistent with the goals of modernization, which so ardently promote technology and science, academic research of all types undertaken now in China, including social and cultural investigations, is mainly quantitative. The work depends on collection of large amounts of data, managing the data via computer operations, and conducting statistical tests as the primary analytical strategy. The methodological range employed so far is narrow:

> The survey method predominates because, like Western social scientists, Chinese researchers derive a sense of security from the 'objective,' quantifiable character of survey data. They feel that such data is more easily analyzed and more 'scientific.' In addition, many researchers feel embarrassed or inhibited by extensive, face-to-face, open-ended interviews.

(Hareven, 1987: 688)

This bias toward quantitative science is also apparent in the training of young Chinese researchers. The emphasis within curricula of Chinese universities is on quantitative research techniques and graduate students who leave the country typically matriculate at schools that provide this kind of methodological training.[3] Ironically, the emphasis on survey and experimental research in sociology, communication, and mass communication is far less in vogue in the West now than it was in the 1960s and 1970s. But for the modernizing Chinese, quantitative research remains very attractive and useful. There is a profound political consideration as well. Many Chinese scholars believe that quantitative research liberates them and their work from the qualitative data-gathering tradition of the Chinese Communist Party; specifically, party meetings and discussions.

CHINESE MASS COMMUNICATION RESEARCH

'Mass communication is a new field in China, a field that is imported from other countries. All of our research institutions are still in the stage of importing foreign theory and methodology. We are weak in using and practicing theory, so we have a lot of work to do.' (Gao Xin-hua, Director, Letter Research Department, Shanghai TV)

'We're behind other countries. We don't have ratings machines attached to TV sets. Most audience members do not have telephones at home so we can't call them to ask what they are watching at any time. We can only walk out to them or invite them in. These are the only methods we can use to make up for our lack of technology. Although we are behind other countries, we have a direct connection with viewers because we deal with them face-to-face. This intensifies our connection with the audience.' (Dou Jian Zhong, Researcher, Propaganda Department, Guangdong Province Television Station, Guangzhou)

Very little theoretically-informed empirical or critical research has been conducted on audience motivations for contact with television, the interpretations and uses that are made of TV, the influence of viewing contexts, or the medium's social and cultural impact. Instead, analyses of mass communication discuss how effectively the media carry out party policy. Other scholarly writing on television in China focuses on the aesthetics and production values of the medium.

There is an image problem too. Social and cultural research in general does not have the same status in China's academic world as does research in the physical sciences. And, just as communication is often thought to be a 'softer' discipline than the more established fields of psychology, sociology, and anthropology in the United States and other Western countries, there is less support for it in China too. In fact, communication is rarely recognized as a separate discipline in China. Most theoretical media

34

audience research is subsumed within large quantitative research programs that are undertaken by academies and institutes of social science or by departments of related disciplines. Mass communication is considered to be more a practical than a theoretical discipline, and so the responsibility for conducting the vast majority of research on television falls primarily on the shoulders of professionals, not scholars.

Applied television research

'We have a principle. If the audience doesn't like a program or if there is not a big enough audience for the program, then we cannot achieve our goals. We expose the audience to a program but *they* determine its success. For this reason we take audience opinion very seriously into consideration.' (Pan Huiming, Deputy Director, Guangdong Television Station)

Every programming or research executive with whom I have spoken in China indicates that there is a growing interdependence between administrative audience research and program decision-making. What this means, above all else, is that audience 'needs,' interests, and desires are slowly being taken into account. Decisions to add, cancel, expand, reduce, combine, reschedule, and change the content of shows have all resulted from recent audience research. And in the minds of the programmers, audience requirements often compete with policy requirements. The implications of this conflict should be abundantly clear.

A national meeting of television executives in 1987 led to the decision to employ a single research organization to determine audience likes and dislikes in China, data which are made available to CCTV and to the directors of all the regional stations. Research departments in the large broadcast organizations produce periodic written summaries of their findings for use by network and station executives, one variety of which I discuss below. In general, research information is being shared now between the national network and the province stations far more than ever before.

Television program producers in China won't lose their jobs if the ratings slip a point or two, but there is still much interest at the stations in knowing how well the programs are received by the audience – a kind of natural competition that broadcasters all over the world experience. The national network and the regional stations in the urban centers all have research departments that are charged with the responsibility to ascertain the size and composition of the audience for various programs. Researchers at the stations also solicit criticism of programming from the audience and analyze comments that are mailed spontaneously to the stations – a research approach I discuss below.

5 Personal letters sent to CCTV are the main form of audience research.

Types of audience data

'In the West, audience research is very quantitative, with a trend toward qualitative now taking place. But in China we began with the qualitative work and now we are trying to do quantitative research. In the future we hope to combine qualitative and quantitative research.' (Chen Rou Ru, Director of Audience Research, CCTV)

Despite the desire to develop quantitative research capabilities, so far the techniques most often used by the television institutions to analyze their audiences are qualitative. Except for the quantitative asssessments of audience size and demographics, the most common research methods used by the broadcasters are the following techniques:

Letters

'Letters from the audience usually don't say anything very nice. There is a lot of criticism, even in the letters we solicit.' (Chen Rou Ru, CCTV)

Audience members send letters by the thousands to the network and to the stations. At least 90 percent of the letters are sent spontaneously; the others are solicited. Letters are the main source of audience response and feedback. While the letters may not statistically represent audience opinion, researchers have found them to be good general indicators of the popularity and utility of television programming. From a standpoint of cost efficiency, a key issue, audience letters are extremely useful as a research method. CCTV receives about 10,000 letters each month. Regional stations in Shanghai and Guangzhou receive between 500 and 1,000 per month. More letters are sent in the winter than in other seasons, certain programs stir up more responses than others, on-air requests for audience input invariably produce an increase in letter writing, and holiday periods – especially the Chinese New Year – stimulate the most written feedback about programming.

Letters are scanned for critical themes (most are complaints of some sort) which are noted either for fresh ideas or recurring criticisms. Statistics on the frequencies of themes present in the letters are sometimes compiled. More commonly, however, tendencies in the letters, or selected letters in their entirety, are published in paperback books, circulated to various departments in the broadcast organizations, and later discussed in meetings. At CCTV a volume that contains audience letters is published every month. Partly because of difficulties posed by the written Chinese language, no attempt has yet been made to use computers directly to analyze the letters despite their importance as a source of information about the television audience.

Special samples

Research teams at broadcast stations in Beijing, Shanghai, and Guangzhou all told me that they have specially-recruited groups of audience members that are regularly consulted and relied upon heavily for information and insights. Viewers in these groups are considered to be especially well qualified to evaluate television programming. These special viewers either write letters to the stations when requested to do so or meet with research authorities in groups to discuss current and planned shows. In Shanghai they even have a name for these consultants – 'TV Friends.'

In Guangzhou a group of television enthusiasts are counted on by researchers at the province station to collect local information about the viewing preferences and habits of members of their neighborhood or work groups which they then pass along to the station authorities. Other self-appointed television experts in cities all over China methodically gather unsolicited data about their neighbors' viewing habits and opinions and regularly send these reports to CCTV and to the regional and city stations. This input is not ignored.

Focus groups

Another qualitative audience research technique used by broadcasters is the focus group. These ensembles are sometimes composed of members of the special samples mentioned above; at other times they are developed according to the requirements of the topic. At the Guangdong Province station, for instance, programmers contemplated changing the scheduling and format of the news programs. From focus group research they found that viewers liked the news very much, but they were 'bored when it went on too long.' As a result, the station inserted a five-minute news brief into the original news time slot, and moved the longer newscast back 90 minutes, to 9 p.m. Then, a series of group meetings was held to determine how the audience responded to the change. Network researchers also conduct informal discussions with viewers. These meetings are held in family homes, collectives, factories, and other work units. No attempt is made in the focus group research to select individual members randomly, although at the network level, at least, participants in focus groups are recruited in neighborhoods or work units that are thought to represent different segments of Chinese society.

According to Chinese television researchers, some people will not or cannot express themselves well during group interviews because they are nervous or concerned about their family background and reputation. So, in order to insure that the focus group sessions are productive, researchers often rely on some agency – typically the local/neighborhood government – to supply willing, opinionated discussants.

Meetings with experts

By far the most common way that Chinese broadcasters make programming decisions is by discussions with experts. Depending on the current issues, researchers, scholars, or technical specialists are summoned. At CCTV, for instance, a psychologist lectured network officials on how to best exploit Chinese traditions in the production of programs for New Year's Eve – a time when nearly all of China watches television – in order to maximize audience satisfaction. Educational psychologists are asked to help determine the level at which instructional programs and children's shows should be pitched – who will watch the programs and how can viewers best be taught? Books or summary reports are published about the deliberations. And, at the time of this writing, CCTV was also organizing its first international conference on television audience research, where foreign academics were to be invited to Beijing in order to discuss television theory and research methodology. If it happens, this will be the first time China has ever reached outside its borders to interact in such a formal way with the world academic community in the field of communication.

38

FOREIGNERS STUDY CHINA

The Open Door policy made it possible for foreigners to study China in the 1980s much more easily than before. Through invitations by the Chinese government, often facilitated by the Fulbright Council for the International Exchange of Scholars in the United States and by similar institutions in many other countries, Westerners have again entered China to conduct research, often in collaboration with Chinese scholars, though, like everything else, these relationships have become less secure in the wake of June 4th, 1989. Before 1980, Western scholars had to study Chinese society from a distance. The most logical location for doing so is Hong Kong. The work of two American sociologists who took this approach is particularly noteworthy.

Martin King Whyte and William Parish established a research center in Hong Kong in the 1970s where they interviewed Chinese immigrants to the British island colony. Transcripts produced by these lengthy interview sessions formed data sets that led to publication of two very important volumes about post-1949 China. Their principal population of interest, the rural dwellers, were subjects of the first book, *Village and Family in Contemporary China* (Parish and Whyte, 1978). China's city population was analyzed in the subsequent volume, *Urban Life in Contemporary China* (Whyte and Parish, 1984).

In the second book, which is of greatest relevance to us here, Whyte and Parish examined the urban political economy, family behavior, and quality of life issues as reported to them by their immigrant informants. Their analyses were developed from 'a series of intensive, semi-structured interviews over two years with 133 individuals who had formerly been residents of 50 different cities, large and small, scattered around China' (Whyte and Parish, 1984: 4–5). The authors didn't ask people directly about their own families, but about their neighbors and others they knew in their immediate environment. The authors also relied on secondary sources such as Chinese mass media, reports from visitors to the country, and literature about Chinese society. Comments taken from the interview transcripts were transformed into 'variables' so that statistical tests could be performed.

Whyte and Parish have been very reflective on the limitations of doing research on China without actually going there. Among the criticisms they have raised are sampling, which was not representative in any sense and depended on informal friendship networks to recruit interviewees.[4] Most of the refugees were from Guangdong Province near Hong Kong. More males than females were interviewed and respondents were younger and better educated than the average for the Chinese population. Even more troubling is that all the respondents had chosen to leave China, and were, therefore, a very biased group. Their 'self-selecting' into Hong Kong was compounded by the way the sampling was done in Hong Kong.[5]

It is not easy to say how much these difficulties misinformed the general conclusions that Whyte and Parish draw, and as Martin Whyte has argued elsewhere (Whyte, 1983) every indirect source of information about life in China is biased in one way or another. Despite all the problems of the Hong Kong method, the work of Whyte and Parish is unquestionably useful. It represents the most comprehensive social analysis ever done on Chinese society, though the work now has certainly become dated. Nonetheless, I was often impressed with the correspondence between the descriptions made in their book and the conditions of life that we observed first hand in China. But to research this book I wanted to enter more ethnographically into everyday life in China and to focus specifically on television's roles in culture and politics. And while most foreign researchers dwell on developments in rural China, I wanted to study the urban situation which is where the bulk of the changes are taking place in Chinese society today. Furthermore, I did not want the American government, the Chinese government, or any other agency to control the research agenda.

THE RESEARCH PROJECT

'We are the people running on the road. We are not afraid to speak out about the government anymore.' (26-year-old female worker in a mint, Shanghai)

'Now we have law. Everybody is equal in front of the law. Two or three years ago we couldn't talk like this.' (27-year-old male worker in a cigarette factory, Guangzhou)

'Things are more relaxed now. We can talk with foreigners. This is part of the reformation. Before we were supposed to protect the image of China. We even had to keep our bedsheets off the clothes lines on the street. Now we show the truth. Now we ask, "where can I put the sheets to make them dry?" ' (49-year-old male manager of medicine factory, Guangzhou)

These were voices of the people in 1986. Chinese citizens were more than willing to talk to us about television – its impact on them as individuals, as families, and as members of the world's most populous nation. The quotes presented above reflect the open, honest, and often critical positions taken (at least semi-publicly) by Chinese people then. Most of them were optimistic about China's economic development and the new cultural openness of the Deng-era government even though many were still fundamentally distrustful of the party and the political system.

Timing was central to the success of our ability to speak so easily and frankly with so many people. Large-scale student demonstrations in Shanghai began just a few months after we left China. Social unrest throughout urban China has continued sporadically since then, creating an atmosphere that makes cooperation between Chinese citizens and foreign researchers much more difficult now.

We tried in advance to arrange formal opportunities to speak with urban families by repeatedly meeting with officials at the Chinese consulate in San Francisco more than a year before we left. It became apparent, however, that we would have to freelance after we got to China. We went to China, therefore, with the idea that we would employ whatever methods we could manage in order to document the impact of television on Chinese society, especially how it affects the thinking and everyday life of urban residents. As it turns out, this informal procedure was a blessing in disguise as we were quite easily able to interview families. We also arranged our meetings with television network and station officials after we arrived.

Except for defrayal of minor costs, we did not seek to have our research funded.[6] This way we did not have to meet any institutional requirements for the work and we were free to create a flexible research plan that could respond to actual conditions and possibilities. I cannot emphasize enough, however, that this research simply could not have been accomplished without the contribution of my primary research assistant, Se-Wen Sun, a doctoral student at the University of Wisconsin–Madison. As a native Mandarin speaker and a person of great insight into Chinese culture, Sun's unending enthusiasm for the project, her disciplined work habits, and her personable interviewing style made the project possible. Certainly no non-Chinese person alone could have gathered the kind of data that is presented in this book. But the Chinese research community itself also has never taken on such a project. Much sociological and anthropological research that is done by Chinese investigators is 'team fieldwork,' a data-collection strategy that is not particularly revealing of the insights I was seeking. Beyond this, we had the advantage of speaking Chinese with our subjects, but not being Chinese citizens (and therefore not representing the government), although technically Sun is considered to be an overseas Chinese.

We worked in China's big cities. These locations – with the exception of a few sensitive neighborhoods – are open to anyone. At the same time, however, the neighborhoods where we conducted our interviews are among those least affected by tourism. Foreigners rarely if ever go into the neighborhoods where we did our work and few of our subjects had ever spoken to a foreigner. The cities and neighborhoods are discussed at length in the next chapter.

6 Se-Wen Sun (left) interviews a family in Beijing.

Sampling

We held several principles firmly in mind when we decided who to interview. First, we wanted to choose our own research subjects. We were unwilling to visit model homes or talk to people who had been prepared to meet us. Foreign visitors to China often are introduced to model workplaces, schools, and homes. On my first visit to China in 1982, for instance, professors and students in our group were driven to the famous Evergreen Commune located just outside Beijing, where we were given a tour of the facility and a briefing on the benefits of communism.

Second, we wanted to represent urban China generally, not to depend on data gathered in any one city. Interviewing, therefore, was to be carried out primarily in China's three major cities – Shanghai (31 families), Beijing (30), and Guangzhou (14). We added a fourth city, Xian (10 families), in order to get additional perspectives from audience members in an urban location that is less developed than the larger, more famous, and more important cities.

Third, we wanted to select families within each of the cities in a manner that we felt could reasonably be considered representative of China's urban population. While we never entertained any idea of collecting a random sample (never in the history of social science has a truly random sample been collected anyway!), we were 'striving for randomness' throughout the

42

sampling process. This means that we interviewed people in all sections of the cities. We used the urban zones represented on bus maps for each city to determine sampling areas. Then, each day, we systematically moved from one part of the city to the next in order to contact families. Although urban Chinese neighborhoods are thought to be comparatively hetero-geneous, we were nonetheless unwilling to limit our interviewing to any one section of the cities. We interviewed three families in each urban zone.

Our daily interviewing began in the mid afternoons as people started coming home from work and ended about 10 p.m., depending on the ease with which we found subjects and the length of the family discussions. After we arrived in the day's designated zone, we simply walked along the crowded streets where we engaged families in conversation. Our work was done during the summer. Chinese people love to sit outside then as the weather is often hot and humid. The people gather outside to eat water-melon and lychee, talk with their neighbors and friends, and play with the children. When we noticed a group that looked like an intact family (our 'unit of analysis' was the *family*; we tried to talk to complete groups whenever possible), Sun would use a 'Chinese way' to initiate conversation. In her characteristic friendly, non-threatening style she would begin talking about a 'small point' (the baby being held by a parent, clothing, the neighborhood, something special to the area) in order to develop 'a relationship' – sufficient rapport to inspire interest and trust. Within five to ten minutes she would slowly and carefully explain our research objec-tives and ask if the family owns a television set. Next, she would ask if the family would talk to us about television. Nearly everyone (87 percent acceptance rate of those contacted) agreed. Chinese people are not faced with the onslaught of business, political, and religious solicitations and exploits that regularly confront Western, especially American, families. In general they were not suspicious or cynical about the purpose of our work. In fact, most families enthusiastically agreed to discuss television, and in several cases they approached us in a friendly way to see what we wanted and if they could help.

The interviews

Family discussions took place inside the homes of the people we met. Non-Chinese visitors to China know that it is impossible to travel outside the tourist paths without attracting considerable attention. Had we attempted to interview people anywhere but in the privacy of their homes, we would have attracted galleries of dozens, perhaps hundreds, of curious onlookers. Even the family home is a semi-public space in China. In a few cases, neighbors and passersby had to be asked not to peer through open doors and windows. In two or three extreme cases, people unknown to the families were asked to leave the room. They had entered unannounced and simply wanted to join the discussion.

The private setting, the innocence of a discussion about television, the openness of China in 1986, and Sun's interviewing style helped families feel free to say what they pleased. A more formal approach, where family discussions would have been arranged by officials, would certainly have been more intimidating. But even under those circumstances, an American researcher reports that in her interviews with Chinese people, the 'accompanying (Chinese) sociologists were surprised that local people would respond so frankly and tell their life stories in such detail' (Hareven, 1987: 688).

Inside the homes, families typically invited us to sit around a small table in the middle of the living space. This table is used for eating and doing various types of paperwork. It is a convenient gathering place that helped establish a democratic tone for contributing to the discussions. An audio-cassette tape recorder with a small but high-quality multi-directional microphone was switched on and placed in the middle of the table. We assured everyone that while we would be using direct quotes in our analysis, we would not identify individuals or families in a way that betrayed confidentiality.

The conversations were spontaneous and free-flowing. According to Sun, my presence also encouraged cooperation as Chinese citizens generally admire Westerners (at least their technological achievements), and the combination of a friendly overseas Chinese researcher and a nearly mute but polite American professor promoted a positive atmosphere for conversation. During the interviews I made notes about the physical details of the homes and families, managed the technical details of the audio recording, and ate endless slices of watermelon that were generously given to me. Eventually I learned to eat the first slice that was provided by each family very slowly. If you eat it quickly, the family will think you must be very hungry and will immediately cut you another even bigger piece, a perplexing development if you really don't care much for watermelon and are in the third home of the day. One does not refuse the offer of watermelon. Watermelon notwithstanding, the most formidable obstacle to successful completion of the interviews was the presence of an activated television set, though nearly every family readily agreed to turn it off during the discussions, even when their favorite shows were on. After each interview was completed, I took photographs of the interior of the home.

Each interview lasted between one and two hours. The sessions were structured according to a common set of questions, beginning with simple queries about demographic characteristics, a listing of favorite types of television programs for each family member, and a brief accounting of the history of television in the family. Family members willingly and interestedly talked about domestic and foreign programs, television's role in family

44

interaction, and the impact that it has on Chinese society generally. The following questions were asked of all families:

1 For each family member: age, education, occupation, favorite type of television show, family history with television.
2 In what ways has your life changed since television arrived?
3 How do you select programs for viewing?
4 How do you resolve conflicts when viewing preferences differ?
5 In what ways is television a communicative 'bridge' between the government and the people?
6 What educational uses do you make of television?
7 What influence does the region in which you live have on your life in general?
8 What other leisure time activities do you engage in other than watching television?
9 How much television do you watch each day?
10 Please evaluate the programming you receive from the CCTV network and from the local and regional stations.
11 (To students) What does your teacher say about television? Are you encouraged or discouraged to watch it?
12 Do you talk about television shows at home, school, work? Which shows? When?
13 Will you please evaluate the role and quality of commercials on Chinese television?
14 What do you think the effects of television are, in general, on Chinese society?

We were pleased to learn quickly that these questions provided a kind of springboard from which family members frequently launched into discussions not only of television, but of individual consciousness, family and neighborhood interaction, workplace relations, as well as the ideological interpretations, uses, and consequences of television programs. So, while we never asked questions about the government, for instance, commentaries about the system of governance were freely given because, for one thing, television and the government are all part of the same bureaucratic structure. And despite tendencies for Chinese to hold back emotionally in the giving of opinion (only fools shoot off their mouths), the fact that some comments could only be correctly understood by carefully examining the discursive context in which they were made, and the fact that certain issues had to be approached indirectly, we gathered a massive amount of data about life in urban China.

Data analysis

We translated the taped interviews into English the following day, thereby preserving as much non-verbal and contextual information as possible about each family. I consider the interviews to be discourses that were constructed between ourselves and Chinese family members. Our research subjects, therefore, were 'narrators' more than 'respondents' (Mishler, 1986). The analysis presented here takes into consideration not only factual information provided by our narrators, but also the reasoning processes that underlie these articulations. Furthermore, the analytical formulations represented in this book emerged at different rates of speed and in different directions from the taped conversations and from our initial interpretations of and discussions about them. Rather than test hypotheses or pose highly-purposive research questions, we attempted to create a context in which Chinese city dwellers, nearly 300 of them, could enter into reflective conversations about technology, communication, politics, family, education, and all other aspects of everyday life. Their verbatim comments are central to the analyses which are made in this volume.

Return visit: the post-Tiananmen Square perspective

I returned alone to China in October and November 1989, during the last stages of writing this book. After watching televised pictures of hundreds of thousands of Chinese students and workers pouring into Tiananmen Square in May (remembering all the while the faces of family members we interviewed in that very neighborhood), following the amazing political developments, seeing the People's Liberation Army evacuate the human congregation, reading every press clipping I could find about China, and speculating endlessly with my friends about what was *really* happening over there during the months that followed June 4th, I knew I had to go back to China to find these things out for myself before I could put this book to bed. Fortunately, I had been invited by the People's University of China in Beijing to do just that.

Residing and lecturing at the People's University, where we had also stayed in 1986, I had the opportunity to speak in confidence, and through arrangements that were made entirely by me, with roughly 50 more people – students, intellectuals, and workers. My overall impression following these sensitive discussions was, indeed, a sad one. So many bright young people have become so hostile to the communist-led government while others have simply disengaged from political thought. On the other hand, there was a sincere expression by some intellectuals that all hope for China should not be abandoned. In general, however, a pervasive, underlying, depressed feeling covers the college campuses and the city of Beijing. One student, for instance, haltingly asked me if I believe in God. When I asked him why he wanted to know, he said: 'We must have something to believe in now.' Another student quietly told of a recent suicide by a classmate who said he could no longer face the future.

I also had another lengthy interview session with executives from CCTV who not only supplied me with verbal information, but (by my request) with videotape copies of the propaganda documentaries that were produced by the network and aired in the summer and fall of 1989. These programs were designed to explain the government's position on the unrest and the military clearing of Tiananmen Square. I will analyze them in Chapter 9. Finally, in order to see the trends in Chinese television programming, I viewed and videotaped for further analysis many domestic and foreign programs that were aired on CCTV and the Beijing Television station. But before analyzing propaganda material, program genres, and specific shows that have appeared on television in China, I would like next to describe how the medium has become part of life at home in the cities, and what that has meant for the quintessential feature of Chinese culture – the family.

4

TELEVISION IN URBAN CHINA
The medium enters everyday life

In China life itself is political. Socialism is not just ideology or a form of government but an all-embracing social and cultural system, providing the ground rules for everything from literature to love and everyday behavior.

(Hooper, 1985: 161)

China's political stresses in recent years reflect tensions between and among the requirements and routines of competing and contradictory 'cultures' within the nation itself. The official culture – the government's prescribed mode of living – has been imposed on the people since the 1949 'liberation.' But Chinese society is grandly informed by its own history, and certain key aspects of the country's cultural contours still are deeply influenced by traditions that long predate and continue to transcend any formalized set of rules for living. Pragmatic responses to the exigencies of everyday life comprise another fundamental part of China's cultural condition. And now, a provocative *imagined* culture has emerged, especially among students and city people, that promotes the possibility of a future that is not limited to governmental provisos, national traditions, or everyday problems. The new visions are of a truly modern China, one that joins the tide of socialist nations everywhere that have come to embrace democratic principles and a less centrally-controlled economy. It is within this cultural complexity that television has entered, interacted with, and influenced Chinese society.

Despite cultural and political orientations that promote ethnic unity and nationalism, there are many Chinas. Some distinctions are demarcated politically (e.g. party members v. others; supporters of the official reformation v. resisters), economically (e.g. state employees v. private unit merchants), and linguistically (Mandarin v. Cantonese and other regional dialects and accents). The biggest gap, however, is between life on the farm and life in the cities. About three-fourths of China's people inhabit the countryside, where everyday life for many peasants, especially those in the outlying regions of the north and west, has not changed much for several generations. Families there have far fewer televisions. Some have

48

no electricity or even candles. Others never travel more than a few miles from home in their lifetime. They may never see a train. Precisely because of their lack of exposure to the modern world, and the unsophisticated political consciousness that results from such isolation, Deng was able to reliably call on People's Liberation Army soldiers from the peasant classes to finally put down the insurrection in Beijing in 1989. In today's China, political activity is an urban phenomenon. Mao Zedong's peasant revolution of the 1930s and 1940s has been supplanted in the 1980s and 1990s by a resistance movement that is based in the cities. Television is a central fixture in the resistance. The influence of television in China's cultural and political milieu can best be understood by first entering ethnographically into the everyday life of city-dwelling Chinese families.

THE URBAN REGIONS

Even though the vast majority of China's population lives in the countryside, there are more city dwellers in China than in any other nation in the world. Most of them live in the eastern third of the country. Differences in lifestyle among the various urban centers are significant – not only to researchers who try to understand this complex society, but first and foremost to Chinese citizens themselves. To be Shanghainese, or Beijingnese, or Cantonese is to be a particular kind of Chinese. Each region has its own cultural traditions and sense of pride, and, in some ways, the regions seem more like different countries than parts of the same nation.

An illegal migrant population comprised mainly of boys and young men has moved from smaller towns and rural villages to the big cities in the north and to the SEZs of the south during recent years. But most Chinese citizens do not move from one city to another except under circumstances that are dictated by the government – work assignments or population relocation. Furthermore, there has been a tightening of security in the cities since the 1989 Beijing violence. Many homeless or illegal residents of Beijing and other big cities have been sent back to their home provinces. This lack of mobility inspires a kind of forced identification with the area in which one is born.

Cultural differences that exist among the diverse regions of China range from food, to language, to courting behavior, and have been the subject of much scholarly inquiry. Some generalizations can be made right away. First, the north differs greatly from the south and the coastal cities differ from the inland cities. Generally, people from northern China can be described as more prudent, culturally conservative, and politically engaged than those who live in the south. It is no coincidence that the political upheaval of the 1980s took place mainly in Beijing and Shanghai. Lifestyles of the northerners, however, are generally more sedate than those of the Pacific coast or south. The southerners have a more lively and diverse cultural environment that has been influenced greatly by foreigners throughout the centuries.

In keeping with these rudimentary distinctions, contrasting social behavior can be observed. First, northerners and inland people tend to defer more to members of the older generation than do those who live in the south or on the coast. Young Chinese in the northern and inland cities are more obedient to their parents and grandparents and are usually less 'wild' outside the home. In Shanghai and Beijing nightlife is still very subdued compared to Guangzhou, where the city is alive at night with open-air restaurants, street vendors, and discotheques. Social and sexual relations between young, unmarried Chinese differ by region too. As one young Shanghainese man explained, 'girls in the north protect themselves more than the girls in the south do.' Pre-marital sex is strongly discouraged by the government and by most parents everywhere in China, though illicit liaisons do take place, often during the day when parents are away at work.

Housing differs by region too. No Chinese city is outwardly poor compared to another and most Chinese citizens live in state housing where the monthly rent is no more than eight yuan (about $2). It is not always clear to what socioeconomic level a family belongs by simply observing the size or interior of the home. We interviewed Communist Party members with white-collar jobs who were living in houses that are inferior to those of non-party workers of a lower level. Private unit merchants have become the gentrified class in China today. They enjoy much greater material freedom, including access to better housing.

Life in Shanghai

Much has been written about the colorful history of Shanghai, China's largest city and long considered to be the nation's center of industry, commerce, and fashion. Rainy and humid during the summer, more mild than Beijing during the winter, Shanghai is one of the world's most interesting and important cities – and the people who live there know it. The streets and sidewalks are crammed with people all day, every day. Taxi drivers speed perilously along the city streets and the buses are always jammed. The primary mode of transportation, though, is foot power – bicycles and walking.

Close your eyes while standing on a Shanghai street during the summer and you'll hear the jingling of bicycle bells, sandals sliding along the pavement, street vendors selling watermelon or tea eggs, crickets chirping from bamboo cages suspended inside homes, water leaking from kitchen drains into the partially-open sewer system, perhaps some music from a cassette recorder and, the most pervasive sound at night, the soundtrack of television programs, often emanating in unison from homes since many families watch the same shows. Light pours through the windows of homes onto the streets in Shanghai, changing color simultaneously with the imagery of television programs.

Although people who live in Shanghai are very aware of their city's reputation as the leader in commerce and culture, one thing is on the mind of every young person there – improved living conditions. The most obvious feature of everyday life in Shanghai is the extreme tightness of space in which people live. There is less floor space per person here than in any other Chinese city and while the people who live in Shanghai may be used to it, they don't like it. One family we interviewed, for example, lives in two rooms, one 12 by 8 feet and the other 4 by 8. The parents and their son, who is 27 years old, sleep in the 'big' room. Their daughter sleeps on the floor in the other room. They share a kitchen with others in the building and use a public bath. The living quarters are located on the second floor of an old apartment building near the downtown area. In order for the inhabitants of the apartments on the third floor to get to their rooms, they must pass through a staircase that is located immediately adjacent to and in view of the family we interviewed. This was not the home of a poor Shanghainese family. The father is an accountant for a hotel, the son is an instructor at an educational institute, and the daughter is an accountant for a petroleum company. It isn't that they cannot afford to move elsewhere or that they are out of favor politically. There simply is no other place for them to go.

The street has a special appeal to adolescents under these circumstances. Shanghai's main drag, Nanjing Lu, originates at the harbor, adjacent to the Bund, and extends through the heart of the business district. This is by far the best place for strutting, and the early evenings are filled with young people walking slowly along the busy street. Before 1949, Nanjing Lu and the other big streets in Shanghai were where all the 'bad' things were happening. In some respects Shanghai's streets still have that feeling. While the streets have been tamed since the Nationalists left, several bars, clubs, discos, and fancy restaurants have opened recently and Shanghai is becoming lively once again.

Life in Beijing

Compared to the bustling, overcrowded conditions of Shanghai and the outwardly social atmosphere of Guangzhou, life in Beijing is quiet. It is not really possible to know China without knowing Beijing. Decisions about all aspects of life are made there. Beijing is the seat of national government and the locus of much intellectual life in China, particularly in the scientific areas. China's brightest young people study at the three prestigious universities located in the city's northwestern suburbs, the area where dissident astrophysicist Fang Lizhi made many passionate speeches

and where the student-led movement for freedom and democracy originated. According to a college professor from Xian who had studied in
Beijing for a year, people in the capital have 'broader sight' than those
outside: 'They have more information than we do. Everything happens
faster in Beijing.'

Beijing is a sprawling, flat, and not particularly attractive city of many
diverse neighborhoods. The city proper has a population of about six
million people but more than ten million occupy the greater Beijing area.
The architectural mixture is striking; buildings in the center of the city
reflect Soviet, European, British, traditional and contemporary Chinese
designs. There are tall high-rise buildings and one-story, commune-style
structures with small courtyards. Some of the apartment complexes are
modern and well designed, others are old and falling apart. Many of the
buildings have no running water. Living conditions in Beijing differ from
family to family, despite a national policy that is designed to reduce
material differences. The inequality is due in part to the slow conversion
of family residences from one-story buildings to high-rise apartments.

Beijing homes have somewhat more floor space than those in Shanghai
and more furniture simply because there is room for it. In Beijing a family
may have a couch and some easy chairs, for instance, instead of the stools
and one or two soft chairs that are found inside Shanghai homes. And
whereas Shanghai families like to adorn their quarters stylishly, Beijing
residents typically make less of an effort to decorate their homes.

Life in Guangzhou

Located in the southernmost region of the People's Republic, Guangzhou
has a far more relaxed and permissive feeling than Beijing or Shanghai,
partly because of the warmer temperatures, but also because of the city's
close proximity to Hong Kong. Guangzhou is China's 'southern door'
through which many travellers pass on their journeys to China. The flow
of foreigners through Guangzhou is nothing new. Commercial and tourist
trade up and down the Pearl River from Hong Kong is an important piece
of China's history. Many Guangzhou residents have relatives and friends
in Hong Kong and in other overseas Chinese settlements. Interaction with
them over the years has given the people of Guangzhou greater insight
into life outside the country than most other urban residents in China
have had.

Materialism abounds in Guangzhou. Although life there seems almost
tranquil when compared to Hong Kong, Guangzhou is a hustle-bustle city
with lots of taxis racing about, privately-owned motorcycles on the streets,
disco music pouring out of audio cassette playback machines, black market
money exchanging, and the presence of many foreign goods including
Japanese motor vehicles, televisions, VCRs, cassette recorders, and cam-

eras. The private unit sector of the economy is far more active and apparent in Guangzhou than in any other major Chinese city.

The way of life in Guangzhou simply seems freer than it does in the north. There are fewer constraints on individuals. Less restrictions are placed on the children. Adoption of Western styles in Guangzhou, including fashion, music (Hong Kong, American, and British pop music tapes are much more available here than in the northern cities), and other cultural elements, has been accompanied by a loosening of traditional values in communication. The personality of Guangzhou reflects the activity of its youth: children argue loudly for the right to view their favorite television programs, couples date and embrace openly, young businessmen spend money as fast as they can because it is illegal to *have* too much money, unrelated young married couples live together in the same house.

The Open Door policy has further enhanced Guangzhou's development. Exchanges of every type can be consummated easily. Many Guangzhou citizens speak of the relative independence and permissiveness of local government as an important part of life there. The southern part of China has always had a separate cultural identity, but in the age of modernization the differences have sharpened noticeably.

Life in Xian

China's three most famous and important cities are certainly Shanghai, Beijing, and Guangzhou. Most of the 85 families we interviewed live in these urban centers. Historically, however, Xian is also one of the country's great cities and, because of its size and location, it is a type of place that I wanted to represent in the research too. Xian is a dry, dusty, ancient city that is located about 200 miles southwest of Beijing. The center of the city is surrounded by a high brick wall, a preserved remnant of feudalist China. Xian has become a popular stop for tourists who are attracted to the nearby Qing tomb, the beautiful and historic Winter Palace, and the startling terracotta soldiers.

Xian's fabled past is much more impressive than its contemporary image. Many residents have immigrated recently from other cities as part of a government relocation program designed to meet national production goals in various industries. Residents are sometimes reluctant to praise the city or think of it as home. But a common theme among the people is that things are improving. Housing in Xian is being renovated, its many historical monuments are being restored, and consumer goods are available in greater abundance. All of this has taken place recently. Several people told us, for instance, that imported Japanese television sets came to Xian years after they were available in other cities.

Street life in Xian is teeming, particularly during the summer. At about 10 o'clock each night the city takes on a distinctive nighttime personality.

53

In a manner far more similar to Guangzhou than to its closer neighbor Beijing, Xian is a lively city at night with thousands of food vendors preparing and serving delicacies from their portable kitchens. People stay up late during the summer here, socializing on the streets. Groups of men sit on little chairs in the middle of the streets to play *mah jongg* or cards as pedestrians, bicyclists, and occasional automobiles pass by. Some people sleep outside their homes on beds that they place there to beat the heat.

The neighborhood

The close relationship between government and family in China has led to the development of orderly and secure neighborhoods. Though economic reform has confused things in recent years, the socialist principle still determines the character of Chinese cities:

> Cities should become spartan and productive places with full employment, secure jobs with a range of fringe benefits, minimal income and lifestyle differences, an end to conspicuous consumption and lavish spending, and with decent consumption standards for all. Crime, prostitution, drug addiction, begging, and other social evils should be eliminated.

(Whyte and Parish, 1984: 16)

These lofty goals have in part been realized in China. The security and control that characterize the neighborhoods are achieved by means of residential registration (a declining practice lately) and the monitoring of activity. Every neighborhood has someone who watches things closely. There is nothing secret about this. Neighborhood monitors, usually older women, are well known to the residents and in the downtown areas they wear armbands for recognition. As a result, people feel quite safe where they live. Women, for example, can walk unaccompanied with little or no fear of attack. An outsider is usually recognized by residents because people know what their neighbors look like.

Some neighborhoods are made up of families of diverse occupations while others are composed of men and women who are employed by the same work unit. Friendships and interpersonal conflicts that develop at work, therefore, are often carried into the neighborhood. Many marriages result from acquaintances made at the workplace because that is where men and women can meet each other naturally. It is also common for the children of these marriages to work at the same place. So, family members often work together, then return home where their neighbors are also their co-workers. These long histories of contact are diminishing somewhat now with the relocation of families into new apartment buildings.

Commensurate with the slow but steady rehousing of families is an alteration of social activity in urban Chinese neighborhoods. The new high-

7 New high-rise apartment buildings near the university area, Beijing.

rise buildings have had the effect of reducing casual social interaction. The effect is exacerbated by the fact that very few buildings have elevators so far more effort is required to enter and depart individual housing units. A substantial reduction in the number of children families now have, and the consequent number of neighborhood contacts they would create, has further contributed to the privatization of life in urban China.

THE CHINESE FAMILY

The very notion of 'family' is itself an enduring cultural value in China. A striking and persistent feature of the culture is the normative presence of intact nuclear families living together. The family is still the heart of Chinese society. Its stability and importance cannot be overestimated. Even the family name signifies a great deal. In China, there are few surnames. Surnames reveal one's geographic origin and status. Some names are associated with high intellectual standing. A person's name in China is usually made up of three parts: the surname is placed first, the generational tag is second (all children of a particular set of parents frequently have the same second name), and the individual's name is third, an ordering that reveals the importance of the family group *vis-à-vis* the individual.

Chinese families differ from each other in many ways, of course, but certain features of family life are characteristic. First and foremost, a strong interdependence exists among family members. One's identity typically is influenced far more by family membership than by individual personality or personal achievement. A family member's earnings, for instance, would probably go into a family account (usually managed by the mother), which would then be redistributed according to the needs of individuals as they arise. Parents take care of their children – even their sons who have their own families – with material and emotional support and they expect to be taken care of by them when they grow old. Traditionally, family responsibility extends even to worship of deceased ancestors.

The socialist system provides guarantees that certain basic needs are met and, in exchange, husbands, wives, and children who are past school age are all expected to work. Employment and living conditions are quite stable for nearly everyone – too stable, according to many, as opportunities for changing jobs or residences are slim.

The conduct of family life has become a major policy issue in China. Broad requirements have emerged: the one child policy, directed mainly at urban families, was designed to limit family size with the eventual hope of reducing the population in the next century. Educational and vocational opportunities are to be equitable for males and females. Equality in living conditions at home for adult family members is another socialist intervention into male-dominated family traditions. As Hareven points out, 'since all property is owned by the socialist state, the father cannot rule his family through control of family property as had been the case in the feudal organization' (Hareven, 1987: 672). Furthermore, elders are no longer to be respected and obeyed simply because of their age.

Of course these goals have not been entirely reached. It is no simple matter to stop hundreds of millions of families from producing babies. In fact, a relative baby boom took place in the late 1980s, requiring that the government give up its goal of limiting the population to 1.2 billion by the end of the century. Many parents, especially fathers, still want to have a son. It has also been no easy task for men to give up their longstanding domestic authority. Women still carry out the bulk of time-consuming chores at home. And despite government policy and the practical difficulties of changing residences, the divorce rate is increasing. Families with private unit status are less required to follow government rules about domestic life because they are far less supervised.

A tremendous emotional and pragmatic investment is made by parents in their children. The hopes of the family often rest on the children, particularly the sons. The one child policy has intensified the great Chinese preoccupation with children. Urban children get a tremendous amount of loving attention from their parents and in-laws now, creating what has been commonly called the 'spoiled brat' syndrome. Children bear great responsibility to carry on the name and reputation of the family. Nothing can damage a family more than to have a child – especially a son – fail at something, have an incorrigible personality, or make a major mistake, such as being caught in a crime. Conversely, the greatest form of flattery is to make positive comments about a couple's child(ren). To tell a father that his son is 'like a little tiger' is indeed a very great compliment.

Some government positions on correct family behavior follow time-worn traditions of Chinese society existing from feudalism through nationalism to socialism. Other official actions are meant to change certain aspects of traditional life that are now considered to be inconsistent with the ideological principles of the socialist revolution. In general, government requirements enforced since 1949 have been designed to piece together the 'best' of traditional Chinese philosophy with the egalitarian contours of socialist ideology. Family harmony, 'taking care' of each other, diligence, and respectfulness are all characteristics of Chinese society that were in place in China long before the 1949 revolution, and still exist in contemporary Chinese communities all over the world.

The sanctity of marriage is emphasized. Getting married is momentous in China for several reasons: the idea of landing a good husband or wife is paramount in Chinese culture; contact between males and females is a subject of moral education beginning in school where boys and girls are discouraged from talking to each other; there still is no real 'dating culture' (Whyte and Parish, 1984); the housing situation militates against unions that require additional space; the work unit of both partners must approve of the timing of the marriage; parental approval is very important; and household items must be stockpiled to equip the new home.

Chinese couples now have the right to marry of their own choosing rather than have the marriage arranged by the parents, as was the feudal custom. The dowry that was expected in earlier times is no longer a part of the transaction, yet it still exists sometimes on an informal level. Couples often have to wait a long time before they can get permission to marry. A young Beijing couple, for instance, eats dinner and watches television together at the home of the parents of the would-be groom, where they will reside after marriage, but they can't move in together yet. They have everything ready – a room, furniture, and a TV – but they cannot get any time off from work for a wedding ceremony and short honeymoon. So, they were waiting for the young man's twenty-fifth birthday to ask the work unit boss for permission to marry since birthdays are considered holidays and a little time away from work is normally granted.

Inside Chinese homes

According to the socialist plan, living quarters are to be functional, not showy. The relatively underdeveloped economy also limits the options, of course. So, the typical urban Chinese home is small and has few

57

decorations or material displays. Most older homes have no flush toilets or no toilets at all. Families use public baths and toilets.

Although the construction of apartment buildings has changed things somewhat in recent years, many families must share kitchen facilities with other families in the same building, a condition that can lead to conflict. There is no alternative to this arrangement, however, until more families can move into apartments that are equipped with separate kitchens. Sharing kitchen and bathroom space necessitates an enduring intimacy between families because neighbors rarely move in and out. In their study of Chinese immigrants to Hong Kong, for instance, Whyte and Parish (1984) found that the average time of residence in the same house or apartment for families on the mainland was 18 years and that only 10 percent of their sample had changed residence during the preceding five years, and only 1 percent during the previous year. Families know each other by the simple fact that they live so close together and rarely move.

Housing conditions affect many social activities, not just neighborhood relations. The prospect of marriage may be a romantic commitment for newlyweds in China, but it is a practical problem for everyone in the family because it typically requires that the couple move into at least semi-private space together. Many young couples first move into the home of the husband's parents. When the couple has children, there will be three generations in the house with the grandmother likely to assume much responsibility for raising the child. This is because both parents usually work while grandparents usually do not (many people retire at the official age of 60 for men, 55 for women, or before).

We interviewed one five-person family in Shanghai that lives in a single room measuring 8 by 12 feet. They sleep outside when it is hot and typically watch television through the front door. The family worries constantly about housing since it negatively affects nearly every part of their lives. The eldest daughter, a 28-year-old waitress in a government restaurant, does not want a romantic relationship until she can realistically expect to find separate housing. The mother says that the family wants to buy a sofa, but asks 'where can we put it?' Their 24-year-old son sleeps on a tiny portable bed that is put in the middle of the room every night. His mother said, 'Foreigners use this kind of bed when they are camping [a belief she picked up from TV], but we use it normally in our home.' There is a chance that the family will be assigned a new home in the future, but that does not help the children much in their effort to start their own families. The father complains, 'we cannot even dream for the children to apply for a home because of the shortage.'

Rooms in many homes are altered by time of day in order to change function. If a family has only one room the space is used at various times to serve meals, study, watch television, and sleep. Furnishings are moved around throughout the day in order to equip the room for its immediate purpose. Some families spend their leisure time and mealtimes at the homes of their parents or other relatives if accommodation there is more spacious.

Urban Chinese homes will nearly always have the following items: thermos bottles for keeping water hot, especially for tea; an electric fan; clothes cabinets and dressers for clothing (few homes are equipped with closets); television sets, radios, an audio cassette recorder; an electric clock; neon lights and exposed wiring; small stools or folding chairs sized to fit under the table in the main room; photographs of the family, either framed or placed under glass on the table where food is served; calendars and other print art hanging from the walls; a clothes horse or wooden hooks on the walls with apparel and towels hanging from them; small mirrors and sometimes a full-length mirror; a hard bed covered with a mat; various bottles, pans, and food-serving utensils; hand-held fans; plants; a newspaper or other publication with the current television listings; clothes, bags, purses, and an umbrella hanging from hooks on the wall; and other furniture or decorations that fit the size of the house, economic level, and tastes of the family.

TELEVISION IN URBAN CHINA

'Television is equipment the family cannot be without.' (51-year-old male personnel director, Communist Party member, Beijing)

The introduction of television into the homes of Chinese families may be the single most important cultural and political development in the People's Republic since the end of the Cultural Revolution. City dwellers now consider themselves to be, among other identities, members of the television audience in China, a self-image that embraces considerable cultural and political power. Television has become part of the Chinese family now, promoting a reorganization of daily activity, an expanded understanding of the meaning of the home, an altered sense of leisure time and how it is to be spent, and a challenge to many cultural traditions and official discourses.

Modes of viewing: stages of adoption

'Life is much better now. Before we were hungry and it wasn't easy to get a radio. We used to watch TV with friends in the city, but that was embarrassing.' (44-year-old female neighborhood monitor (and former farmer), no education, Beijing)

'We had one of the first television sets in Guangzhou. Our work unit [a medical facility] even had to borrow it sometimes. We invited our neighbors to watch. They brought small chairs and sat in front of

8 A Beijing family puts up an antenna for their new color TV set.

the TV in our front room. The house was so full of people we often had to stand to watch programs in our own house!' (70-year-old female, retired nurse, Guangzhou) 'But now they don't come to watch, even though we have a color TV and a VCR. We seldom visit each other any more.' (79-year-old retired male medical doctor, husband to the woman cited above, Guangzhou)

'Families don't join together to watch TV anymore. We don't want to bother our friends.' (26-year-old female waitress in a hotel, Guangzhou)

'A few years ago only a few people had a color TV. We wanted to

60

protect ours so we didn't watch it very often.' (11-year-old girl, daughter of an engineer and accountant, Communist Party family, Guangzhou)

We can identify four phases in the adoption of television in Chinese society. For the vast majority of the people, the first regular viewing took place in work settings and in public locations. The government placed television sets in front of party committee houses that are located in urban neighborhoods throughout the country. Dozens of families brought little stools on which to sit as they gathered around the sets to watch at night. TVs were usually placed out of doors, so bad weather prohibited viewing:

> 'Every alley had one TV set. Families brought chairs and sat there. You had to push yourself into a good position for viewing. There wasn't much on TV then, but we still liked to watch it. Unless it was raining, we watched every night.' (44-year-old female clothing factory worker, Shanghai)

The second phase of television viewing in China was also communal – in the homes of 'early adopter' families who either were able to afford a set or had been given one by their overseas relatives. As the elderly Guangzhou couple describes above, the transition from group viewing on the street and in work facilities to private homes sometimes even crowded out the host families. Those who had television sets may have had the luxury of convenient viewing, but they frequently had to tolerate congregations of viewers who were barely known to them. The tiny front room (sometimes the only room) could be filled with 20 people or more. More recently, many farm families have gone through the same transition. Furthermore, group TV viewing is still an important part of holiday traditions everywhere in China, especially in the rural areas, as is described by a sociologist in Beijing:

> An old woman told me that one Spring Festival's eve, many people went to her home to watch TV. The *kang* (a Chinese heatable brick bed, equal to the size of three double beds) was packed with viewers. Other people sat on little benches in front of the kang. That evening a vat of cold water (about 300 litres) was drunk by those visitors. Because there were so many of them, the hostess was unable to make tea for them ... TV [is] a main part of Chinese recreational activities and it mirrors a close relationship among people in the rural area.
> (Lu, 1987)

Cozy, if uncomfortable, scenes such as this one intensified personal friendships and antagonisms in the cities during this stage of adoption too. In some cases, according to our narrators, access to television was denied to neighbors who were not well liked by the host family.

9 A Shanghai family watches television in their only room.

The next two stages of adoption – saturation of urban homes with television and the transition from black-and-white sets to color models – represent current conditions which I describe in the remainder of this chapter. Television viewing still takes place in public in China but the locations and purposes differ from the early days. Now, some big department stores put television monitors and VCRs that play videotapes of American and Japanese cartoon programs in front of their buildings when the weather is good in order to attract customers. Group viewing is also common in some work settings and in higher education.

Television as a cultural nuance

The impact of television on the everyday life of urban residents can be understood partly by analyzing how people spend their leisure time. To some degree, the patterns of change reflect alterations that are characteristic of any society that gets television. But in China, TV entered an environment where leisure-time options are extremely scarce, where personal mobility is profoundly limited, where there is very little ritualistic activity (little organized religion and few social clubs), and where program content suddenly made the world visible to a society that had lived in near total isolation since 1949.

Television has replaced or altered many non-media diversions. A Beijing

62

viewer, for instance, told us that television viewing is an alternative to gambling: 'TV helps us avoid this problem. Now with TV there is no need to gamble for fun.' This man overstates television's ability to distract people away from gambling, which remains a huge problem in China. But for him, and for others who made similar comments, television is exciting. TV is an alternative to the street as a source of entertainment in urban China too. Some people say they seldom go outside the house after dinner now.[1] Even sleep has become a less prominent leisure-time activity since television arrived. A striking feature of everyday life in China is the uniformity of daily routines. Nearly everyone gets up early in the morning. Still the tendency for many families now is to extend the length of their evening leisure time to include more television viewing.

Of course, television has become a functional alternative for other mass media. Many people have substantially cut back on their movie-going habit as television is so much more convenient and many films appear on TV anyway. Even though work units continue to provide free tickets to movies, many workers do not bother to attend very often any more. Riding a bicycle to a movie being shown many miles away after working all day is no easy way to relax, especially when the weather is bad. One important implication of the availability of television in everyone's home is that the importance of the work unit as a provider of special leisure-time opportunities, and the authority that inheres in the power to distribute tickets, has greatly diminished.

Time spent with radio has also decreased, but not for the same reasons. Radio is just as convenient as television, perhaps more so, but it cannot stand up to the visual medium as an attractive source of entertainment and information. Reading novels is also said to have declined since television arrived as has attendance of live theater, especially presentations of traditional Chinese operas. Television viewing has not replaced newspaper reading; it has altered the time of reading. For many office workers, reading newspapers takes place during the day where they work. There is rarely an objection to this practice, so long as the worker completes the daily tasks and does not irritate the managers.

Family routines and television viewing

Nothing has affected the routines of Chinese families during the modernization period more than television. Very few urban residents believe that their lives have remained the same since television arrived. A 59-year-old neighborhood control attendant in Shanghai claims to have no favorite programs and says he does not like television at all: 'I follow my old habit – sleep. I go outside the house after dinner or I go to sleep.' A hotel attendant in Beijing told us that life is no different with television because 'the shows aren't any good.' Her husband agreed saying that he prefers to go outside or to friends' homes to play *mah jongg*. These firm rejections, however, are rare.

In the vast majority of cases, urban residents believe that their lives have improved considerably since TV came into their homes. Generally life before television is described as 'dead' or 'boring.' A heavy-duty machine operator from Beijing, for example, said that before television 'there was no other thinking except the government's educational meetings. Now, we have something to do with our time, something new to think about, and a way to relax.' Those three dimensions – passing and restructuring time; exposure to and interpretation of novel symbolic material; and changing the mental orientation – are common expressions of the impact of television on Chinese society. The first consideration mainly concerns family life; the second is primarily a matter of ideology; and the third is one of the psychological implications. I will discuss the latter two considerations in other chapters. Of interest to us here is the impact of television on family relations.

There is a time to watch television. A Beijing machinist said 'now we have some consolation after work. Without television you come home and have nothing special to do.' A 66-year-old retired grandmother in Beijing said, 'when it is time, you just want to watch TV.' Before television, families awoke on workdays (six days a week), went to work, returned home, fixed dinner, and occupied the early evening hours with some activity including socializing with family and neighbors, listening to the radio, going out to movies on special occasions, and generally going to sleep very early. Special habits developed within families, but uniform work requirements, the lack of leisure-time alternatives, and low-quality public transportation did not permit or encourage much diversity from family to family in their daily routines. So, what used to be a common routine with three major activities (work, eat, sleep) now has four basic features (work, eat, watch TV, sleep).

Adults don't return home until late afternoon on workdays. Chinese homes are not always vacant during the day, however. Very often the grandparents are home taking care of the child(ren). Daytime television viewing, therefore, is done primarily by retired grandparents and pre-school-aged children. The rapidly growing number of retired people in China has led to development of daytime programming that is designed for them.

Children who are old enough to go to school leave the house at about the same time as their parents in the morning and return in the late afternoon. Most of them spend some time playing with their friends after school. A 13-year-old Beijing junior high school student said, 'I go to school, play with the other kids on the street, and watch TV. That's all there is to do.' Many children run back and forth between their homes and outside after school and before dinner. But as one Beijing parent explained: 'When cartoons are on, all the kids from around here run into their homes to watch. When the children hear the theme songs of their favorite shows, they forget what they are doing and run inside to watch.'

Working adults arrive home about 5 o'clock in the afternoon. We talked with many families where men then look after the children and help with the cleaning and preparation of dinner. But in the majority of cases, families say that women are the ones primarily responsible for these duties in addition to their daily jobs outside the home. The sharing of domestic responsibilities in China is as likely to take place between women as it is between women and men. That is, working women may depend more on their retired mothers or mothers-in-law than on their husbands for help. And, of course, the daughter-in-law must always respect and help her husband's mother. Interaction between women of different generations is a product of shared domesticity that is made necessary by housing and economic conditions. It also follows the tradition of domestic cooperation within the extended family.

The period 5–7 p.m. is when families prepare and consume dinner. Television is sometimes used as a babysitter at that time as neither women nor men are likely to be viewing. Children's TV viewing may conflict with consumption of dinner in some homes, but this is not a big problem for many families because the television set is located in the same room where food is consumed. For young viewers, 6 p.m. is a special time since that is when the children's programs, including the action-packed Japanese cartoon shows, are on the air. The atmosphere of the home changes when the children's programs begin, an alteration of the environment that may be as important to the children as the shows themselves. The situation is very different for teenagers, however. They are far less likely than young children to be drawn to television routinely, preferring to spend time after school socializing with friends or playing sports. At 7 p.m. the CCTV newscast is aired, signalling the beginning of adult viewing. This is the start of 'prime-time' television viewing in China which they call 'golden time.'

Influence of space on viewing

Because of limited space, options for where families can put their television sets are few. Almost invariably the set is located in the largest room and is typically the visual focus of that space. In many homes it is placed in the corner of the room for the best viewing angle. Television sets in China are freestanding; they do not come in wood cabinets and they don't have legs. TV sets, therefore, are usually placed on top of something else, a dresser or desk for instance, and are often surrounded by knick-knacks and small decorations or household items. The area is frequently adorned

10 Men in Xian watch television through the front door to escape the summer heat.

with artifacts that reflect the personality of the family and the region where they live. Families value their television sets highly and often protect them with special cloth covers.

Television simply has an omnipresent influence in Chinese homes. When the set is turned on, there is nowhere to go in most homes to avoid at least hearing it. Chinese family members are just as susceptible as anyone to the medium's magnetism – its ability to capture viewers with constantly changing visuals and sounds. These proxemics create problems. The difficulty of limited space exacerbates television's potential interference with the homework of schoolchildren, for example. Because of this problem, several families we interviewed said they alter their viewing habits to accommodate the more important objective – providing an atmosphere conducive to concentration and study.

Television can also disturb sleepers. A special situation took place during our research period when the national television network carried satellite coverage of the World Cup football games from Mexico City. Nightly action began at 3 a.m. (Chinese time) and men of all ages set alarm clocks in order to watch. This ritual frequently disturbed others at home as it woke them up. On my return to China in 1989, several students I talked to said they were irritated by their parents who turn on television very early in the morning in order to exercise along to a program, *Old People's*

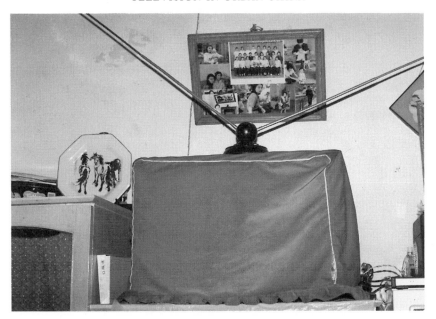

11 Pictures of family members displayed near the TV set.

Disco (*Lao Nian Disco*), a kind of Jane Fonda workout that combines slow-paced disco dance with *tai chi* movement. A college professor at Beijing University told me it is difficult for him to work at home in the evening because his wife and young son enjoy watching TV at that time:

> 'We were living for years in a one-room apartment. TV created a conflict for us. My wife and child like to watch TV after a day of work or study but I needed to work at home at night. I couldn't work there because it was so late when they finished watching TV that I fell asleep. So, for many years I slept in my office at school.'

Watching television

With important exceptions like the CCTV news and the children's programs, very few shows are scheduled for the same time each week. Many programs are one-time-only presentations. The irregular broadcast schedules discourage routinized viewing patterns. And, unlike the individualistic viewing styles characteristic of families in the West, watching television in China is almost always a social experience.

Children, of course, are the most animated viewers, constantly refocusing their attention from television to other attractions and back again. Consider

67

this situation: in Beijing we observed a young mother remind her 5-year-old boy that it was time for the children's program. She checked the printed schedule in the newspaper to see what was to be featured and then turned on the set. She settled him into a viewing position by removing the mosquito netting from a bed located in front of the TV where the child was sitting. The boy was excited to begin viewing. He laughed heartily at the image of a fat foreigner on the screen. Suddenly, after just a few minutes, the boy darted to the refrigerator, took out a bottle of soda, opened it with his teeth(!), and returned to his position in front of the set. He watched for a few more minutes, then ran impulsively outside to play with his pet turtle, bird, and squirrel. After less than five minutes he ran back into the house, watched TV for a few more minutes, then ran outside again to play with friends, leaving the activated television set alone for the remainder of the show.

Some illustrative cases

In the following paragraphs, I will briefly describe some different viewing situations that represent how television is accommodated into the daily routines of a variety of China's urban residents:

The children of a Shanghai family (a 13-year-old girl and a 9-year-old boy) do their homework after school, before dinner. They watch the children's program every night after which they review and do additional homework. The parents allow them to resume viewing until 9 o'clock, providing the school work is done. Since the entire family lives in one room, the parents don't watch TV very much, 'because if we watch, the children will watch too.' The couple sometimes watches reruns of the previous night's programs the following morning in order to circumvent the dilemma.

A Guangzhou family (he is a worker in a bicycle factory and has some elementary education; she is a public food-service worker with very little education) are non-stop viewers of television. They have two children – an 11-year-old girl and an 8-year-old boy. The family lives in a friendly, highly social, but comparatively poor neighborhood. The four of them inhabit one very small room that becomes extremely hot during the summer months. To be more comfortable they move the television set outside in front of their home. They also eat their meals on a table next to the TV. The black-and-white set they have is old (1978) and small (12 inches), so they have purchased a transparent screen enlarger which they place over the front of it. The young boy plays with his friends outside in the evenings and pays attention to television only when something catches his interest.

An 81-year-old man lives with his daughter's family in a Shanghai neighborhood. He awakens every morning very early (about 4 a.m.) and

68

goes for a walk in the park. At the park he performs *tai chi* exercises. He returns home to do 'home jobs' (washing his clothes, cleaning, etc.) and makes his own lunch. He takes a lengthy nap in the early afternoon, and then goes back to the park to socialize with his friends. He then goes home to make his own dinner and watch television in the early evening. He watches whatever is available, usually following the preferences of other viewers: 'It is not important to me to choose television programs.' He falls asleep early every night.

Eight people representing four generations live together in a three-room Beijing home. The old grandparents are retired farmers. Their son, a carpenter, is also retired but does 'neighborly work' now in front of his house. His wife and two adult children also live at home. Their daughter is 33 years old and unmarried. Their son is a year younger and recently married a woman who now also lives with them. This young couple has a baby girl. The family divides according to their interests in television programs. There is the 'old party' and the 'young party.' The old party (the retired grandparents and parents) like the Chinese opera. The young party likes contemporary drama and sports, although none of the women likes football. The daughter said: 'We fight over football. But we all like women's volleyball and China's team does so well. When volleyball is on television it will attract a whole room full of people. It can really cheer us up if the Chinese team wins.'

A fashionably-dressed and articulate 24-year-old Shanghai photographic technician lives at home with his parents, grandmother, and teenage brother. He especially likes foreign dramas and international news on television. He also uses some of the visual imagery that he sees on television to help in his photographic work. Most of his TV viewing is not done at home. He prefers to spend time at his girlfriend's home watching television or, even better, to go out to a video club, one of the latest trends in Shanghai, where current movies are displayed on a large screen. Ticket prices for video presentations are about the same as at the cinema, but the range of films is better, including many imported shows that never make it onto television. He says that 'there are not many good places to go out here. There are too many people.' He thinks that it is appropriate for people of the same age to watch television together because 'we have the same thoughts and interests.'

Fourteen young, male construction workers have come from out of town to refurbish the interior of a department store in Shanghai. They gather around a communal television set placed inside the store every night after work. There is usually no conflict over what is viewed since the group is relatively homogenous and tends to like the same programs – 'we just watch the best shows,' one said. They all sleep in the same room where they work and watch television. Young men like these do not live at home because their work assignments require them to be elsewhere. Married couples are sometimes split up too. For these people, most television viewing is done in work settings.

A mechanic at the Beijing airport lives with his co-workers in a nearby dormitory. 'We don't watch television every night because most of us go out somewhere,' leaving two or three people in front of the set. They never miss viewing football games, however, a scene he describes as 'noisy and fun. We argue a lot.' They vote when there is a conflict over viewing. The same type of situation was reported by a 22-year-old mechanic in a textile factory in Shanghai. He prefers to sleep at the factory rather than in his tiny home with his parents and brother. 'Usually there are about ten of us watching television there. It's more fun to watch TV at work – there are more people, more opinions.'

RULES FOR VIEWING

Generally, explicit rules about television viewing in Chinese homes are for children and have more to do with the amount than the type of viewing that is done. One widespread concern of parents is that watching television hurts the eyes of young children, and for this reason the amount of viewing they are allowed to do is often limited. Some parents, teachers, and children also express concern about children wasting time by watching too much television. A highly-educated Beijing couple voices this sentiment. According to the father: 'I'm worried about the influence of TV on my son. You know, you can watch TV all day long because now, with continuous programming, you can just sit down all day . . . If you lose control, that's dangerous, especially for boys and girls. If parents don't control TV, kids might spend all their spare time in front of it.'

The most common fear is that TV distracts children from their school homework. Many families indicated that rules for viewing are first articulated when the child reaches school age. The typical rule – that viewing can be done only after school homework is finished – is familiar in many parts of the world. It has a special meaning in urban China, however, because the vast majority of young families have but one child, education is highly emphasized in the culture, and the families must manage their overlapping agendas in tight living space. Viewing rules are most vigorously enforced during school examination periods. Also, many families will not allow their school-aged children to view late at night for fear that they will be tired at school the next day.

Let us examine one family's rules for child viewing: the parents are themselves well-educated, high achievers who fear for the future of their 10-year-old daughter. They live in a one-room home in suburban Shanghai. They closely regulate television viewing because they believe TV demands too much attention from everyone and especially distracts their daughter from her homework.

The family comes home from work every day, fixes and eats dinner, and cleans up. After dinner, the man helps his daughter with her schoolwork while his wife studies. They worry a lot about their only child because, according to the father, 'the worst thing about her is that she won't use her brain. She is not self-motivated. She studies only to please us.' The child knows perfectly what the daily routine will be and the mother diligently enforces the expectations.

The parents did not permit the girl to take a singing class because it was 'not useful.' They enrolled her instead in a literary composition class and in an English conversation class. The father said: 'She can already speak a little English. This will be helpful for getting her into a good school.'

Viewing the old (1976) black-and-white television set takes place only at certain times: when there is no schoolwork to do, on the weekends, and during vacations. The television set is regarded by the parents as an obstacle in the way of a good future for the child. According to the parents, the child 'loves to watch TV.' Her parents say that conflicting interests between what should be done and what the child wants to do 'separate the heart.' It is their duty, then, to 'control the situation.' With so much emotional energy invested in the future of children in China, anxiety about their academic performance has led to forms of extreme control in some cases, such as that portrayed above, with regulation of television viewing becoming a central part of the phenomenon. In this situation, such regulation becomes evidence of parental, and cultural, competence.

Many parents and students, however, believe that control over TV viewing should be imposed by the child himself or herself, especially those of secondary school age. As an 18-year-old Beijing student said, for example, 'TV does not affect the achievement level of high school students. It's just not possible . . . kids should control themselves at the higher levels of school especially.' This boy, and several others, claim that students who don't achieve simply don't work hard enough. Many high school students we talked to sincerely emphasized the importance of taking individual responsibility for giving TV viewing a low priority.

Limitations on control

Because television is such a central source of information and entertainment, it is difficult to deny its use to anyone. To ask someone not to view an activated set means that the person must try to find a quiet spot in the home, something that is not easy to do. A Shanghai mother, for instance, claims that she always sends her son out of the main room so that he can't watch TV during examination time. 'But it doesn't work,' she said. 'He always sticks his head around the door' (the family has partitioned its one room with movable flats). Spatial factors influence all aspects of television viewing in China, including parents' attempts to control their children.

Many families say that the interest children have in certain programs is the strongest determinant of their viewing patterns. A Beijing father, for example, said that he has no rules about television for his two school-aged boys: 'If kids have some kind of interest, you cannot stop that interest . . . I suggest no TV during homework time, but there is no absolute rule.' Another Beijing father said, 'During examination time there are some limitations, but during vacation they can watch as much as they want. It's their interest. What can I do?' Time constraints on parents also limit their ability to supervise children's television viewing. Some parents said that their family situations (e.g. long work hours; irregular work hours; a missing parent) preclude adequate control.

Program content rules

Very few parents disallow viewing of certain kinds of TV programs or particular shows, a fact that is best explained by the type of programming China has. Television programs are rarely thought to be a bad influence because of content. In fact, just the opposite is true. Many families encourage, nearly require, their children to watch certain programs. The more ambitious families, of course, are especially likely to call attention to programs they believe will benefit the children. One family referred to these programs as 'necessary' for children and several families said that selective viewing is part of a good education now in China.

POTENTIAL CONFLICT AT HOME: CHOOSING TELEVISION PROGRAMS

Each family we interviewed was asked how it selects television programs, especially when everyone wants to watch something. The question often brought interesting responses, typically accompanied by laughter and little stories. Families handle it in their own ways. Some claim that disputes over viewing are rare, while others say they are common.

Each urban center in China has a kind of *TV Guide* that is published by the local or regional television station. Daily newspapers also carry program listings, although people frequently complain that the listings are incorrect, a troubling condition generally believed to be the fault of the stations. Radio stations also announce the daily line-up of television programs. Viewers depend greatly on these media to find out what's on television. This constant seeking of information helps shape the overall experience that Chinese viewers have with television since, with few exceptions, they don't know what programs to expect at any given time. Consequently, most viewing is very selective.

Many times family members have the same interests, explainable in part by the presence of little attractive programming. Certain programs receive special consideration. These can be regular programs that are automatically viewed because of their excellence or popularity, irregularly scheduled shows that demand attention because they aren't on the air very often, or programs that have compelling educational or instrumental value. The program that most of the country was watching during our data-gathering period in 1986 was the Japanese soap opera, *Oshin*, a drama series of great importance which I will discuss at length in Chapter 8. There simply was no debate in most homes over what would be watched the two nights each week that *Oshin* was aired. Though the program appealed primarily to females, the question of whether or not it would be viewed every week was 'beyond argument,' according to a male viewer in Beijing who himself was no fan of the show.

The frequent consensus about programs to be viewed results not only from a lack of choices in a low-abundance TV environment, it also reflects a cultural tendency toward interpersonal yielding without conflict for the common good. Many families, for instance, cannot explain how they settle disputes, only that they characteristically give in to the desire of the group. To sacrifice a preference is a concrete way to demonstrate concern for others at home. Emotional outbursts, unreasonable demands, or purely selfish interests of any kind are generally unacceptable in Chinese culture, although the lingering resentment of the Cultural Revolution and the competitiveness promoted by economic reform have, in fact, fostered individualist tendencies in recent years. Conflict over television is also less likely to occur in situations where there are fewer people or where viewers are the same age. Old couples, for instance, usually have similar interests and few debates about what to watch.

Family position

Families are divided in their opinions about who among them generally selects television programs. Many family members say they defer to the wishes of older members of the household, though this was more often the case in the traditional northern cities than in the south. At times parents invoke family position as a justification for viewing, like a 56-year-old Shanghai father who said, 'When I'm home, I have priority. When I'm not home, my wife has control.'

Such assertions are rare, however. A fundamental conclusion I have drawn from the interviews is that the stereotypical notion of the male-dominated Chinese household does not characterize Chinese families' negotiations over television. While an underlying theme of parental respect was apparent in the discussions we had with families about this issue, certainly most fathers do not claim to be, and are not typically regarded by others to be, 'rulers' of the television set, a condition that differs greatly from the male dominance of nighttime and weekend TV viewing in Western cultures (Morley, 1986; Lull, 1982, 1988). Furthermore, the remote control device, which has become a symbol of male domination of television viewing in the West (Morley, 1986), is not a factor in China. In even fewer cases, however, is the mother identified as the controller of television viewing, except for the supervision of young children.

There is more agreement that children exercise great influence in choosing television programs (aside from the older ones' responsibility to do homework on school nights). Many parents say that the lives of children in urban China today differ markedly from the past and that the privileges children have with television simply reflect modern times. No doubt, children have a freer and more varied life than their parents had. A Shanghai father with three children, for instance, said: 'We don't hold the feudalist attitude anymore. We let the children enjoy themselves.' In some families, children routinely and unquestioningly control what is viewed at home. In many cases their control seems implicit; no actual decision had been made to grant them such influence. The grandfather of a 5-year-old boy in Beijing said: 'Everybody has to take care of him now . . . to spoil him.' A Shanghai couple said that they nearly always allow their children to choose television programs: 'We take care of them this way.' Most families agree that children 'always' or 'usually' win when preferences are in conflict.

Why do children have disproportionate influence in the choosing of programs? The answer is partly provided above. Chinese families focus a great deal of attention on their children, especially now that the one-child policy has had such a profound impact. 'Spoiling' a child is a positive act. Giving children the 'right' to watch what they want is an extension of this special consideration. Children also often have the most interest in television and are, therefore, motivated to turn on the set, monitor the offerings of the various channels (often without reference to the published program listings), and change the channel to suit their interests.

Of course, children do not always choose the programs. A particularly important consideration in Chinese homes involves in-laws. Some delicate situations arise when a young married couple lives with the parents of one spouse (almost always of the husband). The desires of the older couple, including their television program preferences, are almost invariably respected by the younger couple, and especially by the 'outsider' (normally the daughter-in-law). Troubled relationships between mothers and their daughters-in-law in China are common. Since young couples often have absolutely no choice but to live in very close proximity with the parents of the husband, daughters-in-law are normally very careful to maintain a harmonious relationship. Supporting the parents' TV viewing choices is one way to do this.

There are other family problems with television. Consider this case: a 33-year-old unmarried woman lives at home with her grandparents, parents, brother, his wife, and their year-old baby. She fears that because she has 'passed the marrying stage' and still lives at home, others in the house don't like her. She says that because of her 'unfortunate' situation, she cannot inconvenience her brother and his wife. According to her it is bad enough that she still lives in the house at all. She sleeps in the front room and claims that 'if I were married [and living elsewhere], they could take away my bed and change the whole room into a living room.' She feels very uncomfortable about this and privately told us that she cannot argue strongly for viewing her favorite shows as it could irritate her brother and his wife.

Avoiding the problem of program conflict

Every society deals with the problem of television program conflicts. The most feasible solution, at least in the more economically-advanced countries, is to have more than one TV set at home. In China only a small percentage of homes has more than one receiver. But when viewing conflicts arise, it is often still possible to go unannounced to someone else's home to watch a program. Disagreements, therefore, are often tempered by the fact that the extended family often lives nearby, even next door. Some arrangement can usually be made for one set to be tuned to one channel, and the other set to another channel, with fans of each show choosing their venues accordingly. Since there are typically only three or four channels in any city, chances are good that someone nearby will be watching the program that is not selected at home. This solution is not limited to family visits. A 25-year-old textile worker in Xian, for instance, told us that 'when something like this happens we just talk with the neighbors to find out who wants to watch what, then we go our separate ways. We just blend in with another family.'

THE POLITICS OF EVERYDAY LIFE

In China, nearly everything hinges on government policy. Supervision of family life in such an enormous nation is a management venture of unparalleled proportions. Despite the deep intervention of government into the family, home is still a haven for Chinese people and television viewing is one of few unmonitored activities. Ironically, government policy and national development have contributed, along with television, to the privatization of family life and detachment from the official culture. Family involvement with television came to the cities at the time of the one-child policy and when families started to move into large, impersonal apartment complexes. Furthermore, everyday life in urban China requires negotiating virtually all activity amidst many other people who are trying to do the same thing. Although viewers complain that there are few TV programs that really attract them, television viewing is often much more appealing than re-entering the stressful public space at the end of the day.

The speed of telecommunications media stands in ironic contrast to the historically slow and steady pace of life in China. Chinese citizens have a firm idea of what it means to be Chinese, a kind of lasting self-stereotyping that embodies a wide range of cultural qualities and traditions that persist in spite of technological and political developments and disruptions. The entry of television into the home – where it affects everyone in many ways – has become an important family issue that confronts a basic way of life that has endured for centuries. Everyone's needs and interests must be considered. Sorting through these priorities is family work, influenced by traditional cultural expectations in interpersonal relations and by the realities of the domestic environment.

Some cultural traditions such as sacrifice and yielding, restraint and control, and the emotional and pragmatic interdependence of family members remain fundamentally unchanged, perhaps even reinforced, by the choosing and viewing of TV shows. But there are some subtle changes in orientations toward gender and generation in Chinese families that are melting away partly because of TV. Leisure time for urban families increased at the same time that television became available, problematizing expectations around gender-specific family roles that were based on the domestic division of labor during a far more arduous period in China's history. While men still do 'men's work,' and women do 'women's work' around the home, considérations other than family position determine what TV programs are selected and the styles of viewing that ensue. Men don't exercise absolute authority over these matters. Families also often divide up along generational lines in what they watch and especially in how they construct cultural and political interpretations of TV program content (a topic I take up in detail in Chapter 8). These developments all point to the conclusion that in the process of television being accommodated into the routines of everyday life, it influences gender and generational relations by gradually smoothing out and democratizing these pivotal axes of domestic culture.[2]

Despite the changes, the family remains the centerpiece of Chinese culture, its collective way of life seemingly well suited to the socialist system. As Ju and Chu (1989) have pointed out, however, the family continues to function well while the larger collective enterprises, those of national economics and politics, have 'failed the people' and have fallen into violent disarray. The family, including its newest member, television, buffers the sometimes harsh reality of everyday life. But TV not only provides family entertainment or a way to escape reality; it is a rich resource for the construction of an alternative reality and a new political consciousness. The deep dissatisfaction and distrust that so many urban people have for the political system, as well as the confusion and competition that is promoted within economic reform, have intensified the intimacy and importance of China's 'natural' collective and its natural TV viewing group – the family.

5

CROSSING THE ELECTRONIC BRIDGE

The people and the people's medium

'The function of television is to connect the minds and the hopes of the whole world together.' (46-year-old male nuclear scientist, Beijing)

'A connection between the government and the people is necessary. We are not united, so we need a central information source. Television is better than radio for this purpose. It is more clear, efficient, and revealing than any other medium.' (37-year-old male teacher in an industrial economics college, Xian)

'Television provides direct understanding of government policy. It is especially good for those of us who can't or don't want to read.' (61-year-old male retired construction worker, Guangzhou)

'These days television is the most important influence on people's thinking. The government tries to teach us a new direction all the time. Now they are talking about the "spiritual civilization." Many programs touch on this. But is it successful? It depends. Some of the government's goals fit our situation while others are beyond our living stage.' (36-year-old male news film editor, Beijing)

Chinese mass communication researcher Wang Zhixing describes the official purpose of China's mass media this way:

> The mass media should function as a bridge through which information is delivered between [the Communist Party/government and the people]. This process of information delivery is . . . two-way communication. The mass media publicize the party's principles [regarding] decisions and policies which are in fact based on information [taken] from the masses in the first place.
>
> (Wang, 1988b: 2)

The principle of open and reciprocal communication between government and the people has been advocated in China since the birth of the socialist nation. Hu Yaobang said as far back as 1956 that 'leading the masses to

Communism . . . requires constant back and forth communication between the masses and the party. The party must be flexible in its response to mass demands and adjust its policies according to mass needs' (Womack, 1986: 10). In theory, then, television is the people's medium – the most modern and efficient means for assuring dictatorship of the proletariat. The 'bridge' is much more than mass media hardware and software. It is a way of conceptualizing and putting into practice a relationship between government and the people in a context that explicitly relies on a mutual sense of purpose and consent.

Television in many ways seems well suited for these objectives. It certainly has become the face and voice of government. Television's reach is especially effective for communicating with those who live in the most remote and least desirable parts of China, regions where the people have never had much sense of national identity. Use of the simplified written Chinese characters as subtitles for news and other programs is meant, along with the spoken Mandarin, to help overcome regionalism kept in place in part by linguistic differences. In its role as the government's most sophisticated conveyor of information, television has also replaced the frequent small group meetings that traditionally were called to announce new government policies and discuss problems. Cadre sometimes use television to communicate in work settings too. Near Xian, for instance, the managers of a high-achieving agricultural production unit subsidized workers' income for the specific purpose of buying television sets. The cadre claimed that they could not speak so eloquently as television for passing information along from the government to the workers. According to one of the managers, 'television is the best tool for thought education.'

In line with the proletarian vision of communication, the government should monitor the people's needs and interests, and these concerns should be reflected in programming of all types. Chinese broadcasters have developed special uses of television explicitly to function as an 'electronic bridge'.

EDUCATIONAL PROGRAMMING: THE TELEVISION UNIVERSITY

One of the very first applications of television in China was a direct response to the people's demand for education. The Beijing Television College began over-the-air educational broadcasting in 1960, but the Cultural Revolution interrupted this aspect of media development. The current system – the Central Radio and Television University (often called the 'TVU') – began in 1979. Technical aspects of the TVU fall under the administrative umbrella of CCTV now, but programming is initiated by the Ministry of Education. Lectures are presented, usually during the daytime, on special television channels throughout China. The televised

79

lectures are accompanied by local use of textbooks and meetings with teachers.

The Television University has become extremely popular, now enrolling about one million students, nearly twice as many as are enrolled in all of China's on-campus universities. TVU courses are designed to emphasize science and technology, with degree programs offered in electrical and mechanical engineering, physics, and mathematics. More recent offerings are in social science, economics, and other areas (McCormick, 1986), although the technical disciplines still dominate.

Work units often cooperate with the TVU by releasing certain workers to attend the televised lectures and participate in the related activities. The case of a 40-year-old woman in Shanghai is a good example of how this works. She is the financial manager for a clothing products company and is very hardworking and serious about learning. Her work unit recommended her for enrollment in the TVU. She attends TVU lectures and takes part in a study plan that will eventually qualify her for an accounting license, potentially increasing the quality of her contribution to the workplace. The work unit pays all costs associated with her taking the course. The woman was preparing for a midterm examination when we interviewed her. She claims that it is more difficult to pass the Television University course than regular university courses in her field because the central government makes up extremely challenging examinations. According to her, only about half the students enrolled in her specialty are able to pass the television course.

The Television University system reaches urban dwellers more than rural residents because of the higher literacy in the cities and the comparatively easy access to television, though this difference has lessened with satellite coverage. Despite advances in telecommunications, however, numerous difficulties beset the TVU. McCormick (1986) identifies four major problems that were also raised by our narrators: the perceived negative impact on workplace production caused by the release of workers to study; lack of sufficient local facilities and funds to support over-the-air transmission, especially in the rural areas; the fact that some cadre consider workers who want to enroll in the TVU as 'overly ambitious' (read 'threatening'); and complications that arise in job allocation following graduation.

Despite the difficulties, television is generally regarded by both the government and the people as an effective and convenient educational medium. In addition to college degree and vocational training programs, television has become an attractive alternative to the in-person adult education classes that were popular before. Beyond this, even the non-educational television channels carry much informal educational programming, including self-help and practical advice programs and foreign language training. Mass education has had a high priority in decisions that are made about how television is to be used in China.

12 A model worker display window in Shanghai.

13 'Marry late, give birth late, don't have too many children, have high-quality children.'

14 The government communicates to the people in a Shanghai neighborhood.

MODEL CITIZEN AND MODEL WORKER PROGRAMS

A striking feature of the urban Chinese landscape is the presence of bill-boards, posters, signs, and blackboards that promote government campaigns. These media prescribe everything from the most general goals ('Help build a better spiritual and material civilization'; 'Unite through the party and the four modernizations') to very specific tasks ('Marry late, have one child, have the child later'; 'Don't spit on the sidewalk').

Within this variety of public communication are model citizen and model worker campaigns where individuals are praised for improving themselves and society through dedication to socialist principles and hard work. Model

82

15 Even Chinese money is loaded with ideological significance.

citizen campaigns have been conducted for decades in China. The campaigns become particularly feverish during periods of national crisis – most recently in the aftermath of Tiananmen Square. Bigger-than-life historical role models like Lei Feng, a People's Liberation Army soldier known throughout China for his self-sacrificing, servile personality, are promoted as national heroes by repeated media attention given to their deeds. Chinese people are asked to emulate these government-sanctioned personages. Their very appearance through the media is promoted by the government as evidence of the people's participation in their political governance; that is, socialist ideals can best be represented by displaying the actual achievements of the people.

Model citizen and model worker campaigns are waged on television too. According to our narrators, however, these programs are among the least watched and least appreciated programs on the air. While some viewers allow that there is a place for these expostulative shows, and a few claim that the programs help motivate them in their work, the vast majority of the audience believes that these programs are irrelevant, uninteresting, and patronizing. Many viewers criticize the programs harshly. Typical complaints are that the shows are 'phony,' 'exaggerated,' 'unbelievable,' 'too positive,' and 'ineffective.' Audience members are suspicious of how the model workers are selected in the first place, claiming that special relationships and blatant self-promotion often influence the decisions.

People frequently laugh at what they consider to be the government's naive attempt to get them to unquestioningly follow the conspicuously didactic examples presented in these programs. One man, a 53-year-old male worker in a Shanghai boat factory, for instance, said: 'The model citizen programs are too strong, but then again we don't expect anything else. We're used to it. Before they *tell* us what they want us to do, we already *know* it.'

TELEVISION NEWS

'Freedom of the press means destruction of the absolute power of the government.' (21-year-old female university student, Beijing)

Just like many societies all over the world, Chinese people rely on television more than any other media source for news. Television news in China, however, is much different from that in most Western nations. For the most part, news is not meant to be objective and the people do not labor under any belief that it tries to be. The term 'propaganda' is used without apology in China. Journalism students are trained to write stories that promote the goals of the government. So, news should be selective and instructional more than objective and reportorial. Journalists should find facts to support official positions.

Journalism in China was originally used to establish the legitimacy of the Communist Party, promote the party's policies, and combat illiteracy. Journalistic practice has been irregular since 1949 (Womack, 1986). During the Hundred Flowers Movement of 1956, for instance, citizens were encouraged to voice their opinions on national issues and, caught up in the fresh spirit of openness, many journalists began writing more objectively and critically. But the Anti-Rightist suppression of the following year ended the brief period of permissiveness. Of course, objectivity was out of the question during the Cultural Revolution. Following the death of Mao Zedong and the fall of the Gang of Four, however, the trend has been toward unprecedented journalistic freedom and an implicit redefinition of 'news.'

The Thirteenth Communist Party Congress in October 1987 was attended by domestic and foreign reporters and the opening ceremony was telecast live for the first time on CCTV. This was a significant moment in Chinese political history, because a fundamental form of political control in China is accomplished not by the manipulative rhetoric of government authorities on television and the other mass media, but by their absence. By putting distance between themselves and the people, Chinese government officials over the years have been able to wield tremendous political power by elevating and mystifying their actions. Until recent breakthroughs on television, Chinese people have never had the opportunity to follow the actual process of their governance. Since television, politicians have had to become more accountable to the people. The most extreme cases involve Li Peng. In response to foreign and domestic journalists in April 1989, Li agreed to respond directly to questions about his political positions and personal history at a press conference, a situation that proved to be very uncomfortable for him. Li also faced up to striking students later that spring in a televised debate, a crucial turn of events in the midst of the political turmoil. I will take up these matters again in Chapter 9.

Today, of course, China is still rebounding from the shock of 1989. Journalism suffered a drastic setback. The widespread desire within the ranks of practicing journalists to continue the liberalizing trend crescendoed during the last few weeks of the resistance activities in Beijing, but the subsequent military-backed political repression has cut to the heart of press freedom.

China's news coverage of the last days of Tiananmen Square and the trials and executions of the alleged counterrevolutionaries – subjects which I also take up again in Chapter 9 – are but the most recent examples of how the Communist Party still ultimately determines what the people will learn through the public channels. This iron fist control is less apparent when things are going well for the government. But when China faces a crisis, reactionary forces once again assert their power, as Wang has shown in Chinese media coverage of natural disasters: 'Disaster coverage is like a thermometer of the Chinese media through which we can see clearly the media policy, the trend in media practice, [and] the conflicts between the mass media and other social groups' (Wang, 1988a: 21).

In a very interesting case study, Wang analyzed journalistic coverage of a 25-day fire that raged in northeast China in 1987. An advocate of journalistic reform, Wang was encouraged by the fact that journalists were allowed to give more details about the disaster than ever before. Even Li Peng, who was then Vice Premier, stated publicly that the incident should be reported more openly. But Wang also uncovered some troubling aspects of the coverage. People who were allowed to be interviewed were mainly government authorities and local citizens who praised the government for putting out the fire. Journalists were kept out of many areas and their reports had to be approved by a local authority. When one journalist was caught taking pictures of local leaders 'gluttonizing' at a dinner, he was beaten and accused of 'acting like a Western journalist' (Wang, 1988a: 20).

Invariably, CCTV and other television news outlets are late with their stories in crisis situations. Details of the Tiananmen Square incident were not reported for several days after the massacre and, of course, coverage was blatantly distorted. Similarly, an earthquake in Yunnan Province that took place in November 1988, was not reported by CCTV in a timely way and the eventual coverage was extremely brief. The overarching policy of the party becomes clear in cases like this: responsible journalism should not alarm the people. It is better to cover stories late, or not at all, than to confuse the people by not sufficiently explaining unsettling developments. Bad news is to be kept largely within confidential government channels (the 'internal channels') while the mass media (the 'public channels') are to be filled with positive reports. This stratified approach means that audiences for news in China occupy different informational 'classes.'

CCTV's 'international' news

Viewers watch the network news on their local CCTV affiliates and many also watch local or regional newscasts on other channels. Television news, especially the CCTV evening telecast, is one of China's most popular programs. Our narrators repeatedly said that television news is the most effective way for the government to communicate with the people.

Though viewers frequently refer to the evening CCTV broadcast as 'international news,' in reality the program is dominated by national 'news.' Domestic news occupies more than 80 percent of the international news program. When the big stories were breaking in Eastern Europe in 1989, for instance, CCTV focused its attention on domestic information. The lead story of one newscast I watched during that time was the announcement of a new bicycle tire that had been invented in China. The second story showed Taiwanese swimmers visiting China. The increasing production rate of a fishery was featured for more than five minutes. But it is the 'meeting story' – where hundreds of men are pictured taking notes as they sit in government meetings – that is most characteristic of Chinese television news.[1] The international stories are safe too – the San Francisco earthquake, a successful United States spacecraft launch, a bus accident in Australia, Laurence Olivier's funeral. Furthermore, there is nothing 'live' about the news. The entire program, including the segments where the anchorpersons are featured, is videotaped and edited hours before it is transmitted.

According to a study commissioned by the News Broadcasting Department of the CCTV Editor-in-Chief's office, television had become the preferred news medium of urban residents, at least in Beijing, by 1986. About two-thirds of the people surveyed said they watch CCTV news every day and 84 percent claimed to watch at least three times per week. Just two years earlier, Beijing residents said they relied on newspapers and radio more than television for news. By 1986 viewers described television as the most 'impressive, comprehensive, authentic, and convenient' of the mass media. In our interviews, many people praised television's immediacy, visual appeal, and ability to reach the rural areas.

Despite the popularity of television news, audience members are very critical of it. While some people said that TV news gives them a chance

16 The 'meeting story' on CCTV news.

to learn what the government is doing, far more said that news is propaganda, nothing more. One man, who is himself a news film editor in Beijing, defended this policy by saying that the instructional style of news is appropriate in China since the country 'still has so many illiterate people who don't have the ability to analyze . . . so, in this way we need leadership from the government.' But the majority of audience members are sharply critical, and many of them quite cynical, about television news in China. They are fully willing and prepared to analyze news events for themselves and simply do not accept the news as it is framed by the government. Instead, they pay close attention to the most subtle details of stories about what the Communist Party Central Committee is doing, for instance, so they can render their own alternative interpretations of what is really going on in China. It's a challenge for viewers to do so, a bit like trying to solve an ongoing political puzzle where new pieces are given out each night. The most common criticism, which recurred in the interviews we held in all four cities, is that the government promotes itself too much and that the emphasis is almost always on good news. Others complain that news comes late:

'Television news stays away from sharp problems. They hold the news down for a while. They send the good news out immediately and repeat it over and over. Sometimes in order to know the truth

87

about our own country we have to get the news from outside radio stations [for example, from Hong Kong, Voice of America (VOA), British Broadcasting Corporation (BBC), and others]. That's a pity. Foreigners might know something about our country that even we don't know. It is embarrassing for us Chinese not to know the problems with China.' (28-year-old male worker for a cigarette company, Guangzhou)

AUDIENCE INVOLVEMENT PROGRAMS

Many television stations give their audiences opportunities to participate in locally-produced programs. The Beijing station, for instance, answers letters on the air from its viewers. Variety shows all over the country feature local talent and have local studio audiences. One program pits families against each other – a kind of Chinese *Family Feud*. Shanghai viewers are asked to nominate local talent to be featured on a variety show.

The audience may also become involved through national appeals made by CCTV or individual stations. Funds were raised to help feed the starving people in Ethiopia, for instance. One of our female narrators, a neighborhood monitor in Beijing, said this is a particularly effective use of the electronic bridge, permitting instantaneous, widespread information to help solve a problem: 'We have to be thrifty because we are poor. But if a little money is collected from a lot of people, it could help.'

The innovative Shanghai station has a weekly program it calls *From the Audience*. The program begins with a request: 'Tell us what your problems are!' Viewers are asked to write letters to the station. Of course, if a viewer responded by saying that communism has outlived its usefulness or to complain about a national leader, the input would be quickly ignored. Still, viewers respond by the thousands. Problems that are mentioned reflect Shanghai's troubles – housing, traffic, garbage collection, pollution, crime, and health. The station staff sorts through the letters to select certain ones to be featured on the program. Sometimes the station responds directly to the problem. In one case, for example, a viewer complained about the service and cleanliness of a local restaurant. The station sent a camera crew there to investigate. Officials at the TV station claim that conditions at the restaurant improved greatly after the program was aired.

Programs such as this one resemble shows telecast in the United States and elsewhere. But in China the context in which these programs are produced and received is very different. The programs are meant to reinforce the fundamental idea that the people have a right to participate in the people's medium, that television should be their advocate. But common complaints among viewers of *From the Audience* type programs are that only a few viewers can participate, that only a small number of issues are raised, that sensitive issues are not touched, and, in many cases, that nothing constructive happens as a result of the program anyway.

CAN THE PEOPLE CROSS THE ELECTRONIC BRIDGE?

'I'm just an ordinary worker and my wife is just a housewife. We only want to watch our favorite programs and try to enjoy our lives. We have no reason to speak to the government.' (27-year-old male metal fabricator, Beijing)

'CCTV always tries to give you some little lesson. Talk, talk, talk, all day. It's always the same. We turn it off immediately sometimes.' (26-year-old female private unit fruit seller, Guangzhou)

In early 1988, a study was undertaken by the Public Opinion Research Institute of the People's University of China to investigate citizens' attitudes toward Chinese mass media as political instruments. The results point to a high demand for media reform. Some 62 percent of 200 people interviewed said that mass media performance in China is 'unsatisfactory' or 'not very satisfactory.' Viewers identified three major problems: the media are unable to check or criticize the government; government authorities are featured too much; and the 'voice of the people' is not heard on Chinese media. This official study – which probably underestimates the true extent of the negative perceptions held by citizens – resonates clearly with the comments of our narrators. Chinese people do not consider the electronic bridge to be a two-way medium.

Although the government itself originated and still advocates the official version of reform, many viewers believe that television programming does not realistically reflect the problems that must be addressed in reform or suggest effective alternatives to the status quo. The overall sense is that China has long been on the brink of reform, but that the government, in part protecting itself through television rhetoric, has refused to take the necessary next steps to advance the country. The critical sentiment of the people – as best it can be characterized in such general terms – is rarely present on Chinese television, a known-to-all fact that violates the most basic principle of the electronic bridge.

The exceptions have great symbolic value. *New Star* (*Xin Xing*) and *River Elegy* (*He Shang*), two astounding domestic drama series that were aired on CCTV, will be discussed at length later. 'Crosstalk' ('*xiang sheng*') exchanges, which usually appear as part of variety programs, also reflect the thinking of reform-minded and otherwise politically-engaged viewers. Crosstalk is a unique form of Chinese television entertainment where two interlocutors hurl rapid-fire verbal jabs at each other. It is an animated, comical debate. Each speaker tries to outperform the other through clever insults, puns, and jokes. During crosstalk debates participants attack their adversaries with biting criticisms that viewers recognize are actually indirectly meant to insult government officials, policies, or events. To use a simple example, if an interlocutor were to say, 'you are too old, you have no wisdom, it is way past time for you to retire from your job!' the remark would be widely interpreted by the audience as advice given to Deng Xiaoping, not to the debate opponent.

Another possible way for the people to cross the electronic bridge is through direct feedback to the image makers. But China's electronic media, especially CCTV, are very distant from the people. Criticism of all aspects of life in China, including media performance, is best given through letters to the editor of various newspapers, a common practice in recent years. Work unit and neighborhood meetings are also intended to be forums wherein the people can contribute directly to discussions of public issues. But this arena has changed since television arrived too. Before television, government policy proposals would be announced at meetings where discussions would follow. Now there are far fewer meetings and they serve mainly as a place to respond to policy that is first announced through television and the other media.

The diminished frequency and importance of group meetings has had a broad impact on the way the people view their own involvement in the workings of the government and society. Now they are rarely required to attend long meetings in order to talk over points of policy, discussions they feel would probably have little or no impact anyway. In that sense, television liberates viewers by greatly reducing a dreaded requirement. According to one Beijing woman, 'Since television came, they don't try to gather us up for meetings. Less people try to catch us and personally control us.' In certain ways, then, the government's plan to use television as a unifying force actually works to the opposite end. Home television viewing, unlike group meetings, cannot be required or supervised.

In most Western capitalist societies, television viewers are accustomed to the one-way tendency of the medium. Except for ratings research, which only measures viewership of shows that already exist, we don't expect to influence the development of television programs or policies. But in China, where the mass media are supposed to reflect the concerns of the people, much television programming has only reinforced widespread disdain for the heavy-handed, pedagogical manner in which information is generally given. The original concept of using television for 'constant back and forth communication between the masses and the party' has become hopelessly lost and abused. One effect of the bureaucratic and technological coldness of television in China is to remind the people of their nation's longstanding tradition of autocracy and the styles of communication that accompany it – from the imperial edicts of the feudalist era to the policy directives of the Communist Party today. Television technology and programming theory – transmitters that send, but don't receive; programs that are strategically developed to gain compliance for the objectives of an unresponsive government – mirror the worst of China's political past and present. Even today, high-level officials in Beijing are unlikely to realize all this, accustomed as they are to theorizing communication along the lines of a transportation model wherein information given out is thought to be information received, properly interpreted, and acted upon.

6

CHINA'S *NEW STAR*
Reform on prime-time television

Until *River Elegy* appeared on CCTV in late 1988, no television program produced in China had ever created a reaction among viewers to match the response given to the political drama, *New Star* (*Xin Xing*, pronounced 'sheen sheen'), a 12-part series that was telecast on the national network a few months prior to our arrival there in 1986. We had no knowledge of this program beforehand, but its importance became apparent to us very early during the interviewing. By the time we had talked with half a dozen families in Shanghai, our first research site, the name of the program had been mentioned spontaneously so often that we knew we had to explore the significance of the controversial show in detail. We added two simple questions to our list of open-ended inquiries that were asked of all families: 'Did you watch the drama series *New Star*? What did you think of it?'

From these questions families often launched into lengthy and sometimes very emotional descriptions of not only the program, but the sensitive political questions that are raised in the show – the viability of the government-backed reform movement and, specifically, a questioning of the morality and competence of the country's middle-level bureaucrats – the managers, officials, cadre – known in Chinese as the *ganbu*. Family members spoke freely about these matters, an openness that was enhanced by the fact that we had inquired about a television program and had not asked for their opinions about political matters directly. While Chinese citizens in the cities spoke critically without fear of reprisal in 1986, I believe that their remarks about the politics of the workplace, for instance, were far more freely forthcoming when placed in the context of the subject matter and storylines of a hugely-popular television program. This was a fortunate methodological circumstance that revealed in detail some of China's most pressing political and social issues – themes that were embodied passionately in the program itself.

By presenting *New Star* on the national network, Chinese television achieved a rare degree of relevance. The program was aired during a period of great public support for Deng Xiaoping. *New Star* will be remembered as a positive symbol of the Deng era, especially the decade of such great optimism following the Cultural Revolution culminating in the late 1980s when, by means of television, virtually all urban homes, and many in the countryside as well, had simultaneous access to the same story – a development that was without precedent in the country. *New Star* is a piece of electronic literature that touched nearly everyone.

New Star is a story about China's modernization but it does not focus mainly on technological or economic reform. The program is a blunt criticism of the heavy bureaucratism that plagues China and the horrible social consequences that it brings. At one level, *New Star* is an introspective attack on the current management dilemma in China, an exposé of the widespread incompetence and abuse perpetrated by many *ganbu* that has discouraged millions of young Chinese workers who are intimidated by their bosses in a system that rarely allows for the willful changing of jobs. At the same time, *New Star* symbolizes the 'new feeling' in China, in the words of one of our narrators, the spirit and consensus of a people who demand meaningful change.

The drama of *New Star* turns on the fictional encounters of a young communist political and economic reformer – Li Xiangnan (pronounced 'Lee Shan-nan'). Li's heroism stems from his courage to implement effective reform in the face of stiff resistance from China's conservative old guard. Li is a warrior against the muddled Chinese bureaucracy, its history of inefficiency, corruption, and reputation for placing profound constraints on the development of human potential. The program was popular mainly because the story resonates so well with the conditions and frustrations that workers and peasants routinely experience in their own lives. The production format also fitted the story. *New Star* was a political soap opera, replete with intricate interpersonal relations, a love triangle, family intertwinings, and traumas and tragedies of unbelievable proportions. The constant use of close-up and extreme close-up shots of the actors and actresses created an intense intimacy that enhanced the show's significance and impact. The contemporary reformation in China is a kind of soap opera in real life. Television's treatment of the story within the formulaic conventions of the melodrama was appropriate and compelling.

New Star is a story about two fundamental and contradictory issues – the potential progress that is promised by reform and the negative influence of a steadfast bureaucracy that stands in the way of change, personified by the old *ganbu*. It's an honest and straightforward critique of the Chinese system that was written by a Chinese man, appeared on the Chinese TV network (and on many regional outlets), was viewed, at least in part, by nearly everyone in the country who has access to a TV set, and stimulated an enthusiastic reaction by viewers. A major achievement of *New Star* is that its very appearance on the nation's television system gave credence to public complaints about the incompetence and corruption of many *ganbu*, while it cast an image of the possibility of a radical new style of party leadership.

The success of the program also helps reveal how television, the great storyteller of our time, can radiate its influence throughout a society. I shall tell the story of *New Star* from several perspectives – the producer, the originating broadcast station, the network, researchers, and most important, the audience members. The analysis includes many verbatim descriptions and opinions that were expressed by viewers.

THE CHINESE REFORMATION: CAN IT REALLY HAPPEN?

'During the Cultural Revolution the government told us, "You are good, you are good." But we were hungry. Why did they say we were good when we were hungry?' (42-year-old male battery salesman, Beijing)

'Look at my body. I am healthy. Deng took control and now we have a higher standard of living. You can eat whatever you want. In the past even peanuts were rationed by the government. Now nobody likes to eat peanuts.' (33-year-old male worker in a boat factory, Shanghai)

'In many ways the Communist Party has not helped the people at all. The party leaders work only for their own privileges. Big policy changes take place, but nothing changes at the local level.' (45-year-old male wood craftsman, Beijing)

The economic improvements that took place in China in the early 1980s are widely recognized by the people. Since then, of course, the economic picture has dimmed, but even in the mid 1980s the people were demanding more than economic reform. From their own experience, however, they know that an immense and corrupt government bureaucracy works against their great hopes for a radical restructuring of the system and for more personal freedom:

'We need to take true advantage of socialism and apply it to our real life. Even Deng Xiaoping says that the style of the party must change. They have had this disease (bureaucratism) for a long time.' (45-year-old male furniture factory worker, Beijing)

'The idea of the reformation is well matched with young people now.' (16-year-old female radio factory worker, Xian)

'In my office everybody thinks that China needs to be reformed. Young people especially think it's very important.' (22-year-old male hospital administration clerk, Beijing)

'Now everybody realizes that we need to reform. But it's hard to walk a step ahead in my own job, so I can imagine how difficult it is to accomplish the reformation. Still, with no change, there is no future for China.' (49-year-old male English teacher at a business college, Xian)

'To "think" the reformation is much easier than to "do" it. We haven't done it.' (28-year-old male taxi driver, Guangzhou)

Within the rhetoric of reform, the government has admitted the problem of China's unmanageable management system, the human penalties it imposes on peasants and workers, and the need for revision of management procedures at the work unit level. Deng himself outlined the problem as early as 1980:

> Bureaucratism is expressed in sitting high above the people, using power in an indiscriminate way, becoming divorced from reality and the masses, being fond of keeping up appearances, a liking for uttering empty words, mental ossification, sticking to old ways and conventions, swollen bureaucracy, delaying the handling of matters, paying no attention to inefficiency, failing to take responsibility, failing to keep one's word, endless circulation of official documents, and mutual passing of the buck. All this results in a stuffy atmosphere, reprimanding others on the slightest provocation, retaliating against people, suppressing democracy, cheating those above and hoodwinking those below, acting in an imperious and despotic way, engaging in bribery and corruption, and so on . . . all this has reached an intolerable stage.
>
> (Nathan, 1985: 75)

These formidable problems have been heightened by China's lack of a legitimate legal system, the uncertainty that surrounds processes of political succession, the equivocations of national agencies of information and socialization, and, especially, contradictions that exist between officially prescribed ideology and what happens in the real world. Nowhere are these contradictions felt more strongly than in the workplace.

Ganbu in service of the status quo and the *Guanxi* problem

'China is not like other countries where you can make money or be famous because of your talent. Here the relationships make it much more complicated.' (19-year-old male art school student, and son of parents who are party members, Beijing)

'I work with no opinion.' (29-year-old female worker in a VCR factory, Shanghai)

The positive impact of China's concrete achievements in the early 1980s and, ultimately, the viability of the communist system are confounded and diluted by the day-to-day experiences of the vast majority of urban workers. They made it clear to us that improvements promised by reformers in Beijing have not filtered into the workplace. I want to illustrate substantively the depth of this problem by recounting actual conditions of work that were described in detail by our narrators.

A key feature of the problem is the practice of *guanxi* (pronounced 'gwan shee,' meaning the reciprocal giving of favors) and the formation of *guanxi wang*, interpersonal networks that are based on this practice. *Guanxi* originates in the Chinese tradition of interdependence and sharing and is consistent with the Chinese habit of family members and friends 'taking care of each other.' It derives from the Chinese concept of *bao*, or 'social investments,' where the giving of a favor carries an unspoken, but firmly understood expectation that the giver will receive something of equal weight in return (Gold, 1985). *Guanxi* is an informally institutionalized 'I'll scratch your back if you'll scratch mine' way of doing business that, while officially discouraged, is widely practiced. One builds *guanxi*. A person has good *guanxi* with somebody else. *Guanxi* is pragmatic relationship capital. Economic scarcity and a system that provides limited opportunities for individuals to advance through legitimate, official channels breeds dependence on informal, personal connections – *guanxi wang*. Furthermore, the potential for benefitting from *guanxi* is not evenly distributed within the population. People who supervise official functions (for example those who assign housing, promote workers, permit marriages, or admit students to universities) are in positions to require favors in return. Although their salaries may be low, cadre in these positions can live relatively well by demanding personal favors and goods (food and alcohol, for instance) in trade for material resources or administrative actions that are under their control. *Guanxi wang* reinforces and expands bureaucratism while it promotes corruption at every level of government in China:

> 'There is no way to close the back door. You even need a relationship with a store clerk to get what you want. It's not fair.' (26-year-old female travel agent for river tours, Shanghai)

> 'There are two ways to buy good products in China – with a lot of money or with *guanxi*.' (28-year-old male export trade specialist, Beijing)

> '*Guanxi wang* is just like the Mafia.' (26-year-old male graduate student, Shanghai)

Ganbu politics

The *guanxi* problem is but part of the delicate nature of interpersonal relationships in work settings in China. Workers are at the mercy of their *ganbu* – the middle-level managers of China's factories, farms, offices, and agencies. Many workers consider their *ganbu* to be members of a privileged class. This is not a recent development. Cadre and worker statuses were very different during the Maoist era too, despite the egalitarian rhetoric of the time (Dietrich, 1986: 278).

There are many problems inherent in the worker–*ganbu* relationship, beginning with the fact that many managers are not respected much by their workers. The difficulty begins with a questioning of the qualifications and competencies of the *ganbu*:

'My work unit leader is a party member and a Vietnam veteran. He got a special government award and was given a leadership position because of it. Otherwise there is no special quality to this man. He is of terrible ability. He cannot control production.' (28-year-old male worker in an automobile factory, Shanghai)

'The old *ganbu* are too conservative. They miss the contemporary way of thinking and they have no guts. They "look left and look right." They create problems for young people. That's the problem of our entire society.' (22-year-old male hotel employee, Beijing)

'Middle-level *ganbu* are very conservative and stubborn. This is because they never had a chance to see how fast the world is developing. They only think, "we are so good." They are narrow-minded. They say, "follow me," but no one is willing to take responsibility.' (63-year-old male school administrator, Shanghai)

The negative stereotype of China's middle-level managers is that they are inefficient, lacking in ideological vision, poorly educated, old, abusive, corrupt, jealous of young workers, vindictive, protective of their private interests (in traditional China and even now it is considered a disgrace to flaunt one's private interests), and often gained their positions through political favoritism – hardly the right type of leader in the era of reform. They reward the 'yes' man and woman and punish troublemakers – people who disagree with them. Workers' rights are few and there is no effective system for fair redress of grievances in any case. As a result, many workers fear their bosses and develop strategies for coping and not standing out:

'I don't work too hard. If you are a good worker the *ganbu* won't give you a day off. So, I just fool around and pass the time at work.' (26-year-old male factory worker, Shanghai)

'They give you a job and you just work the job. We are not

97

naughty . . . we don't fool around or make trouble. We come to work on time and we don't leave too early. We just try to blend in.' (32-year-old female electronic assembly worker, Beijing)

'Generally the attitude at work is, "you don't bother me and I won't bother you." ' (33-year-old male factory worker, Shanghai)

'In our daily life when we find a problem with our *ganbu* nobody wants to say anything. Everybody is afraid to wear the small shoes (to be eternally punished). So we don't always see the problems of our *ganbu*. We open one eye, but we close the other eye.' (30-year-old female accountant in an electronic products retail store, Shanghai)

'When we think about why someone in our department is *xian jin* [considered to be outstanding: literally, 'first, keep going'] usually it is because of his relationship ability.' (49-year-old female accountant for a redistributable products company, Shanghai)

'If you have a good relationship with the *ganbu* you don't have to work very hard. Even good workers who don't have a good relationship will never have a chance to be *xian jin*. In your whole life you just work.' (26-year-old female television factory worker, Shanghai. She is the daughter of the woman who made the comment quoted directly above)

The way so many Chinese people describe the atmosphere at work reminds me of military life. Low and middle-ranking officers rise to their institutionalized level of incompetence where, in a system of highly-structured statuses and a constant threat of punishment, they unleash their authority in a way that rewards mindless compliance and discriminates against progress. In many Chinese work units, as in the military, the supreme value is conformity.

Another problem frequently reported concerns the higher education and specialized training of ambitious and bright workers. Many *ganbu* don't want these workers to study abroad, for instance, because the student-workers often have high unofficial status when they return to China, an automatic credibility that makes some *ganbu* jealous. There is a Chinese expression, 'to keep someone short,' meaning that people in power are often jealous of 'taller' people (meaning smarter, better educated, or more clever) and will find ways to limit the taller ones' potential. This is one reason why so many Chinese who have studied overseas have not returned to China. Lucien Pye describes this problem and recounts an interesting story:

Even more troubling are the reports that students trained abroad in technical skills appropriate for China's modernizing effort are not effectively used when they return to China. The problem does not

98

lie with the top leadership, who apparently want to upgrade the Chinese pool of modern trained talent, [but with] [l]ocal cadres, who have less education, may be resentful and may exploit China's egalitarian system by making petty demands on the returned students. In a particularly noteworthy, but not untypical case, Xiu Rui-juan achieved the remarkable distinction while at Stanford of publishing her research, which became known in medical literature as the Xiu Theory; but upon getting back to China she was assigned to the modest position of 'deputy research fellow' in her medical institute until the scandal came to the attention of Hu Yaobang, after which she was made a research assistant.

(Pye, 1985: 194)

Obviously I have painted a very bad picture of China's middle-level bureaucrats. But the themes outlined so far were repeated over and over by Chinese family members. Of course, some favorable reports were given by workers about their bosses. Several people spoke proudly of the accomplishments of their work units, the talents of the *ganbu* there, and the hope that this offers Chinese society. Typically, however, favorable accounts were given about young or well-educated *ganbu*. Many new management positions in China require high or specialized education.

Eradicating or, more realistically, reducing the *ganbu* problem cannot help but be an extremely slow process, regardless of high-level intentions and instructions. Many cadre consider the reformation to be a personal threat. They fear a loss of power and possibly the loss of their jobs. Most *ganbu* believe that they deserve to keep their positions. They won those jobs often through sheer loyalty to the system. They are hard-nosed 'old boys' (most are men) who cannot be moved out easily. Regardless of how they got their jobs (political maneuvering during the Cultural Revolution is an often-mentioned and hated reason), it seems impossible to deconstruct the structure in which they are embedded, regardless of ideological pronouncements. The party, then, is stuck with the image of the incompetent *ganbu*. Some people say that ultimately the best hope for reform is to simply wait for better-qualified men and women of the next generation to take over these positions. Others are unwilling to wait.

THE REFORMATION WILL BE TELEVIZED

'Most people want reform. We must reform, otherwise we cannot be a strong and rich country ... [*New Star*] ... really shows how the old *ganbu* cannot follow the new thinking ... [also] *New Star* reflects people's problems and criticisms. This is the main reason why we put *New Star* on the air.' (Wang Chuanyu, Director of Production, CCTV)

99

'Without reform we cannot continue to move our country forward. So, this is the most popular current issue among audience members. *New Star* just matches the tendency that everybody is talking about – the reformation.' (Pan Huiming, Deputy Director, Guangdong Province Television Station, Guangzhou)

The world's largest television audience watched a fictionalized version of the reformation unfold in their homes when *New Star* was telecast in China. The appearance and appeal of the young reformer – Li Xiangnan – and the bold critique of the bureaucracy and bureaucrats was most timely. Li became television's version of the vigorous leader who is expected to guide China on its way to meaningful reform. The setting for the story, rural China, was appropriate since early economic reform was directed toward revamping the concept of collective labor in the countryside in hopes of minimizing bureaucratic sluggishness and increasing agricultural production. Just as the Cultural Revolution had legitimized and strengthened the bureaucratic structure that paralyzes the country today, *New Star* is a feature *sui generis* of a new Cultural Revolution, a struggle to overcome some of China's most deeply-entrenched and debilitating social and political practices.

Development of the television series

Ironically in a system that is based so fundamentally on planning, the most important television series to have ever been produced in China found its way onto the air via an irregular and controversial path. *New Star* was not intended originally to be a television series and it was broadcast on the national network almost by accident.

The story on which the television series was based was written by Kuo Yunlu, a factory worker who had lived in Shanxi Province, an arid expanse of land located in the northeast part of the country. The author is a member of the 'lost generation' of Chinese men and women whose most formative years were interrupted by the Cultural Revolution. Kuo was dispatched to the countryside in 1968 before he was 20 years old. That awful experience, combined with his extreme interest in the structure of leadership in China and his contact with persons in power who were sympathetic to his viewpoint, inspired him to begin writing a story about the carrying out of reform in China. The result was a novel, *New Star*.[1]

Kuo's unpublished novel first appeared in 1984 as a series of articles in a literary magazine (*Contemporary*) and was also produced as a radio drama, but neither the articles nor the broadcasts received much attention from the public. In late 1984, however, a new television station operating in Shanxi Province began to transmit programs for the first time. Operating out of an old building with little equipment and only 1,000 watts of radiating power, the station transmits from the city of Taiyuan, located in the middle of the province, about 200 miles southwest of Beijing. Programmers at Taiyuan Television (TYTV) had little experience developing locally-originated programs, but *New Star* seemed to be an excellent candidate because the author is from that area and the story had already been written. The station's only previous attempt to air an original drama (*Jin Ein Wan*, a story about the life of a miner) was criticized as 'too plain' and had not attracted much of an audience. Fully aware of the sensitive nature of the story in *New Star*, the managers of TYTV decided to produce an uncompromising TV docudrama miniseries based on the novel. Although it can be argued in retrospect that the basic version of reform that is presented in the program is one which is advocated by the Communist Party itself, the political consequences of producing such a scathing critique of the system were certainly risky for officials at the Taiyuan Television station. Their decision to produce and air this program – the first ever about reform and by far the most critical television show to have ever been made in China – was a courageous act.

There was not much money or equipment available to produce the 12 hour-long episodes. In the end, the program was produced for about 250,000 yuan – the equivalent of roughly $800,000 US, about half of what it would have cost to make just one feature-length film in China at the time. Still, the series came in under budget by 50,000 yuan. Originally the production company had only one box of stage property and a single camera that was borrowed from the Taiyuan Iron and Steel Company. Station personnel and the producer of the program – Ching Darli – admit that the challenge they faced in producing *New Star* was a sobering one at the beginning. The station was a start-up operation and financial resources were slim. But excitement and a positive spirit surrounded the production of *New Star* from the very beginning.

High-ranking government authorities in Taiyuan agreed with the strong, activist perspective on reform that is portrayed in the story. They enthusiastically endorsed the series and raised more than 300,000 yuan in support of the production and promised more money if needed. Volunteers were everywhere. The province police department donated uniformed guards and a doctor to work on the shooting location. When 'extras' were needed on the set, the uniformed workers changed into farmworkers' clothes and became part of the production. In order to keep costs down, virtually everyone associated with the program, including the producer, director, stage manager, even the stage hands, also had roles in the story. Hundreds of local villagers and farmers also volunteered to assist in the production and were dumbfounded when the production company tried to pay them for their services. To the very end, the extras refused to accept money for their parts in the production.

New Star was directed by Li Xin, a little-known director from the talent pool of the Beijing Film Production Company. He made the decisions about who would be given the major roles and he carefully selected actors and actresses who were not particularly well known but who were caught up in the spirit of the project – both the ideological nuances of the story and the idea of helping to establish a new television station. When the production contract for *New Star* was first negotiated, two other companies (Chang Cheng Film Production Company and the Chinese TV Drama Production Center) also came to Shanxi Province to compete for the right to produce the show. But officials from TYTV settled on the small production unit whose leaders had so aggressively pursued the project and refused to be intimidated by the presence of the larger production companies during the negotiations.

The 12 episodes of *New Star* were produced in 102 days, averaging less than 9 days shooting time per installment, a remarkable achievement given the variety of locations and number of actors involved. The series was first broadcast on the local province station, TYTV, beginning on the first anniversary of the new station. Audience response far surpassed expectations, attracting the attention of the entire city. Based on its overwhelming success at TYTV, *New Star* was bicycled to dozens of other stations in China where it also became very popular.

Ching Darli and the others from the production team would not be satisfied, however, until *New Star* had a national audience. They wanted the show to be distributed throughout China on CCTV and tried to convince the broadcasting officials in Beijing to put it on the air. There was no serious question at CCTV about the ability of the program to attract a viewership large enough to justify presentation on the national network. However, concern was expressed about the sensitive political content of the drama. Despite the potential difficulties, CCTV broadcast the series in winter and early spring 1986.

The decision-making process that led to airing *New Star* on the network remains something of a mystery. As the story has been told to me, the series was received and supported by a ranking network official who was only filling the position temporarily. A question remains even today as to whether or not top officials at the network ever previewed and approved the program. Still, at least one meeting was held about *New Star* after which approval to air the show was granted. Precedence was extremely important. The series had already been presented on many city and province stations throughout China. Had the program not been aired by other stations, or had it been aired only by TYTV and rejected by other province stations, it is unlikely that the network would have touched it. The fact that few high-quality drama series are produced in China also helped *New Star* find a network slot. Television is a medium with a voracious appetite and producing original programs is extremely expensive. It is an attractive proposition, therefore, for the network to broadcast programs that have already been produced.

Circumstances surrounding the way *New Star* was produced further enhanced its chances for being aired on CCTV. Content of the original novel and the shooting of the series in Shanxi Province were never under serious scrutiny by censors. There was little chance for interference or termination of the project during the making of the show. *New Star* arrived at CCTV as a finished product. Compared to film, which can be evaluated in one sitting by government officials, a 12-part television series is far more cumbersome to review. Some Chinese scholars have speculated that had *New Star* been a film instead of a television series, it would not have passed the censors or would have been greatly toned down. Despite all the mysteries and complications, a decision was reached to put *New Star* on the air at CCTV during peak viewing time in the evenings. *New Star* appeared on the network during the dead of winter when family members are inside their homes at night – watching television.

The national exposure thrilled people in Taiyuan. According to one account published in China, when the familiar theme song from the show pierced the airwaves and the TYTV logo appeared on the CCTV channel in Taiyuan, the local television contingent excitedly ran outside their offices and ignited a firecracker to celebrate its appearance on the network (Wu, 1986).

Additional meetings about *New Star* were held at the network offices in Beijing *after* the first two episodes were broadcast. The program had created a national controversy soon after the first episodes appeared. While feedback from audiences throughout the country was overwhelmingly positive, high-ranking government officials were divided in their view of the appropriateness of the program. Some were adamantly opposed to it. Clearly, however, a decision to pull the program off the air would have damaged the credibility of the government which was heralding reform at the time. *New Star* had become at once an extremely popular show, a topic of conversation throughout the country, and a public relations problem for a government that was trying to display a more open and self-critical attitude. A new decision was reached to allow the series to continue. One family member with whom we spoke said that, in fact, one of *New Star*'s best effects was to influence China's government leaders who he reasoned correctly were as likely as anyone else to be watching.

NEW STAR – A STORY OF THE CHINESE REFORMATION

The television series has many characteristics of Chinese literature. The story is complex and slow developing, full of double meanings and innuendos. In the following paragraphs, I will outline the basic storyline, episode by episode, in order to reveal its major themes and to provide

17 Li Xiangnan and Gu Rong talk about the future of Gulin County.

interpretations of the cultural and political subtleties that are woven into the program.[2]

The drama hinges most basically on an ideological conflict between the two main characters – Li Xiangnan and Gu Rong – and the intricate relationship between their families. This meshing of political circumstances and social histories, embedded and embroiled in the controversies that surround China's reformation, is part of what made *New Star* so popular. It is exactly this atmosphere of personal interdependencies and politics that so many Chinese people complain about. Several subplots and stories – not just political struggles, but family traumas and love affairs too – emerged throughout the series. But the heart of the story, and the theme that was discussed by audiences everywhere in China, is the conflict between the handsome young political reformer, Li, and the guardian of the status quo, the old *ganbu*, Gu.

I will now describe in greatly abbreviated form what happens in each episode. The main characters, story developments, and the most important underlying implications will be introduced along the way. The two main characters, Li and Gu, will be referred to by their family names only. Others who have the same family name, Gu Shaoli and Gu Heng, for instance, will be called by their generational/personal names (e.g. 'Shaoli' and 'Heng'). The program does not move along chronologically. Rather, simultaneously developing subplots are presented, in soap opera fashion, and my accounting reflects this fragmentation. In order to comprehend the complexity and depth of the problems explored in *New Star*, it is extremely important to read this summary carefully.

Episode 1

Li arrives by train in a village said to be the capital of fictionalized Gulin County, part of a poor, dry farming area that bears a strong resemblance to Shanxi Province, home of the author. Li is a young Communist Party member from Beijing. He has been sent to Gulin County to become Party Secretary there. He is met by the Party Vice Secretary, Gu, a much older man, who will become Li's antagonist throughout the series. According to the bureaucratic structure, Li is Gu's boss. But Gu's older brother, Heng, is Party Secretary of the province in which Gulin County is located. To make things more interesting, Li's father, Haitao, has an even higher administrative post in Beijing. Beyond this, the old men all know each other from the days of the communist revolution.

Li and Gu must work together in Gulin and there is much work to be done as the county has a very poor reputation for productivity. Upon Li's arrival, Gu advises him about protocol in accomplishing their work: 'Don't talk too much . . . don't criticize past work . . . proceed slowly, listen, and follow me. You may have trouble if you go too fast.' Gu further advises that no changes should be made immediately, that 'research' should be conducted first. Li politely disagrees: 'No, we can do both at the same time.' Gu confides to a friend, 'Li cannot be controlled by anyone.' We begin to see big differences in their personalities and leadership styles. Li is the straight-talking intellectual who is concerned with fairness. Gu is the manipulative veteran bureaucrat – the classic stereotype of the incompetent *ganbu*.

In their first concrete struggle, Li orders analysis of a problem revealed by a woman who claims she has been discriminated against in her work by her *ganbu*. Li wants to know how many cases like this exist. To Gu's great embarrassment, his own son is implicated in the problem as a smuggler of antiques, as is the son of one of Gu's fellow cadre, Feng. A continuing theme throughout the program is that Gu is somehow involved in many corrupt activities in the county. There is a constant blurring between bureaucratic privilege and illegal activity for Gu. He appears to be motivated by personal interest while Li is the people's advocate.

A town meeting is held where Li is introduced and is obliquely criticized by Gu for his aggressive style. Li then addresses the crowd: 'The work here is not done efficiently. You don't serve the people. The Communist Party says "Take care of the heart and soul of the people." We must support the people.'

Lin, Li's former girlfriend from their teenage days during the Cultural

Revolution, arrives in Gulin. So does the attractive Xiaoli, who is Gu's niece. Lin is portrayed as soft, while Xiaoli is tougher – aggressive and ambitious. Lin is a journalist. Xiaoli, who is ten years younger, also wants to be a writer. Xiaoli meets Li and immediately begins arguing with him, testing him. An intriguing tension between the two develops. There are some things to explain. Li is not married. At his age, apparently in his early thirties, this is unusual in China. If someone is not married he must have some problem. A bad temper or incorrigible personality? Too personally ambitious? Why isn't Li married?

Episode 2

Li appoints a new director of policy research to replace an old *ganbu* who would not do the work the way Li wanted it done. Li then walks among the villagers to get the general feeling of the situation. He meets Xiaoli on the street. During their conversation, Xiaoli asks Li if he likes the clothes she is wearing and he tells her that they may be too modern, not appropriate for the farm country. A romance, however understated, seems to be blooming.

Li meets a poor woman who has come to tell him a story of the tragedy of her husband's death. She pleads for financial and medical help and says that she has walked 25 miles from her home to the county government headquarters more than 50 times in her previous efforts to get help from Gu but received no attention. She claims that she had been unable to prove to Gu her need for help. Li comforts her, assuring her that she need not prove anything, saying that all those trips by foot are proof enough. This is a critical incident in the story because it reflects Li's personal caring and his ability to cut through the bureaucracy and to act immediately. This leadership style contrasts with the old style personified by Gu, and suggests the potential of reform. Word circulates quickly among the people in Gulin that Li is a true friend of the common people. He is becoming a cultural hero. Xiaoli watches Li from a distance, obviously becoming more and more interested in him.

Another mass meeting is held. By now the people are aware of Li's work and some of them have developed high expectations for the future. But Gu has been an official in the county for more than 30 years. They fear his power. Gu addresses them: 'Raise your hand if you are a Communist Party member!' Many hands are raised. Gu then indirectly criticizes Li (who is also present) by claiming that experience, not youth, is what China needs. He reminds the group of the failure of the Great Leap Forward of 1958, attributing the problems of that era to the lack of wise leadership. He praises the comrades for their 'good recent work' and reminds them that he has 'never moved from this county.' He asks, 'Might someone else neglect our success here?' This episode ends with Li moving

18 Li listens to a woman who has been ignored by Gu.

to the podium where he begins to address the group. Li gives a kind of pep talk, encouraging the people to try to be the top-producing county in China. He suggests that the great hopes for the future can only be accomplished through reform. The battle lines are clearly, but politely, drawn at this meeting as Gu and Li vie for the support of the party membership and for the confidence of the rest of the people of Gulin County.

Episode 3

We resume with Li still addressing the Communist Party meeting. He says that the old leaders have made a fine contribution to the county, but now it is time for new challenges.

In the next scene, Gu is at home when the director and assistant director of the county police department arrive. The police have come to Gu's house to arrest his son (who is not at home) for smuggling. A long conversation ensues where Gu tries to convince the police to 'go easy' on his son. Thinking that the police may have been buoyed in their confidence to arrest his son by the presence of Li, Gu reminds them that Li is likely to leave: 'When he leaves, you will again be under my control,' he tells them. The situation becomes further complicated when the police director's assistant asks Gu for help moving his wife from the countryside to the city to join him. And when it is revealed that the police director's son is ill, Gu offers to find help for him, but suggests that in return his own son should be taken care of as well: 'You should understand my feeling for my son!' Later, Gu falls ill at home under the pressure of the situation and is rushed by ambulance to a hospital. Li arrives at the hospital to pay his respects to the older, and apparently infirm, Gu.

Li walks among the people of the city, stopping to advise many of them how they can improve their personal finances through profit-driven, incentive-based work. He meets an old man, Se, who he promises to help build a well to provide the much-needed water. The old man prefers to build a 'dragon temple' in order to pray for rain, but Li gently recommends that science is a better bet. Xiaoli is watching Li during all these interactions, and she tells him, 'I want to write about you in my book.' He replies: 'No, you should write about Se instead.'

A loud dinner party is being held at the county electric company facility. The party is given in honor of the district leader of electric power who is visiting Gulin County. Li arrives and the festivities stop. He criticizes the electric company *ganbu* for inviting so many people to this party because the food and alcohol are paid for out of the department budget. He blames the *ganbu* for his failure to provide electricity to farmers who needed it for their harvests. By spending money on the party, Li said, 'You drink the people's blood.' A discussion takes place about how farmers have had to bribe the *ganbu* with gifts in order to get electricity. Li instructs that this practice of *guanxi* must stop.

In the meantime, Gu is holding an unauthorized meeting in his hospital room with friends, many of whom are older *ganbu* who feel threatened by Li's presence in the county. They unite to oppose Li and agree with Gu's assessment that Li 'does not respect older officials.'

Episode 4

Several short scenes begin the episode. Gu telephones the district Party Secretary to complain about Li's 'troublemaking.' Li has a positive talk with the *ganbu* of the electric company, whom he had scolded previously, signalling that Li is winning respect from at least some of the managers. Li also solves a problem at a school where coal was needed to heat the children's food and drink.

The relationship between Li and his former girlfriend, Lin, is revealed at a public meeting. Li agrees to go public about their history and he goes to Lin's house but she isn't there. They meet by chance in the woods. With romantic music playing in the background, Li and Lin walk their bicycles along a path in the woods talking intimately about their past, about the situation in Gulin County, and about their life philosophies. Li is optimistic about changes in the party and in the country; Lin is cynical.

They reach Lin's house and go inside. Li is smoking Winston (American-made) cigarettes and they share a Western beverage, cocoa. Lin cries about her suffering during the Cultural Revolution. Li, expressing sadness that he had not taken more responsibility for Lin when they were young, listens to her sensitively as they discuss their roles in life – past, present, and future. It is clear that they do not have a romantic relationship anymore, and Lin asks Li not to return to the house for fear of damaging both their reputations. They touch hands as he leaves.

Xiaoli, meanwhile, has been following Li and Lin and appears to be very jealous when she sees them touch. In another brief scene, the police have arrived at Gu's house where, after all, they arrest his son.

Episode 5

Li and Xiaoli walk together in the village, their growing involvement becoming quite clear. They talk about the politics of the county and Li credits Xiaoli for her maturity. 'To accomplish the reformation,' he says, 'we must be strong.' Xiaoli kisses Li on the cheek.

In brief scenes, Li visits the home of a retired *ganbu* to solicit support from him in his reform efforts. Gu contemplates writing a letter to Li's father to ask him to recall his son from the county. Li and Xiaoli visit Gu to ask his advice on a small matter and Gu refuses to cooperate: 'I have no advice for you. Do what you want.'

Li travels to an outlying farm area by bus. He stops the bus to settle a fight between two female merchants. On the bus he discusses with others the problems that old Guomindang officials face in China today and he recommends improving their lot. A long discussion takes place at a water storage area in the countryside. Li wants to use the water that is contained by the dam to breed fish, a plan the party had already approved. The *ganbu* in charge of the dam is a former party official who was dispatched to this undesirable job by Gu. The *ganbu* says that no progress has been made at the dam site in the plan for fish breeding because of bureaucratic hassles created by Gu.

Episode 6

Li continues to discuss the fish-breeding plan with Zhu, the official at the site. Li tells him, 'Before, it was the harder you worked, the more you got hurt. But with me here now this won't happen again.'

A struggle erupts between Li and the leader of a commune in the county, Pan, who was promoted to his position during the Cultural Revolution and is an old friend of Gu. Pan attempts to turn the people of his commune against Li by blaming him for the shortage of water suffered by the people of the commune. The people yell their disapproval at Li when he arrives.

Li and Pan have a confrontation. Li tells Pan: 'It is your responsibility to solve the problem here. If you cannot do it, I will find another commune leader.' Li tells him that he is aware of the many awards that Pan received during the Cultural Revolution: 'But now is now. You must do your work. What research have you done?' The confrontation continues as Li and Pan visit a school house that has been destroyed by bad weather. Shoeless children and their teacher are forced to endure unbearable conditions at the school. Showing great concern for them, Li asks Pan: 'Why haven't you fixed this problem?' Pan responds that it is not his responsibility. Li tells him, '*You* are the director here. *You* are responsible!' Li turns to the teacher and the children and gives them a little speech, saying that the problem must be solved right away. The Li/Pan entourage continues to inspect the commune facilities. Li finds another room that could be used as a classroom, but Pan says it can't be done right away. Li asks Pan if he is really qualified to be a commune director. We also learn that Pan's nephew wants to marry the teacher and, if she doesn't agree, she will be reassigned to an even more undesirable place.

Episode 7

Another problem develops. Not only is the farming area in Gulin County lacking rain, Li discovers that the peasants have not been managing the land properly. The farmers explain to Li that they prefer to exploit the fields for immediate profits permitted under the new incentive policy. Conserving the land, rotating crops, and guarding against erosion are long-term approaches to farming. But because the peasants fear that the incentive policy will be revoked or changed in the near future, they have made the short-term decision to get as much immediate gain as possible. This scene reveals another serious problem that plagues the country – the lack of faith that people have in the consistency and stability of government policy. To solve this problem with respect to local farming, Li appoints Hu, a *ganbu* with whom he had disagreed earlier and who had called Li's attention to the land management problem, to a high-level research position. This appointment reflects on Li's fairness (appointing a former opponent) and his practicality (appointing a talented and hard-working person to a key post – a key contrast to the stereotype of positions held by unqualified *ganbu*).

We briefly meet Uncle Meng, a shabby old man who lives in the forest and advocates protection of the woodlands (he will return later). Li goes back to the village where the elementary school is located to see if Pan had made the improvements he demanded. As Li approaches, the old school collapses, injuring many children. The teacher lies nearly dead. Emergency vehicles are not available as they are all being used by the director of the hospital for unauthorized personal reasons.

Throughout these scenes we see that several local committee members of the Communist Party are gradually beginning to support Li. They vote to fire Pan from his position as secretary of the commune – a major show of confidence for Li. Li then makes a speech at a party meeting where he appoints Hu, the former adversary who had already been promoted, to the vacated position. Further demonstrating kindness and fairness, Li consoles Pan in the speech, reminding the group that 'every *ganbu* should learn a lesson from what has happened here.' In the final scene, Li is back on the bus headed to the countryside when a storm breaks out and a tree falls across the road.

Episode 8

We resume the story back on the road where it is apparent that there has been much illegal cutting of trees. This is a big problem in China as about one-fourth of the nation's forests have been destroyed since 1949. Young men are using a government truck to haul the stolen wood. Li busts them at this, but he patiently explains to them that what they are doing is wrong. The way Li handles the situation stands in stark contrast to the heavy-handed tactics typically used by the old *ganbu*.

Uncle Meng, the old man of the forest, is in his little house. He is portrayed as a kind old man with a habit of conserving everything – he will take nothing for himself and his love of the woodlands is evidence of his selflessness. He is later shown in the forest admiring the birds and animals, when he encounters a group of boys. He asks them not to hunt or smoke so as to protect the trees.

A struggle takes place when many young men prepare to return to the forest in order to illegally cut trees again. Uncle Meng tries to stop them, but falls and badly hurts himself on some rocks. In another location, Li discusses with experts the wisdom of tree cutting. Another former adversary of Li contributes to the discussion, a subtle indication of his growing support for Li. The *ganbu* who allowed the tree cutting is fired.

Episode 9

In the firing of the incompetent *ganbu*, Li lectures the gathering about protecting the forest. At the same time he praises the contribution made by the old *ganbu*, but he says that 'You have lost control here,' and he tells him 'Now you can do other important work.'

Xiaoli brings her uncle Gu a letter that was written by Li's father, the head of a central ministry in Beijing. We find out that Gu had written a polite letter to the senior Li previously, complaining about his son. Xiaoli is upset with her uncle's actions. Hu, the *ganbu* who twice had been promoted by Li, shows up and he and Gu begin to discuss the younger

Li's performance in the county. Hu: 'We should take care of the people.' Gu: 'We are politicians. We should take care of political problems.' Xiaoli and Gu fight after she reads the letter aloud. In the letter, the elder Li allows that his son may not be competent for the position he has assumed. Xiaoli angrily departs to find Li. She runs into Lin along the way and they have unpleasant words.

Pan, the fired commune secretary, cries at home about the loss of his job. Some children from the village laugh at him and a man tries to collect money from him for some painting that had been done. This scene makes the point that when Pan held his position as secretary, he would not have had to pay for the work, but instead would have granted the painter a favor – an act of *guanxi*.

We resume action in the forest. Uncle Meng has fallen gravely injured but many young men are still intent on cutting trees. Meng's son begs the men not to do it. Li arrives and he and Gao, a *ganbu* in charge of the forest, have a confrontation. Gao offers to resign and there is a taking of sides over him. A generational difference emerges as he is supported, at least tolerated, by the older men but is opposed by the younger ones. Li tells him, 'You have worked hard, but the masses oppose you now. You should absorb a lesson from this.' Li then addresses the young men about the history of the county, and they admit that they are wrong.

Li now realizes that he knows who old Uncle Meng is. Forty years ago, the old man had saved Li's father's life. After that, Meng had singlehand-edly planted all the trees nearby, turning a bare mountain into a forest. In the final scene, Meng is dying from his fall. Meng refuses to admit that he had helped Li's father (another indication of his selflessness), but requests that a box full of money that he has saved throughout his life be used for protecting the forest, not for his son or grandson. Li promises that the money will be spent accordingly.

Episode 10

Uncle Meng dies and many people come to his little house to pay their respects. A variety of short scenes follow. Xiaoli gives Li a letter from his father. Gu and his wife go to the jail to visit their son. The jailed son asks his father to get him out, and old Gu answers: 'I can't do more under the law. Your daddy's heart is very sad.' Pan later comes to Gu's house, crying pathetically (an unacceptable show of emotion in this situation for a Chinese man) and looking for sympathy.

Xiaoli is plotting for a way to convince her father to support Li. Gu notices that Xiaoli has written Li's name on some papers in her room (she lives in her uncle Gu's house). Gu asks Xiaoli of her feelings about Li:

Gu   : 'There have been lots of rumors.'

19 Li and Xiaoli share a light moment together.

Xiaoli: 'I don't care.'
Gu   : 'Do you have a special feeling for Li?'
Xiaoli: 'I want to live with him.'
Gu   : 'And what of Li's feelings about you?'
Xiaoli: 'He is kind to me.'
Gu   : 'But there are political considerations . . . '
Xiaoli: 'I don't want anyone else to take care of me.'
Gu   : 'But what about Li's relationship with Lin?'
Xiaoli: 'I don't care. What I want to do is up to me.'

This exchange is a clear illustration of an extremely untraditional position taken by a woman in the People's Republic and contrasts vividly with the style of the older and far more conservative Lin.

The next day Xiaoli goes out to find Li, but runs into a friend who warns her that Li may be leaving the county soon. Xiaoli yells, 'No!' She runs to the outskirts of town where she finds Li walking with Lin. She jealously watches them. They notice Xiaoli and Lin touches Li as she departs from him, asking him to visit her. Li asks Xiaoli why she came there. Xiaoli is nearly hysterical, threatening to kill herself. Li asks her to sit and talk. He tells her that he wants to contribute something positive to the history of China. She says that she will ask her father, General Secretary of the Province (the next administrative level), to help him,

113

saying she has designed a clever strategy for doing so. Li tells her he doesn't want this kind of help. Xiaoli threatens Li, telling him that she can hurt him by revealing his relationship to Lin who now is revealed to have been married to Xiaoli's brother and as having been sexually abused as a teenager! Li angrily stands up and asks her why she must be so hard. Why can't she take pity on a divorcee? He asks Xiaoli why she cannot understand another person's position. He tells her that she is very lovely, but that she also makes people suffer – 'this is such a contradiction.' Xiaoli runs away. In the final scene, a train arrives in Gulin County carrying Zheng, a high-level party official and the former secretary of Gulin County, a man who once held the position that is now occupied by Li.

Episode 11

Zheng has arrived to check Li's work and he immediately gets bad impressions. Xiaoli runs into Zheng and Li and acts as if she doesn't really know Li. They meet workers from the electric company who had their privileges curtailed by Li earlier for their excessive partying. Gu invites Zheng home for dinner where they meet with other resisters to Li to discuss a strategy for possibly removing him. Zheng claims that he (Zheng) is democratic. He says, for instance, that his wife and children decide about what food is eaten in his home. Despite his politeness and apparent correctness, however, Zheng opposes the reformation and asks Li to give it up.

An executive party committee meeting is held to discuss Li's future. Li, who is present, is criticized on two counts. First, one of his adversaries claims that Li has failed to acknowledge contributions made by former officials (including Zheng, but also Gu) to the progress of the county. Second, Li is called a 'dictator,' that he makes all the decisions by himself and as a result the people feel oppressed. Li denies the charges.

Hu speaks on Li's behalf, giving an account of his own transformation and outlining the problems with Gu's son. He asks Zheng to be objective. Another man, an intellectual, supports Li, saying, 'Some officials do nothing,' a remark that Zheng takes personally. Several other key committee members speak in support of Li, including the *ganbu* from the electric company who earlier had been busted by Li. This is a crucial moment in the drama as it is nearly impossible to imagine in real life that a *ganbu* who had been embarrassed and punished as this man had would support the person responsible. The portrayal of many *ganbu* in *New Star* is ultimately favorable, showing their potential for acceptance of the new leadership style embodied in the character of Li Xiangnan.

Li explains the reasoning behind his decisions during the two months of his governance in the county. When questions are directed to him about his involvement with Lin and Xiaoli, however, he abruptly stands and leaves the room. Later, friends privately encourage Li to speak out and extinguish the rumors about his relationships with the women. Li loses control emotionally in front of his friends, but calms down and quietly remarks that 'we must continue our work here, otherwise we fail.' At the end of the episode, one of Li's confidants finds out from the director of the police station that Zheng has ordered Li transferred out of the county.

Episode 12

Several short scenes introduce the last episode. Li's friends try to convince Zheng to support him. Li arrives at the room where Zheng is staying but cannot talk to him because Zheng is watching a volleyball match on television and ignores him. Feng is at home celebrating the news of Li's departure as he thinks this will clear the way to have his son, who had been incarcerated with Gu's son for smuggling, released from jail. Xiaoli and Li meet briefly. She is leaving by bus and Li asks her to say 'hello' to her father. Zheng and Li finally meet to discuss the situation. Zheng tells him he is going to 'change his position' and also advises him to be more careful with his girlfriends.

Li and one of his closest friends, Kang, have coffee together, then take a walk. Kang consoles him, telling him he is 'too good' and threatens people like Zheng. Li claims that he himself is not competent for political work, but Kang insists that his talent is both theoretical and practical and urges him to stay and contribute. They discuss Li's romantic situation, and Li admits that perhaps he should be married. Kang says someday he will write a novel about Li. He says the title will be *Ambitious and Loving*.

Li goes to visit Lin who receives him warmly. Their relationship has changed now with Li's firing. Lin is a 'damaged woman' because of her past (especially the divorce) and Li is damaged now too. They are closer as a result. Li tells her he wants to find a more quiet environment and continue to do some research on Chinese social and political problems. They walk together to visit an old woman who had taken care of Li when he was a young boy. They greet the woman who then prepares Li's favorite food which she remembers from years ago. Li gives her a present of clothes and distributes little gifts to the other neighbors. Everyone knows that Li is leaving and they are sad.

Again, Li and Lin walk together. They discuss their philosophies and recall the time they had spent together as teenagers. They talk about the political realities of making an impact at the highest level in China. Family politics are discussed too and Lin clearly explains her past marriage, a description that upsets Li. They meet a group of *ganbu* who support Li. The *ganbu* ask him not to leave the county, but he asks them to support his work, not him. Much support is shown for Li by his former opponents and by those who previously had not taken a position.

A bicyclist approaches with a letter from the Province Secretary, the brother of Gu and the father of Xiaoli. The letter praises Li, saying 'You have some good ideas and good proposals [for reform]. I have given a copy of your proposals to all province party committee members to read.' So, ironically, Li is being dismissed from his position, but receives praise at the same time.[3] *New Star* ends ambiguously. Li is celebrated as a 'new generation leader' and reform has been implicitly endorsed. Still, Li's personal future is in doubt and the potential for reform in Gulin County is completely unclear.

NEW STAR FEVER

Reaction to *New Star* came from everywhere. Most of it was favorable. Audience members spontaneously sent an unprecedented number of letters to the network praising the broadcasters for airing a program of such great relevance. The stunning response to *New Star* motivated one Chinese sociologist, Zhou Yong-ping, to conduct a large-scale audience survey about the program. He labeled the phenomenon '*New Star* Fever':

> The people endured the whole winter sluggishly, and now they wake up to the sound of thunder (*New Star*) . . . When we are awakened . . . we cannot stop thinking why *New Star* can have such a huge influence, from children to old people, from the masses to the *ganbu*, from the workers to the professionals, the professors, and the intellectuals . . . In our memory, it seems that no other literary or artistic production has had such deep influence and popular appeal.
>
> (Zhou, 1986: 1)

The program was a critical success, winning several prestigious national awards for excellence in a television drama series. When the lead actors were not nominated for individual awards, the oversight became a minor scandal in the country. Although the program was criticized by some network officials who claimed that the artistic quality and production level were not high (attributed to the 'lack of experience' at the Taiyuan station), and was faulted by some audience members (to be explored below), the consensus was clear: *New Star* was a television series of unmatched political importance. Television was not only the political agenda setter, but also the popularizer of the story. The success of the television series led to publication of *New Star* as a book that has sold out several printings and is still in demand.

VIEWERS RESPOND TO *NEW STAR*: REFORM IN FASHION

'This is a program that discloses a problem. It's not just a positive representation or a funny escape.' (28-year-old female cellist in orchestra, Guangzhou)

'We were happy to see this program. Now we don't have to hold this feeling inside anymore.' (61-year-old female retired textile worker, Xian)

'*New Star* helped encourage young people to fight the problem. The program reflects the will of the people.' (62-year-old male teacher in a telecommunications institute, Shanghai)

'It was a show about ordinary people. If someone can support us, we like to watch it.' (40-year-old male machinist, Beijing)

'This program shows the truth – the mistreatment of farmers and workers.' (28-year-old female unemployed worker, Beijing)

'We didn't watch it. We didn't like it. I don't even like the *New Star* theme song.' (33-year-old male driver for the post office, Beijing)

Almost everyone in China had an opinion about *New Star*. The great majority of the comments were favorable and many reasons were given for liking the series. But there were lots of criticisms too, even among the program's supporters. One point is clear: the program caught the attention of the world's largest television audience because of its subject matter. The sociologist who coined the term '*New Star* Fever' described the program as 'acupuncture that touched the contemporary social dilemma in China' (Zhou, 1986).

Zhou's study

I was told by faculty members at the People's University in Beijing about a graduate student in the Department of Sociology at Beijing University who was about to publish a major piece of survey research on the audience's response to *New Star*. This man is Zhou Yong-ping. We met with Zhou to discuss his study and to translate into English an article he was writing about his research that was subsequently published in a Chinese journal (Zhou, 1986). Zhou's work is important for two reasons. Not only does it disclose systematic information about this television series, it is one of very few comprehensive audience studies ever published in China.

Zhou sensed from the beginning that *New Star* was important. Word of mouth about the series was so strong that he quickly developed a survey questionnaire in order to measure public opinion about the program. He met with officials at the Taiyuan Television station, the author of the story (Kuo Yunlu), and workers at various levels (farmers, factory and service employees, technical specialists, professionals, and students) in order to decide what items should be included in the questionnaire. He mailed copies of the questionnaire to a random sample of 1,300 people in Beijing and Shanghai, including the outlying regions where farmers live. Slightly more than three-fourths of the completed questionnaires were returned and, according to Zhou, unrecovered questionnaires were missing because of administrative problems in the research rather than lack of enthusiasm for the program.

The overall response to *New Star*

New Star's enormous popularity was clearly evident both in my research and in Zhou's. Nearly every family we talked to knew about the program and most had watched several episodes. The national television network had never received so many letters about any program and some 92 percent of the opinions expressed were favorable. Zhou reports that 91 percent of the people who answered his survey watched at least one episode and that about half his respondents watched them all. Of Zhou's respondents who watched, 91 percent said they liked the show.[4] Chinese print media published countless positive reviews. People throughout China talked about the program at home and at work.

Zhou found that the program was popular among all viewers including, believe it or not, most *ganbu*, though they and high school students (for a very different reason – lack of interest) were least favorable toward the program. Besides the relevance of the program to life in China, the two major factors that encouraged viewing were the series format (audiences became hooked after viewing one or two episodes) and interpersonal influence attributable to the favorable talk that the program stimulated. While the program was widely appreciated throughout China, *New Star* was not received with equal enthusiasm everywhere. The most interest and favorable response came from the northern part of the country, as determined by the origin of letters sent to CCTV, the high ratings it received in Zhou's research (which was conducted there), and the interest and knowledge expressed by our narrators from this area. Still, *New Star* appeared twice on television in Guangdong Province and, according to broadcast authorities there, the program was popular overall and had a significant impact.

How realistic is *New Star*?

'Realism' is a key evaluative criterion raised by viewers. Various realisms emerged. First, the audience frequently told us that the program is realistic because it reveals actual, deep, nagging problems of Chinese society. In Zhou's survey, 78 percent of the respondents agreed that 'a realistic picture of the main conflict in contemporary Chinese society was presented (in *New Star*).' Even more (79 percent) agreed with the statement: '*New Star* revealed the necessity of reform; it reflects the people's strong desire for reform.' Zhou's study also shows that viewers (77 percent) thought that the program realistically depicts the obstacles that the reformation faces.

And, respondents did not agree that the 'political conflict in the Communist Party' was 'too exaggerated' in the program (3 percent).

After this general endorsement of *New Star*'s realism, however, many audience members said that the way in which reform was portrayed in *New Star* is far less true to life:

'Our family watched this program from our hearts. But this kind of reform is not possible in our department.' (26-year-old female worker in publishing company, Beijing)

'The direction of the reformation is correct but from an economic standpoint we can't promote the living standard very fast. The drama was exaggerated.' (44-year-old male *ganbu* for harbor workers, Guangzhou)

'If you try to act this way (Li's style), you won't survive in my department. The social pressure is too strong. A friend of mine made a proposal titled, "Making the Unreasonable Policy More Reasonable." He was criticized by his *ganbu*, pushed out of the picture, ignored, and considered to be a troublemaker who was breaking up harmony and morale at work. But in reality my friend made a very good suggestion about management and economic development.' (22-year-old male hotel service worker, Beijing)

'I didn't like *New Star*. The leader corrected the problems in one or two days. That's impossible and unrealistic.' (15-year-old male high school student, Beijing)

So, while *New Star* was thought to be realistic in its portrayal of problems that are close to home, *the way the problems were solved* in the drama was far less convincing. Certainly one reason for the audience's discomfort with this aspect of the story results from the adaptation of the novel into a television series. Key scenes are portrayed in a very concentrated way. The program often seems to be a sequence of incredible disasters or sticky situations that are almost always effectively solved quickly by Li. His brusque efficiency, intensified by the compression of time and action characteristic of television drama, made this aspect of the story seem unbelievable to some viewers. While some people fantasized about how China could benefit from such an uncharacteristic speeding up of change, others were less certain of the possibility. Consider this difference of opinion:

'The problems [that are raised] in the show are true and are part of our daily life. This program should be repeated. We need a wide ax to do the reformation work. If the country can do it this way, then we can develop fast. We only have a strong policy on paper. It seems like we can never really do it, finish it. Are we lazy? Always delayed?

119

Slow? This may be our Chinese habit, our personality.' (56-year-old female retired seamstress, Beijing)

'The program is not true. Not all of the new generation of leaders are like Li. His behavior is too strong and he is not part of the people. The reformation must take place from the top down. Li's behavior was too radical. My friends and myself make our contribution by doing our jobs well. What Li did was not realistic. He was not like most people in his position.' (37-year-old female medical doctor, Beijing, and daughter of a high-ranking Communist Party official)

Li Xiangnan – personification of reform

Not all the families we interviewed in China remembered *New Star* by its title, but as soon as we mentioned Li's name there would usually be instant recognition. His name was synonymous with the program and, in the minds of many viewers, with the reformation. Of course, Li *is* the 'new star.' And while most people said they admired him, his heroism was considered by some to be flawed. Ironically, many viewers complained that he got his executive position in the province because of his father's influence, a kind of relationship abuse that only reinforced the bad feelings that viewers hold about this problem. Because of this, Li's accomplishments were considered by some viewers to be tainted or, to continue the theme I am already developing, unrealistic.

'If we put this story into our real life it is not possible. He had power because of his father.' (28-year-old male food store worker, Beijing)

'An ordinary-status person cannot accomplish what Li did. His father was a high leader. Only in this kind of situation can someone do what he did. If somebody else tried this, the person would be stopped. Most people support Li, the character, but the reality is far more complicated.' (36-year-old female accountant, Beijing)

'There should be examinations for young leaders. Who can solve China's problems? Nobody should depend on their father or the status of the Communist Party to occupy a job they would not otherwise have.' (42-year-old male battery salesman, Beijing)

There were other criticisms of Li too. One Beijing woman, a 55-year-old retired cook, called him 'wild, stubborn, and unreasonable. He tries to give a little lesson to anyone he can find. Anyway, I never met anybody like him in my whole life.' True enough, Li is different – an exceptional leader who stands out because he so aggressively pursues a policy and course of action he believes is right. Traditionally in Chinese society,

120

individuals who promote themselves or their points of view too strongly are disliked or thought to be foolish. But most viewers of *New Star* praised Li for his aggressive and rather self-righteous personality. They often spoke of him as a friend. They said that they could participate vicariously in reform through him.

Li's role as a leader in the reformation, together with television's penchant for making stars through repeated exposure and the feeling of intimacy produced by the melodrama's close-up style, had created a media hero. The image of Li easily surpassed the constructed model citizen personae that originate in the Department of Propaganda:

> 'I respect Li. He is so successful. When he says something he never changes his direction. He is a real man . . . a strong personality. Li has so many qualities in one person. He is a symbol of many virtues.'
> (22-year-old male military vehicle mechanic, Xian)

This remark reflects the primary perceptions that audience members held toward Li: strength and fairness. Our narrators described Li's strength this way: 'decisive,' 'had courage . . . he dared to say and dared to do,' 'powerful just like he should be,' 'clear and strong,' 'didn't hesitate,' 'grasps situations tightly,' 'strong mind,' 'says what is right and doesn't care about pressure,' and 'not afraid.' Furthermore, some 92 percent of Zhou's respondents agreed with the statement: 'Li is a confident, powerful, and talented person; when he handles problems he is strong and insistent.'

Just as important, he was considered to be fair: '[he] . . . listens to public opinion . . . doesn't just make decisions by himself,' 'keeps his promise . . . he can really bring the "higher spirit" to the low workers,' 'fair . . . works on behalf of the ordinary people,' 'honest,' and 'made mistakes, but corrected his mistakes.' In Zhou's report, 74 percent of the sample agreed that 'Li never takes advantage of the system; he is a good official to protect the people.' Only 2 percent agreed with the assertion that 'Li is politically devious; he wants private profit.' Several of our narrators complimented Li highly by referring to him as a *Bao Chieng Tien* personality. Bao was a famous judge who lived during the Song Dynasty and was known for his absolute fairness. *Chieng tien* means 'clear sky' or 'blue sky.' Li Xiangnan protected the rights of uneducated farmers and workers, just as Judge Bao had done centuries before. So, Li had earned the honorific title from history, *Bao Chieng Tien*.

Li's role in the drama was central to China's political struggle. He gave symbolic hope to many viewers that the Chinese reformation might someday begin to resemble in reality what took place in *New Star*. Nearly eveyone we talked to said they believed that the direction of reform as it was displayed in *New Star* is correct. After that, however, opinion was divided between those who wishfully believe that it is possible to accomplish the work in a manner similar to what was shown, those who

121

believe that it is absolutely unrealistic to expect anything of the sort, and others who think that reform can take place, but that Li's leadership style was inappropriate – an opinion held by many Communist Party members. This matter of style was discussed by several of our narrators:

'Li was like an idol . . . his image was that of a moving idol, not a person. I like his power and the way he worked against an unfair system . . . In all of China we have had only one real leader like Li [Ma Senli, a factory reform leader of the 1970s]. Before he became famous he had a miserable life. Do you realize how much difficulty and frustration he experienced?' (33-year-old female electronics assembly worker, Beijing)

'I want the country to be strong. Everybody should support the reformation, but whether Li's style is correct is another question. In some ways I disagree with the way he did the work. He may have acted too fast.' (37-year-old male teacher in an industrial economics college and a party member, Xian)

'The actor's style was not typical of a Communist Party member. When he first got the job he fired lots of people. The Communist Party does not act this way. We cannot do our work without thorough thinking . . . [Li] had a new solution for the situation, that's good, but the personality of his character is not good . . . The reformation needs a method to be effective . . . the party method must be structured, stable, and flexible.' (51-year-old male personnel supervisor, a *ganbu* and party member, Beijing)

'In reality we rarely even hope to have a hero like Li because this kind of person will have a lot of power directed against him.' (49-year-old male English teacher at a statistics college, Xian)

'[Li] is persistent, tenacious, and never discouraged, although he was short-tempered at times. But he is young. His technique is not sophisticated. So people criticize this part of his character, but nobody can deny that he is a model for the reformation. In the mind of the audience, he has an excellent reputation. People hope that all reformers can be like him – brave, intense, and able to push away all the stones that stand in the way of the reformation.' (39-year-old female college history professor, and Communist Party member, Guangzhou)

Gu – personification of the obstacle to reform

The audience also reacted strongly to Li's antagonist, Gu Rong. His role in the television series as the conservative, old *ganbu* represents a type of leader in Chinese society that is far more recognizable to viewers than the image of Li had been. Whereas Li represents the ideal *ganbu*, Gu is the reality. The audience responded to Gu as a kind of composite *ganbu*, a fictionalized character who possesses all the bad qualities of the middle-level bureaucrats, a man who combines the worst of Chinese tradition with the most corrupt and inefficient elements of the communist system. Respondents to Zhou's questionnaire agreed strongly (83 percent) that 'In the real world we seldom see a person like Li, but we see many people like Gu and Pan' (the commune director who was dismissed by Li in the program).

CONCLUSIONS

From Confucius to the feudal emperors, to Chiang Kaishek, Mao Zedong, Deng Xiaoping, and Fang Lizhi, China calls out for heroes. Li Xiangnan was China's first television hero. Many viewers admired him deeply, considered him a friend, and engaged him to do vicariously what they themselves cannot do in their work situations. Even those who considered him a 'dictator' frequently thought that his progressive ideas about reform were far more important than his character flaws.

One critical argument that can be made against *New Star* as a symbol of reform, however, relates precisely to Li's popularity and the traditional reliance in China on a great leader. The program may have focused too much on Li as an individual and on his personal triumphs. The villagers and farmers of Gulin County thought Li was their savior – an authentic, modernday judge *Bao Chieng Tien*, and many viewers reacted to him in this valiant role. This focus takes away from the more compelling political issue in China – the necessity for *structural reform* that is far less amenable to the dramatic conventions and visual gloss of television. The repressive system stayed in place during *New Star*. The rules were the same before and after Li's tenure in Gulin County.

Battleground of the generations

Differences of opinion that were expressed about *New Star*, and about Li's leadership style, were often divided by age and generation within families. When the program appeared in 1986, many young people still hoped that real reform could take place within the communist system, that somehow young cadre like Li would be appointed to key positions and lead the way. At the same time, many older people were frightened by the prospect of reform as it was portrayed in *New Star*. The concept of reform is often interpreted differently by the young and the old. For the young, who often compare the situation in China to what they perceive to be the realities of the West and Japan, 'reform' means a fast and dramatic change. For the old, it means to modernize according to the government plan in a gradual, stable way. 'Reform,' therefore, can be used to signify very different positions. During the 1989 uprising, for instance, both the government and the demonstrators rationalized their actions in the name of reform. Our narrators provide additional perspectives:

'Well, there *is* a generation gap in China. Older people literally have different ideas from younger ones. The new generation wants reform and the old generation sometimes doesn't even recognize the problem.' (40-year-old male cybernetics engineer, Beijing)

'The old generation thinks that young men like Li are trying to steal power from the old. The young generation thinks that Li's attitude and actions were appropriate for the job.' (37-year-old male *ganbu* in a plastics factory, Guangzhou)

'Our father does not agree with us (the narrator and his 22-year old brother) so he kept quiet while we all watched the show.' (26-year-old male roofer, Shanghai)

'When the program dealt with the relationship between the young and the old generation, it was not mature.' (36-year-old male news film editor, Beijing)

In other cases, however, members of the older generation support the reformation while their children completely distrust the motives behind government-sanctioned reform or are profoundly cynical about China's ability to transform such an entrenched system. Zhou's study casts light on this situation. He found that people of all ages and work categories were favorable to reform, positive about *New Star*, and supportive of Li. He concludes that the generations overlap more than they differ in their desire to change China. But consensus among audience members on these issues masks a crucial difference that is typically demarcated by age and generation. The fact that nearly everyone wanted the country to change is not surprising, even in 1986. The sharper question is *how* should it change? On whose terms? Can the government be trusted to lead the people into the future? Does anyone really expect that leaders like Li Xiangnan will replace the Gu Rongs of China? Won't Li become the Gu of the future anyway? Can *guanxi* and *guanxi wang* ever become things of the past in a communist system?

Provoking political discourse

New Star not only harshly criticized the abuses of power that are so rampant throughout the country, it did something that good art should do in any circumstance. It caused people to discuss and take positions on larger questions – especially the matter of the efficacy of government-sponsored reform. The very appearance of *New Star* on CCTV was a victory for Zhao Ziyang (who had yet to emerge from the politburo as party secretary) and the 'Western faction' of the CCP. Other viewers were less optimistic. Opinions differ:

> 'The reformation is new . . . we don't fully understand this stage in our history. For China, we construct and experience reform all at the same time. We walk, we touch, we discover problems.' (Wang Chuanyu, CCTV)

> 'Media reports about the reformation are not really true. The party just follows a form. Every department claims that it is evolving, but it's just not true – it's just a hollow image.' (44-year-old male worker in electrical power plant, Beijing)

Many people believe that not only is China developing too slowly, but that citizens are subjected to endless government hyperbole that is designed to create an artificial image – an unrealistic, overly positive picture of current conditions, including the status of national reform. For most people, the certainty of media representations fails to reflect the tentativeness of government policy and the profoundly frustrating conditions of everyday life.

Furthermore, real reform implies democratic participation, a sensitive historical issue in China. The people remember well that Mao's Hundred Flowers Movement in 1957, which was designed to promote robust criticism of the government and its leaders in order to produce democratic dialogue, was followed later the same year by the repressive Anti-Rightist Campaign, where many people were persecuted for expressing political sentiments. 'Democracy Wall' in Beijing, a place where citizens at one time were encouraged to express political opinion, was closed unceremoniously in 1978. The student uprisings in late 1986 and early 1987 in Shanghai and Beijing were temporarily snuffed out by the government at the height of excitement about the Open Door policy, and we all know what followed in June 1989. Unclear and constantly changing policy, backed by hollow rhetoric and the constant threat of military force, greatly demoralizes the people.

New Star left everyone with lots of questions. First of all we don't know what happened to Li or to Gulin County. Although Li was heroic, in the end he was not clearly successful. His removal from the county presumably left the fate of the people in Gu's hands once again. Many viewers liked the program but didn't like the ending or preferred not to accept the hopelessness of the final scenes. Others saw the concluding scenes as typical of what would really happen in China – nothing.

Still, the very appearance of *New Star* on the national television network is one of the most important political developments to take place in China since the end of the Cultural Revolution. By 1986 no domestic program had ever stirred viewer interest like this one did. Although not everyone shared in the enthusiasm, very few people were cynical about *New Star*. Viewers took the program personally. One woman remarked incredulously, 'finally somebody did something for us!' People discussed not only the artistic merits and dramatic intrigues of the show, but its relevance to their daily lives and to the future of the nation. Chinese men, like males all over the world (Lull, 1988), rarely discuss television dramas with each other, but they frequently talked about and debated *New Star* with their friends. *New Star* was much more than a television series. How people reacted to the program revealed not only their feelings about the show, but about the prospect of reform and the very future of communist China.

7

THE FREEDOM TO HAVE FUN
Popular culture and censorship in China

China's Open Door and expanded economy have brought more than trade, tourists, technology, and expertise into the country. A contemporary popular culture that is shaped in part by foreign television, film, music, and other media material, has also developed during the modernization period. But China's contemporary cultural dynamics are not just the products of foreign influence. The artifacts and ideologies of Western popular culture were being imported into China at the same time that writers, TV producers, filmmakers, musicians, and other artists *inside* the country were winning unprecedented freedom and having great impact themselves. These foreign and domestic influences have been unleashed under the terms of an ambiguous and inconsistently applied cultural policy – a situation that has fueled many hopes, dashed many dreams, and generally contributed to the great confusion of contemporary China. Furthermore, the turmoil of 1989 has *not* led to a thoroughgoing cultural crackdown. The cultural influences that helped stimulate unrest in the first place are still fundamentally in place.

Western culture has seeped into China through many channels, leading in some cases to stunning developments. American cosmetics companies entered into joint agreements with local merchandisers to sell beauty products that were once anathema in Chinese society. California surfers were hired to introduce the sport to China in order to entice tourists to Hainan island. Colonel Sanders' Kentucky Fried Chicken became an alternative to *kung pao* chicken in Beijing and New York-style pizza came to the city shortly thereafter, though Chinese people had trouble adjusting to a central ingredient with which they are not familiar – cheese. The Harlem Globetrotters slam dunked the country. Billy Graham promised 5,000 faithful in Shanghai that religion can help speed the modernization along. Bodybuilding and bikinis became stylish. American Peace Corps volunteers were finally accepted by China. A United States' navy ship docked at a Chinese harbor for the first time since before the communist revolution. The spectacular motion picture, *The Last Emperor*, became the first American-produced movie ever shot in the People's Republic.

20 Colonel Sanders' American fried chicken franchise in Beijing.

21 Taiwanese, American and British pop music stars have become part of China's youth-oriented contemporary popular culture.

22 The Rambo syndrome, Beijing, fall 1989.

Famous foreign television serials from the United States, Japan, Mexico, Brazil, Taiwan, Singapore, and Hong Kong were big hits on the Chinese system. The popular *Follow Me*, a program produced by the British Broadcasting Corporation to teach English to Chinese people, began its long run on the national network in 1982. The hostess of the program, Kathy Flowers, became a pop culture heroine. A spinoff, *Follow Me to Science*, is still on the air. American movies, including *Rambo, Love Story, Superman, First Blood, Taxi Driver*, and *Waterloo Bridge*, were shown in theaters all over China. People copied and traded videos of every imaginable film smuggled in from the West and from Hong Kong.

Popular music may be the most striking example. Music was mentioned many times by our narrators as an important part of the developing youth-centered culture in China. Parents frequently told us how much their young children love music. One family described how even the musical soundtrack to an ice skating routine on television provoked their young daughter to dance wildly in front of the screen. Students and other young people became fascinated with disco music as public dance halls grew popular. For the first time, couples were permitted to dance without harsh, fluorescent lights shining on them.

The most common delivery system for pop music in China – the audio cassette recorder/playback unit – has become an extremely important piece of cultural equipment. In our home interviews, we found that nearly every urban home in China has an audio cassette recorder/player. Most of the machines are dubbing units that make it easy to copy music tapes. But even by the late 1980s few Western pop music tapes were available in the little music stores that dot the country. Singers and groups from Taiwan, Hong Kong, and Singapore (music that is itself influenced by the West, however) are far more abundant and desired. When I visited China in late 1989 a Taiwanese pop star was performing in a Beijing concert hall with the price fixed at 15 yuan, roughly one-eighth of a government worker's monthly wage. The demand for pop music in China encouraged the managers of the conservative national radio system, the People's Broadcasting Station, to air a twice-weekly Anglo-American show that features artists such as Madonna, Lionel Ritchie, and (oh no, not China too) John Denver.

Breakdancing also found its way into China in the late 1980s, thanks mainly to the release of the movie, *Breakdance*. An American teacher at the People's University in Beijing told me in 1989 that his students often practice breakdance moves and Michael Jackson's moonwalk in the hallways between classes. Because he is an American, the young teacher is often asked by the students to evaluate their proficiency. The positive reponse to the film prompted the English-language *Beijing Review* to explain that breakdancing is acceptable in China now because the reformation permits the 'freedom to have fun' too. Indeed, the wild contortions of

131

breakdance deviate completely from normative life in China. But young Chinese women and men also love to do foreign social dances, especially the waltz and tango. Schools and work units often hold social dance contests in the cities. Dance is thought to be healthy. Even during China's most austere periods in history, the idea of body movement for physical and mental exercise has been considered a good thing. The Mao Zedong-endorsed *tai chi* exercises, for instance, are part of this tradition. Today, *tai chi*, which is performed mainly by older adults, has been supplemented by 'old people's disco' (*lao nian disco*).

The practical limits and symbolic value of popular culture

Cultural change is one of the undeniable byproducts of China's moderniz-ation, but there are limits to the extent that people can practice the new media-inspired activity. Western media often sensationalize China's new popular culture. Simply put, everyday life in China does not lend itself well to any profound revolution in popular culture, even among the young. First of all, most of the new activity is confined to the cities and to certain groups. Furthermore, cultural traditions, family life, work routines, and basic economics all militate against cultivation of a far-reaching, youth-oriented popular culture in any case. Except for the relatively few young people who have been able to enter private business, there is not enough disposable income to buy music tapes, video cassettes, or the clothes, cosmetics, and the other accoutrements that are normally associated with youth culture. Media policy also interferes. Chinese media do not set out to make pop culture heroes or, for that matter, to even distribute basic information about pop singers, film stars, or television personalities. Exposure to even the most attractive elements of popular culture, foreign and domestic, is fragmented and short-lived.

Still, the new influences have affected the entire society symbolically, offering refreshing, exciting cultural vistas whose attractiveness is enhanced by comparisons that the people readily make with the drab official culture. The unaffordability of pop culture materials also enhances their appeal. Despite the practical limitations, China's new and exotic worlds of popular culture, originating inside and outside national borders, have contributed greatly to the cultural crisis and political upheaval of recent years.

THE CONFUSED CENSORS

'The Communist Party principle is to encourage cultural opening . . . we must be open to the outside, but protect the inside.' (Liu Jing-qi, reporter, Shanghai Television station)

'The content of television should be more open. It's not dangerous to show hugs and kisses. We see this sometimes in foreign programs, but not in Chinese dramas. Why?' (46-year-old female accountant for a printing company, Shanghai)

'China is still not open enough and there is no freedom of the press. We must have the freedom to import books, too.' (63-year-old male president of a continuing education college, Shanghai)

'Our family prefers the newspaper that is least controlled by the government.' (22-year-old male teacher of population education, Shanghai)

'Government policy requires cutting up TV shows. This ruins the continuity and destroys the art, especially of imported shows that the government thinks could influence our thinking. In some ways the censorship isn't so bad, though, because it protects young people. Our customs are different from foreigners. TV programs represent the customs of different cultures.' (60-year-old male retired farmer, Shanghai)

'China's television policy is generally open now and more foreign input is good. Some people could not accept the openness at first, especially older people who don't like Western ideas. But, imported programming is slowly becoming more acceptable to the people. Still, we must evaluate the values of foreign programs. Some Chinese values will never change.' (62-year-old male professor in telecommunications specialty school, Shanghai)

'Chinese television programs cannot reach a high level of art but they don't entertain the ordinary people either.' (18-year-old male student, Shanghai)

Cultural policy has been so inconsistent over the years that the main impression people have of the whirlwind cultural changes in China is one as much of confusion and frustration as it is of excitement. Just as the economic modernization and political reformation sprinted and stalled throughout the 1980s, state policy about cultural life has been likewise unsteady. Standards loosen when the economy is going well. But when it stumbles, crackdowns in culture and politics are again instigated, repeating a pattern that is all too familiar to the people under communist rule. The government typically justifies the negative sanctions by claiming that they are necessary to halt 'spiritual pollution,' 'bourgeois liberalization,' or something of the sort. The crackdowns often come on the heels of a political flareup. Management of cultural life and promotion of the elusive spiritual civilization is accomplished not only by promoting 'positive' ideas and images through the media, but by censoring cultural products too. Because of political uncertainties and bureaucratic inefficiency, however, censoring is inconsistent.

Especially since 1978, China has found it difficult to censor foreign materials effectively. Overall, the government has relaxed its standards during the modernization period. But foreign occupation and influence have hurt China before. The government, therefore, tries to regulate what comes into the country by applying some vague principle of cultural acceptability. This has not been easy to do during the era of the Open Door policy. Edward Gargan describes the problem well: 'The continuing dilemma confronting China is whether it can absorb technical accomplishments without embracing the ideas that gave rise to those achievements. The fear, simply put, is that somehow Chinese culture will be undermined and destroyed if Western culture intrudes' (Gargan, 1987: 26).

Scientific and technical information coming from the West and from Japan generally is not considered a problem. Social themes are more likely to stir controversy. Sexual permissiveness, for instance, is simply not allowed, though the specific limits are never clear. Even steamy romantic novels can be considered pornographic. So, in a famous case, the Chinese translation of Jackie Collins' novel, *Lovers and Gamblers* was banned, but because of confusion in the censors' offices it wasn't taken off the shelves until more than 300,000 copies had been sold. The classic novel, *Lady Chatterley's Lover*, was also inconsistently banned. But censoring erotica does not put out the fire. A black market for pornographic magazines and videos has developed steadily during the past several years, despite the passing of a law in 1990 that can punish porn sellers with death or life in prison.

Another troubling source of information from outside China is foreign broadcasting, particularly signals from the Voice of America (VOA) and the British Broadcasting Corporation (BBC) that are easily received in most parts of the country. Until the 1980s, exposure to foreign radio was considered unpatriotic. Listeners were subject to reprimand. But, in the 1980s, before the student-led demonstrations began to heat up again in 1989, China had gradually relaxed restrictions on listening to these stations. A more specific case is Hong Kong television. Located within telecast range of China's southern provinces, Hong Kong television has always posed a distinct threat to the mainland government. For many years Chinese residents were forbidden to construct tall antennae in order to receive Hong Kong TV signals, a policy that was also relaxed during the 1980s. The Hong Kong viewing is an important issue that I take up in depth later in this chapter.

Some types of domestic cultural products are also difficult for the government to manage. These 'unstable artistic possibilities' include literary journals, poetry, modern and abstract art, critical journalism, and critical, historical films (Gargan, 1987). But finding programs to put on national televison can create problems for China's censors too, as the standard of what is acceptable cultural and political information is never completely clear and changes with the direction and force of the political winds. Just when television gradually started to show programs that depict romantic entanglements, for example, the government insisted that love relations 'should conform with reality, national customs, communist morality, and the socialist legal system' (Hooper, 1985: 180). Toward the end of 1988 the first Chinese-made film to feature scenes of (unexplicit) sexual activity (*Widow's Village*) was released and drew big crowds. At the same time a large gathering attended an all nude art exhibit at the Beijing National Art Gallery. But an avant-garde art exhibit opening in Beijing in early 1989 was quickly closed. And while books written by George Bush, Mikhail Gorbachev, Nancy Reagan, Sylvester Stallone, and Lee Iacocca became best sellers in China, a host of other imported and domestic volumes were being destroyed.

The 'people's appreciation of beauty' which, rhetorically at least, has been rekindled since 1979, also led to conflicting and uncertain developments by the late 1980s. A fashion show was telecast nationwide from Beijing's Great Hall of the People, for instance, 'in order to give correct guidance to consumers of different levels.' But at the same time, beauty pageants held in Shanghai and Beijing, both of which also were scheduled to be telecast, were abruptly cancelled. The case of Chinese pop musician Cui Jian pointedly illustrates the ambivalence of government cultural policy. Cui developed a large youth following in Beijing and Shanghai for the concerts he gave on days off from his regular job with the Beijing Song and Dance Troupe. But after the student demonstrations in late 1986 and early 1987, his concerts were officially eliminated in a wave of cultural straightening and then suddenly permitted again in early 1989.

Even more curious in the socialist nation is the positioning of hard-sell advertising on television – messages that feverishly encourage audiences to promote their individuality by purchasing all kinds of products. Among the products promoted in TV commercials are beer, wine, motorcycle tires, icecream, sandwiches, medicines, champagne, soap, pimple cream, baby shampoo, crackers, men's cologne, mouth freshener, 'permanent' hair styling kits for men, all kinds of electronic equipment, cars and jeeps, and cameras. The Industrial and Commercial Bank of China hypes a credit card that can be used to buy all these things. Many TV commercials now try to sell fashion-oriented and beauty items including jewelry, perfume, and personal-care products that are designed far more for show than for health. Sex is frequently the vehicle for persuasion. In one commercial, for instance, a group of young men notice an attractive woman who is walking alone. As the men turn to stare at her, she tosses her head sensually and her long, silky hair blows in the wind. It's a hair conditioner commercial. Other cases are more extreme. The female form – dancing, romancing, flirting, seducing – is used to sell refrigerators, electric fans, and huge industrial appliances. Images like these never stopped flowing from Chinese television during or after the trouble of 1989.

Imported commercials blatantly promote materialism. Messages sponsored by Coca-cola, Pepsi-cola, Gillette, Maxwell House, IBM, Procter & Gamble, MacDonnell–Douglas, and Boeing, as well as a whole host of famous Japanese labels, are common on Chinese television. Chinese people are being introduced to the hazards of Western life in the commercials. The Chinese commercial for Head and Shoulders shampoo, for instance, shows a young mother being publicly embarrassed by her young son who notices flakes of dandruff on her blouse, the very same persuasive appeal that this sponsor uses to heighten consumer anxiety in Western countries. A Hong Kong commercial shown in China displays a totally bourgeois setting – men dressed in tuxedos riding around in limousines to push the product. A Hitachi commercial shows an Asian family in a spacious, luxurious home watching TV – an environment that is completely at odds with the living conditions of Chinese people. Commercials such as these do more than sell products or even a way of life; they stand in fundamental, competitive contrast to the stark reality of China. Their messages surely are interpreted emotionally even in unconscious ways that have contributed to the people's confusion, frustration, and dissatisfaction.

It is also significant that some of China's most widely-acclaimed media accomplishments have provoked the most severe criticism from the government. During the 1980s, producers and directors from China's film and television industries made some powerful statements with their media. The films of Zhang Yimou, Chen Kaige, and Wu Tianming became favorites of critics and audiences around the world, bringing unprecedented attention to China for cinematic achievement. *New Star* and *River Elegy* were milestones in Chinese television programming, drawing enormous, adoring audiences. Despite their artistic achievement and widespread appeal, these films and television programs were harshly criticized by government hardliners.

CHINA'S CONTROVERSIAL FILMMAKERS

'This is the time for China to produce great works. Only by giving [film] directors greater creative freedom can they produce better films, not by telling them what to do. There is a saying in China, "If there is no tiger in the mountains, the monkey will be king." These young directors will be our kings.' (Wu Tianming, former director of Xian Film Studio, Xian)

'I'm Chinese. I love my people . . . But every time I make a film I get into trouble . . . Great films are made by filmmakers who see the

23 Wu Tianming (photo courtesy of Xian Film Studio).

24 Zhang Yimou (photo courtesy of Xian Film Studio).

world through their own eyes . . . I do what I can under censorship.' (Chen Kaige, director of *Yellow Earth*, the first of China's 'new wave' films)

'The basic thing is that you can't make films that are anti-communist.' (Zhang Yimou, director of *Red Sorghum*, winner of the West Berlin Film Festival)

'Some people are for this film (*Red Sorghum*) and some are against it.

138

We'd best not interfere.' (Zhao Ziyang, former General Secretary of the Chinese Communist Party)

One truly remarkable accomplishment of Chinese mass media since the mid 1980s is the production of a handful of spectacular films and the rise of the country's 'fifth generation' filmmakers, a small group of producer/ director/actors who have brought unprecedented national and international acclaim to China's film industry. The success of the new filmmakers peaked in 1988 when *Red Sorghum*, the first feature film directed by Zhang Yimou, won the coveted award for best foreign film at the West Berlin Film Festival. Despite the favorable attention that *Red Sorghum* and the other contemporary films have received, there are serious objections in Beijing to their cultural and political implications.

Debates about the proper role of film in China reflect the longstanding desire by the government to control the ideological agenda via public communication and entertainment media. The film industry in China was quickly appropriated for promotion of China's propaganda efforts after 1949. Until television arrived in full force, film was the most popular entertainment medium. Even in the early 1980s Chinese citizens attended about 30 movies per year on average, far more than their counterparts in the United States and Europe (Bishop, 1989).

Very few films were produced during the Cultural Revolution. Those that were made fell under the strict ideological and artistic control of Mao Zedong's wife, Jiang Qing, whose authoritarian vendettas against disagreeable directors, actors, and artists of all types are well known. Jiang and her supporters considered film to be the most effective medium for distributing ideology and for unifying the people. Lock-step ballets presented in films such as *The White-Haired Girl* and *The Red Detachment of Women*, and the self-congratulating ideological haranguing of *Mao Zedong – Greatest Revolutionary of our Time* and *Breaking with Old Ideas* are striking examples of the extreme Cultural Revolution era propaganda.

Jiang's fall from power in the mid 1970s opened the door for China's new wave cinema to develop. The Beijing Film Academy admitted students to its first post-Cultural Revolution class in 1978. Four years later, the star directors of today's Chinese cinema scene graduated and began their careers. Three men – Wu Tianming, Chen Kaige, and Zhang Yimou – have been the major figures in the production of China's superb recent films. The story of these men is worth telling briefly here. Their struggles and successes are a significant part of the development of China's contemporary popular culture, a microcosm of the essential national ideological conflict.

Like everything in China, film is to serve purposes of the national modernization. But it is never obvious if any particular film meets this criterion. Judgments that are rendered by members of the film review board in Beijing are based on highly subjective perceptions about the political correctness of art, a process that has led to considerable quarreling, censorship, and favoritism. The films of the fifth generation directors have forced the authorities to ask sensitive questions. Should China confront its problems head-on by raising troubling issues that will be seen by millions of people throughout the country? Is it appropriate to openly criticize periods and personalities in the history of China and problematize the inefficiency of the current system? Does a story that is set in pre-socialist China and reveals much of the backwardness of the rural areas bring shame to China today? How will Chinese audiences react to films that are more abstract and open-ended in their implications than the straightforward propagandist movies that cinema goers know so well? Generally, what images should China project to itself and to the rest of the world?

The driving force behind the contemporary cinema scene is Wu Tianming, known to film buffs as the director of *Old Well* and *Dislocation*, two successful new wave films. But Wu's main contribution to the changing film industry derives more from his five-year tenure as director of the Xian Film Studio, located in northern China. Dedicated to overcoming what he calls the 'tired didacticism' of Chinese filmmaking, Wu took control of the studio in this out-of-the-way part of the country and created an atmosphere where great films could be made.[1]

The story of Wu's success in Xian is legendary. He became director of the disreputable Xian studio in 1983. Fighting what he calls 'extreme inefficiency and laziness,' the ambitious Wu retrained the studio staff and worked to inspire innovative filmmaking. He took advantage of Xian's strategic geographic location. In order to give some of the young filmmakers a sense of rural northern China, he arranged trips up and down the Yellow River to the remote areas – the desolate plains that later became the places where *Yellow Earth* and *Red Sorghum* were filmed.

The film *Yellow Earth* (1985), directed by Chen Kaige at age 32, is often cited as the breakthrough piece in China's new wave cinema. The story is set in the late 1930s. In the story, a soldier from the Chinese revolutionary army comes to a mountain village to collect peasant songs to be used by the Communist Party for propaganda. He becomes involved in the everyday life problems of a peasant family, where he finds himself powerless to help a 12-year-old girl avoid a forced marriage. Very subtle cultural, social, and political themes are explored by Chen in *Yellow Earth*, creating a sophistication and daring that go beyond the limits of previous films made in China. But the trademark of this film, and of Zhang's *Red Sorghum* too, is not just the sophisticated treatment of a story, but the rich cinematic textures of carefully selected scenes of northern China that lend a panorama of historical authenticity to the work.

Red Sorghum explores pre-liberation, rural China too – the late 1920s and early 1930s – focusing on the lives of peasants who operate a sorghum winery. The tone of the film is lighthearted and playful until a Japanese military unit invades the area, capturing the village and torturing its inhabitants – among them the workers from the distillery. The quiet, peaceful cinematic textures and the comical, endearing personal developments in the story are replaced at the end by a violent splashing of red blood and wine in a series of gripping experimental effects.

While foreign critics loved the film, *Red Sorghum* was harshly criticized in China, not only by wary censors but also by some older people who did not understand the movie or thought it cast China in a bad light. Nonetheless, the film drew a record 200 million viewers. The film's themes provoked controversy. Sexual relations are shown much more openly than usual. The backwardness and poverty of rural China at the time (and now) are frankly portrayed. And, contrary to the conventional heroic images of Chinese peasants that have appeared in previous films, literature, and art, *Red Sorghum* realistically portrays what was the inability of the people to defend themselves against the ruthless Japanese during their occupation of the mainland.

From the point of view of Chen and Zhang, the use of desolate scenery and the depictions of the simple life of the rural peasants in their films is done not to demean the people, but to show what a struggle life was for them. These directors say that, far from dismissing or ridiculing their own culture, they have embraced and romanticized it. In *Red Sorghum*, for instance, many scenes positively characterize the egalitarian spirit of socialist China. There is, for example, an insistent focus on the lead character, 'Nine,' who inherits the distillery. She is portrayed as an extremely strong and independent woman, resisting the authority of her father and her forced-marriage husband, assuming a non-stereotypical aggressiveness and confidence in consummating a physical relationship with her lover, and managing the brewery with great skill and concern for the well being of the workers. Furthermore, the symbolic imagery that permeates the film – the strong woman, a solar eclipse, the survival of her son, even the bean of the red sorghum, suggests hope for China's future.

Despite their great successes, Wu, Chen, and Zhang have been at odds with the censors all along. Wu resigned his administrative post at the Xian Film Studio in late 1988. On a trip to the United States that year, he told *San Francisco Chronicle* movie critic Judy Stone that he considers the Chinese film industry to be 'stagnant, archaic, and bureaucratic.' Wu has had to struggle to produce films efficiently and to treat controversial themes. He claims that officials in Beijing believe that the fifth generation directors have turned their backs on China in a quest for international recognition. Wu has been the subject of three investigations for 'lifestyle mistakes' and 'insubordination.' He insists that the Chinese system of employment militates against excellence: 'You can't fire anybody . . . talented artists who do great work often are not rewarded properly whereas those who do not work at all or are loafers still insist on their share of whatever profit has been made. This has seriously affected the motivation of artists to produce quality work.'

RIVER ELEGY – CHINA'S DEATH POEM TO ITSELF

This yellow land cannot teach us the true spirit of science, nor can the fierce Yellow River reveal the true consciousness of democracy.
(line from the television miniseries, *River Elegy*)

'As I see it, this program (*River Elegy*) curses the Yellow River and the Great Wall and vilifies our great Chinese people. I fought for many years to rule this country, yet now I run into this band of professors and graduate students [who created the television series]. I have never been so angry in my life. Intellectuals are dangerous.' (Wang Zhen, Vice Secretary of the Chinese Communist Party, in remarks made during the closing session of the Communist Party Central Committee meetings, October 1988. From a story released by United Press International)

'*River Elegy* was propaganda for bourgeois liberalization . . . the broadcast of *River Elegy* gave theoretical and emotional preparation for the recent turmoil and rebellion.' (Hong Minshen, Deputy Director, CCTV, quoted from *Beijing Review*)

Wang and Hong's remarks about the television series *River Elegy* reflect an ideological position that has never wavered in some quarters in China. Media successes are perceived by the hardliners more as threats than achievements. Artists and intellectuals are considered necessary but troublesome and in need of constant evaluation and correction. This autocratic, paternalistic management of culture is justified in the name of protecting the people against their own ideological lapses – whims that are blamed on the work of artists and political 'counterrevolutionaries.'

River Elegy is a six-part television series that appeared on CCTV twice during 1988. It created a major controversy at the time and has frequently been blamed for helping stir up the unrest the following year. The principal scriptwriters are Su Xiaokang, a 39-year-old former teacher at the Beijing Broadcasting Institute and Wang Luxiang, 32, an instructor at Beijing Teacher's College. The director was 26-year-old Xia Jun, a reporter at CCTV. The writers, producers, and directors intentionally set out to use television as a transmitter of subversive ideology. Su said that he hoped the series would 'stimulate conscious self-examination throughout the country in this time of social transformation' (Li, 1989: 47).[2]

That it did. Relying on visual imagery and metaphor rather than didactic narration, *River Elegy* attacked traditional Chinese culture by claiming that some of the country's most revered symbols – the Yellow River, the Great Wall, the dragon, mythic Confucianism – actually represent China's backwardness and passivity, not its greatness. Through beautiful visual representations and a lyrical, non-linear storyline, the series argues that China fell behind other nations in the development of a modern civilization because of a persistent inward orientation, a fixation on the land which led to isolation from the rest of the world. The Yellow River, with its sulfur-colored, silt-laden water, was used by the writers as a metaphor for China's steady, but unprogressive and agriculture-based society – a nation that still remains fundamentally trapped within the cultural and ideological confines of its feudalist past. Though the point is delicately made, the communist government of today is also implicated in the regrettable tale of China's continuing decline.

Audience members became intimately involved with *River Elegy* in part because of the inviting, open-ended structure and tone of the series, an approach to television production that contrasts sharply with the explicit propaganda messages to which viewers are so accustomed. So, while *River Elegy*'s 'oratory narrative lacks a logical argument . . . the viewer [was able] to *see* [italics mine] the conclusion' (Lau and Lo, 1990: 17). That conclusion insists on sweeping and immediate economic, political, and cultural change. Celebrating the intelligence and ability of Chinese people, the series' last episode dreamily sentimentalizes the symbolic 'azure blue' of the ocean as the direction China must go to reach its vast potential.

For ideological hardliners like Wang and Hong, the program irreverently chastized mythic China and failed to show sufficient deference to its current leaders. The television audience, however, did not interpret the series that way and even the government's official publications recognized the program's widespread influence. The program was praised in the Chinese press for creating a dialogue between intellectuals and ordinary people. Just as *New Star* had stimulated viewers to discuss the complexities of reform two years before, the critique that drives *River Elegy* provoked the very 'collective self-reflection' that its originators hoped it would (Lau and Lo, 1990) and, again like *New Star*, served as a symbolic rallying point for the liberal faction within the Communist Party. The fact that the government has attempted to stop sale of video copies of *River Elegy* has only increased its appeal.

In the next pages, I describe three other key areas that have created problems for the Chinese government in its attempt to manage the cultural and political agenda. I will return to the subject of Hong Kong television now, then discuss the phenomena of American television programming and foreign advertising in China. The consequences of this cultural invasion are immense. I discuss them in detail in the next chapter.

25 The TV program *River Elegy* questions romanticized views of Chinese history and tradition.

WATCHING HONG KONG TELEVISION

'Government policy about [Chinese people watching] Hong Kong television has changed and softened. Before the government might come into your house and take your antenna away. Now they don't do much to stop us from watching . . . it's useless for them to try.' (29-year-old female worker in a bicycle factory, Guangzhou)

'We'd like to receive the channels from Hong Kong but we can't. Every family in the building must agree to build an antenna. It's easier to do this in a new building. With a small antenna inside your apartment you cannot see the Hong Kong programs clearly.' (29-year-old male cartographer, Guangzhou)

'The Hong Kong programs are very diverse. That's good. But someone is always fighting on those programs . . . especially kung-fu – some people act like they are out of their minds.' (79-year-old male retired medical doctor, Guangzhou)

'We especially like the kung-fu programs from Hong Kong. And the Hong Kong stations use the Cantonese language. Hong Kong programs are usually of better quality too. The emotions are stronger and more clear. The language and the action are more alive.' (26-year-old female worker in a battery factory, Guangzhou)

'We have a different speed of living. Hong Kong is so fast and so is their TV. We prefer to slow down and relax our minds after work. We can't adjust to programs of that speed.' (32-year-old female surgeon, Guangzhou)

'Hong Kong television is closer to our real life than Chinese TV. Guangzhou TV shows are more concerned with political teaching. We shouldn't focus on this so much any more in China. We need to get information from the government, but we don't need so much emphasis and repetition. Hong Kong programs are more varied and fun. They don't try to teach you something all the time. They just tell you stories.' (28-year-old male taxi driver, Guangzhou)

The comments of our narrators in Guangzhou reveal the basic issues related to viewing Hong Kong television in southern China – government policy, signal quality, program quality, language, and cultural appropriateness and appeal. The remarks also reflect the lack of a dominant opinion about Hong Kong television. The Hong Kong channels, which broadcast a lively spectrum of Chinese, British, and American entertainment programs, have irritated Chinese authorities for years. Before the modernization, viewing Hong Kong TV shows was not approved. Southern Chinese people were told that the content of Hong Kong television is not of high moral character, in particular that it is 'too sexual.' But during the optimism of the 1980s, the government stopped trying to discourage viewing. In fact, several families told us that the government helped residents of their apartment buildings install antennae that facilitate viewing distant TV signals. Now, following the political upheaval of 1989, viewing the Hong Kong stations is again controversial, though the government has not prohibited viewing.

Exact statistics on the issue are not available, but it is safe to say that the vast majority of Guangzhou residents cannot reliably receive Hong Kong television stations in their homes. Three factors limit reception. The distance between the two cities (about 150 miles) makes reception inconsistent at best. Weather also interferes. And, especially in recent years, the signal of one of Guangzhou's television stations (Channel 14) occupies spectrum space so close to one of the Hong Kong stations that it distorts the distant signal.

Hong Kong television programs

'One good thing about Hong Kong TV shows is that they are very popularly-oriented and lively. So, our audience frequently tells us that the hosts of our shows are too boring and always try to teach them something, tell them this or that. But in China we feel that television should educate, not just entertain.' (Pan Huiming, Deputy Director, Guangdong Province Television station)

Despite the technical and cultural difficulties, some Hong Kong TV shows are very popular in Guangzhou. A weekly schedule of Hong Kong television programs can be purchased in China. Generally, Chinese audiences believe that Hong Kong television is more professional looking and has a wider variety of programs and more interesting content. Some viewers complained, however, that the Hong Kong shows begin too late at night and last too long for the more conservative lifestyle of mainland viewers. The biggest complaint is about commercials. Although Chinese viewers think that Hong Kong commercials, like the programs, are more professionally done than the Chinese advertisements, viewers don't like the fact that many commericals appear on Hong Kong television and that they are scheduled during the shows.

Our narrators were clear about the kinds of programs they prefer from the Hong Kong stations. It is not news from the 'outside world,' although that was also praised. What Chinese viewers really like are Hong Kong's drama serials. Viewers said they don't care if the TV serials come from their own stations or from Hong Kong, they simply love to watch dramatic programs. One family told us that a Hong Kong show was the only television program that could make them 'give up everything else just to watch.'

Hong Kong-produced commercials and drama serials portray upper-class and middle-class lifestyles of Chinese in the colony that contrast sharply with life in Guangzhou. For instance, there are frequent images of Chinese businessmen in modern Western-style suits with fashionable wives and girlfriends living in spacious, beautifully-decorated homes, driving around in cars, drinking in bars, and so on. Mainland Chinese people do not have or do most of these things. Cultural values also clash. In one Hong Kong serial that we viewed in Guangzhou, for instance, the mother in the story secretly marries a family friend *before* she divorces her husband. When her daughter finds out about this, the girl runs crying out of the house to find her boyfriend. When they meet, he excitedly tells her that he has just been promoted at work by his boss who is, of all people, the new husband of the girl's mother. The boyfriend supports the new marriage, asking 'why not?' This sequence of events in unthinkable in China. Not only does it conflict with values promoted by the government, it is utterly impractical. Perhaps it is just this impossibility that appeals to some Chinese viewers, who can only fantasize about such a social reality, even if many of them would not care for such a lifestyle. Our narrators also said that the spicy stories of the Hong Kong dramas are frequently discussed at home and at work, especially by young people.

Hong Kong television programs are broadcast in Cantonese, the native spoken language of people who live in southern China. Programming sent throughout the country on CCTV, on the other hand, is in China's official language, Mandarin. Consequently, many southern Chinese viewers prefer to watch the Hong Kong shows simply because they are telecast in the more familiar language. This is especially true of older people who have been less able and willing to follow the government's campaign to national-ize Mandarin. Furthermore, some viewers believe that the Hong Kong Cantonese accent has become more prevalent in Guangzhou in recent years, attributable, according to them, to the influence of Hong Kong TV.

AMERICAN TELEVISION PROGRAMS IN CHINA

'There are financial exchange problems and television is in its infancy there, so China has to be treated differently from other countries . . . [The Chinese] don't quite understand the significance of airing a commercial at an allotted time period. And China is highly motivated politically, so anything can change at any moment.' (Bert Cohen, Senior Vice President, International Sales, Worldvision Enterprises; from Sobel, 1987: 72)

'The Open Door policy gives us the chance to import good programs from foreign countries. We are interested in having programs that can have a positive cultural or artistic impact in China.' (Wang Chuanyu, Director of Production, CCTV)

'We are selective about what programs we import. We are not going to pick up programs that are too violent, too sexual, or too religious.' (Pan Huiming, Deputy Director, Guangdong Province Television station)

In order to develop the TV system and fill airtime, China has looked to other countries as sources of programming since the system began. The abundance of television programming that originates in the United States has become a logical resource. The first American show to be aired in China was *Man from Atlantis* in 1979. Shortly thereafter the government arranged to pick up American-originated international news from com-munications satellites. The CCTV evening news invariably features clips from foreign sources accompanied by Mandarin-language voiceovers from the network anchorpersons in Beijing. Some of this material comes from America's Cable News Network (CNN). Dozens of American drama serials have appeared in the past ten years. Speciality programs are also imported. The Chinese preoccupation with learning effective business techniques, for

147

26 American television comes to China.

instance, encouraged them to import *Global View*, an American-produced program that features executives from several huge corporations – including Hewlett-Packard, AT&T, Polaroid, and United Airlines – discussing capitalist economic philosophies and business practices.

Although a few cash deals are struck, nearly all American programs that appear on Chinese television result from barter agreements. Because of China's relatively low economic status, its government is unwilling to spend hard currency on imported television programming. Instead of buying programs outright, they sell airtime on the system to foreign advertisers. Under these agreements, the American producer/syndicator provides programs to China at no cost in order to receive airtime on the Chinese stations, which they then sell to American advertisers. In effect, these barter agreements allow American syndicators to become sales agents for the Chinese television stations.

In 1982, for example, CBS Productions gave China 60 hours of American programs in exchange for 320 minutes of advertising time. Among the shows were *Count Basie in Concert*, *NBA Basketball*, *60 Minutes*, and the *Tournament of Roses Parade*. Advertisers who bought airtime include IBM, Boeing, Weyerhauser, Procter & Gamble, Kodak, and Stauffer Chemical. Twentieth Century Fox later agreed to let CCTV choose 52 feature films from more than 3,000 titles. MCA/Paramount/MGM has provided 100 hours of programming, including *Star Trek*, to CCTV in exchange for commercial time.

Some contracts are for a single show or series while others are for a package of programs. In some cases, syndicators send samples of programs to China for consideration. China also dispatches delegations of representatives overseas to consider programs, and at times the cultural departments of Chinese embassies make recommendations. The manner for selecting programs is not consistent. Managers at CCTV told me in 1989, for instance, that even some non-CCTV delegations who travel overseas have the authority to choose programs, bring them home, and place them on the air directly.

China's big regional and city stations also have authority individually to import shows on barter terms. Lorimar Productions signed a five-year agreement with Shanghai Television (STV) in 1986 where more than 7,500 hours of famous American TV shows were made available. The Shanghai station was able to choose from a list that included *Falcon Crest*, *Knot's Landing*, *Hunter*, *Alf*, *Perfect Strangers*, *Valerie*, and animated programs such as *Thundercats* and *Silverhawks*. Lorimar was particularly interested in signing with STV because it was able to sell more advertising time there than would have been permitted at CCTV.

China imports much sports programming. Viewers like to watch sports in which Chinese teams participate – soccer and volleyball, mainly – but they enjoy watching all sports, including American football and basketball.

I spent time one afternoon in Shanghai with a group of Chinese men watching an American National Basketball Association game. The men reacted excitedly to the game, not realizing that the contest was being transmitted from videotape, not live, and that one of the teams – the Kansas City Kings – had moved to Sacramento several years before. Barter agreements have put the Super Bowl on Chinese television since 1986 and the Entertainment and Sports Network (ESPN) has placed its international program, *Global Sports*, on regional networks in China during prime time.

The most famous and controversial barter agreement between American program producers and Chinese television is the Walt Disney production, *Mickey Mouse and Donald Duck*, a compilation of Disney cartoons dubbed into Mandarin. Resonating perfectly with China's cultural orientation toward children and family, *Mickey Mouse and Donald Duck* quickly became the country's most popular television program after its initial airing in late 1986. The program is presented on Sunday evenings at six-thirty on CCTV. Two minutes of commercial airtime is retained within each half-hour program by the American distributor, Buena Vista.

A financial problem developed, however, when several companies in China began to use images of Disney characters as promotional vehicles to sell various products, a turn of events that prompted the Disney company to temporarily withhold episodes of the show. Disney's lawyers insisted that China pass comprehensive laws to protect trademarks and patents. To settle the problem, a joint venture was proposed that would allow Disney to capitalize on the enthusiastic response in China with the marketing of Disney memorabilia and the formation of a Chinese Mickey Mouse club.

ADVERTISING IN CHINA

Advertising – including foreign advertising – has been part of China's economy and media operation since the post-Cultural Revolution reform movement began. Virtually all mass media, even Communist Party publications, carry advertising. Television stations have become more and more dependent on advertising revenues to maintain their operations. According to the official view, advertising serves socialism by letting the people know what is available to buy and where. Television advertising in particular is thought to motivate consumer activity and invigorate the economy.

China's first television commercials appeared on the innovative Shanghai Television station in February 1979. Before the year ended, CCTV and regional stations throughout the country were airing commercials and virtually all other media began to permit advertising. In terms of money spent, television is still second to newspapers as the top advertising medium. The steadily growing size of the television audience, however, and the comparatively inexpensive cost of advertising on Chinese television, make it an attractive advertising medium. How much money clients pay to advertise on television in China depends on who they are. Domestic 'businesses' (government or private; government firms have budgets that are to be used specifically for 'promotion') pay only about one-third of what foreign sponsors must pay. But the cost of foreign advertising, in terms of cost per thousand (CPM: the ratio of money spent to persons contacted), is also very cost efficient. A one-minute television commercial on Chinese television, for instance, might cost $5–10,000 and could reach 300 million viewers. In the United States, by comparison, a 30-second spot might cost about $400,000 and reach, at most, 65 million viewers. By 1987, American advertisers were placing about $16 million of advertising on Chinese television yearly. And Americans are not the biggest spenders on advertising in China – the Japanese are.

Despite the recent economic setback, Chinese families have realized greater spending power and have been able to choose from an unprecedented number of desirable consumer items. Until the confrontation at Tiananmen Square, American and other foreign advertisers were optimistic about the future of advertising, and business in general, in China. Enthusiasm peaked when the Third World Advertising Conference, a gathering of more than 1,000 high-level advertising executives from all over the world, met in Beijing in June 1987. By that time, many major United States agencies, including J. Walter Thompson, McCann–Erickson, and Ogilvy & Mather, had established offices in the capital city. The general consensus by the end of the conference was that advertising, and the capitalist tendencies it embraces, would continue to grow in China. In fact, by 1987 advertising had become one of China's top growth industries. Statistics released during the conference revealed at least a 50 percent increase in demand for advertising in China every year since 1979. In 1983, China's first public relations firm also opened in Beijing, and soon after advertising and public relations companies began to spring up throughout the country. They now number more than 6,000 with a heavy concentration of the firms located in the SEZs of the south.

The 'China market'

For many years in the United States and in other Western capitalist countries we have heard talk about the 'huge China market.' The international business community has been licking its collective lips in anticipation of enormous profits that presumably could soon be made from the newly-enfranchised Chinese consumers. The troublesome realities of doing business in China, however, became apparent long before the 1989 crackdown sent everyone's plans into disarray. There are many drawbacks to placing ads and doing business in China. Most fundamentally, trade agreements and market realities have limited the number of American products that are available in China. Chinese consumers generally are unfamiliar with imported products. The stores are not full of these goods and when they do appear on the shelves they are often priced out of reach. Most of the imported items that the Chinese people want are not American or European, but Japanese – especially TVs, cameras, cassette recorders, refrigerators, washers, and other domestic equipment. So, until exports to China increase, the strategy taken by most foreign companies is to advertise general features of product lines, company names, logos, and slogans rather than trying to sell specific products.

Furthermore, while consumer spending generally has been on the upswing for the past decade, the amount of disposable income that Chinese families have remains very low. While many people may see a television commercial in China, each of those viewers is 'worth' very little as a consumer. And, of course, the volatile political and economic environment deterred many foreign companies from investing and advertising in China even before the summer of 1989.

The Chinese way of doing business

As Jane Ferguson, director of advertising sales for CBS, has said: 'the Chinese are interested in forming their own policies and evaluating world-wide advertising practices on programming rather than just copying the way it is done in America' (Sobel, 1987: 73). Foreign companies who have entered into joint ventures with China have done better than outsiders who have tried to go it alone there. The investments seem to work out fairly well when Chinese firms share marketing and advertising objectives with foreign companies. However, many foreign companies, including numerous large American firms, are unwilling to enter into joint ventures that do not allow them to dictate the terms of how business will be done.

Problems that affect foreign advertising on Chinese television also crop up in the way broadcast stations are managed. Scheduling of commercials is frequently imprecise and commercials are sometimes not aired at all or not 'made good' when problems occur. Commercials are clustered together at the end of program segments, not during the programs, a policy that does not please American advertisers. Booster stations around the country also sometimes cut off or cover up network commercials by inserting their local ads over the national or regional spots, thereby reducing frequency of contact between message and potential consumer.

THE GAZE AND THE FALL

Chinese emperors throughout the centuries had the habit of destroying all vestiges of cultural life that preceded their dynasties' rise to power. This cultural defrocking, including burning the books of Confucius, was done in the name of cultural and political unity. The emperors, claiming that divine intervention was prompting them, each tried to establish or maintain a single cultural system (*ru*), and declared that the *ru* of previous eras were simply false. In more modern times, the ancient stories of the beloved Chinese opera were rewritten to put into place the political values of Chinese communism, a new variety of *ru*. The challenge for China's managers of culture today is television. In this chapter, I have introduced several considerations about the production of popular culture, particularly television, in China. We now consider how it is received by the audience.

8

LOOKING IN AND LOOKING OUT
Viewing habits and cultural consequences

'Without television you are blind and deaf. You don't know anything.' (53-year-old male food supply worker for military unit, Shanghai)

'We just bought a new color TV but the programs aren't very good.' (54-year-old female personnel manager for an electronics factory, Xian)

'TV was fresh before, but not now, especially for the young generation. The shows are boring. Chinese TV has not improved over the years.' (22-year-old male worker in a medicine factory, Guangzhou)

'From books we learn about the policies of other countries, but from television we learn about everyday life outside of China . . . and it is so vivid.' (20-year-old university student, Beijing)

'Since television they can't fool us anymore.' (24-year-old college student, Beijing)

The power of television rests not only in its ability to influence people by exposing them to particular ideas, thereby serving the interests of those who control programming, but also in the personal evaluations, interpretations, and uses of program content that are made by viewers and the ways that those audience-initiated actions engage and transform political, economic, and cultural realities. This collective cooption of television is an act of cultural construction, and the cultures that are being created in China now draw from a pool of resources that were not available before information from TV became part of the popular consciousness. Given all this, several central questions must be asked. What television programs appeal to viewers? How do people feel about what they get from TV? And most important, what have been the social and cultural consequences of television's presence in China?

154

VIEWERS' FAVORITE PROGRAM TYPES

During the first few minutes of the family interviews we asked each person to tell us his or her favorite type of television program. For family members who were not present, we asked the others to identify the program type that is preferred by the absent person. We accepted multiple responses when viewers had more than one favorite. Some people did not have a favorite type and nothing was recorded when there were disagreements about the preferences of an absent family member.

I have constructed basic statistical representations of the responses. I hasten to point out that these data reflect preferred types of programs – not particular shows, amount of time spent viewing, or impact. Furthermore, there is greater opportunity for some program types to become popular simply because they appear on TV more often. Interestingly, however, some of the least abundant programming (e.g. sports and drama serials) is the most preferred. Program types divide into four essential categories shown in Table 1. In order of overall popularity, these are drama, sports, information, and light entertainment programs. Situation comedies, by far the most popular American prime-time genre, do not appear on Chinese TV.

Drama

Nearly half of the viewers prefer drama, underscoring the fact that Chinese viewers, like people everywhere, watch television primarily for its entertainment value (Lull, 1988). The various drama series are favored most, but traditional Chinese operas are also well-liked.

The age of the viewer makes a difference in the type of television drama that is preferred (statistics not shown). Clearly, young people like contemporary drama serials while older viewers lean toward the Chinese operas. This difference symbolizes how members of the old and young generations think. Contemporary dramas, especially foreign productions, are regarded by many older viewers as irrelevant (outside their experience and interest) or confusing. Similarly, young people are bored by the traditional operas. While the Chinese operas present only the history and traditions of old China, the modern dramas project a progressive, international mood. A retired grandfather in Xian explained that he cannot watch contemporary dramas: 'I love, but I don't talk about love anymore. These new dramas make me very uncomfortable. It's not appropriate for us to watch modern love stories in front of our children and grandchildren.' His wife, a retired metal fabricator, agreed: 'It's so embarrassing if we watch this together. The daughter-in-law and the grandfather should keep some distance between themselves.'

155

TABLE 1 Family members' favorite program types*

Program type	No. of mentions	% of mentions
Drama	183	46
Drama series/specials	84	21
Chinese opera	61	15
Foreign drama	14	4
Movies	10	3
War dramas	8	2
Foreign movies	3	1
Historical drama	3	1
Sports	87	22
Sports (all)	66	17
Kung-fu	21	5
Information	75	19
News	46	12
Educational/TVU	12	3
Travel	9	2
Documentaries	4	1
Language	3	1
Political	1	0
Light entertainment	52	13
Variety	29	7
Children/cartoon	6	2
Animal shows	5	1
Crosstalk	4	1
Game shows	3	1
Music shows	3	1
Comedy	2	1
TOTALS	397	100

* Excluding children 11 years old and younger
Slight discrepancies in column totals are due to rounding error.

Many older viewers use Chinese operas to stake out cultural space in a world that is changing before their eyes at an unprecedented pace. Some of these viewers claim to have 'old style' personalities that resonate culturally with the operas. Furthermore, fans of the opera can watch the same show many times, a reassuring cultural experience. As a Beijing devotee said, 'We watch the operas because of their good values. Chinese people like the Chinese opera like Western people like their Jesus . . . Chinese believe in their old heroes and their history. So people like to watch it again and again just like Western people think that the Christian story never ends.'

Sports

Sports is second only to drama in overall popularity, though there are relatively few sporting events presented on television and Chinese teams rarely appear. The fact that many televised sports presentations are video-tape replays of old contests played outside China doesn't matter much to Chinese viewers since they do not normally follow the status of foreign teams anyway.

European-style football is the favorite television sport. Women's volley-ball is also popular, though it is not televised enough to be named a favorite. Kung-fu is a substantial favorite among viewers too. Although kung-fu action is typically set within a dramatic context, young fans usually appreciate the physical aspect more than the story.

Information

News is the most popular of China's informational programming and exposure to it is actually greater than its popularity suggests. Many family members are regular news viewers, for instance, but do not regard it to be their favorite type of television program. Television is the most access-ible news medium for urban people. Less-educated and older viewers frequently say they benefit from the explanations that accompany the visuals.

Other categories of informational programming elicit far less enthusiasm, though a few viewers say that educational, TVU, travel shows, documen-taries, language-learning programs, or political programming are their favorites.

Light entertainment

This is a catch-all category comprised of comedy, music, dance, and other performance arts. Variety shows, the most popular light entertainment programming, usually include some combination of these elements. Among the most popular light entertainment programs is *Foreigners Sing Chinese Songs* – a rare peek at how the outside world deals with Chinese society, one that flatters and greatly amuses viewers. Other favorites are children's programs (especially cartoons which are sometimes viewed by older view-ers), animal shows (which also appeal to some older viewers), crosstalk, game shows, music and comedy specials.

Gender differences

Males and females differ in their preferences (Tables 2 and 3). Drama is far-and-away the preferred television genre of women. Exactly two-thirds of the female viewers rate drama as their favorite while slightly less than one-third of the men do so. Sports preferences are even more lopsided. Overall, sports is the second most popular type of television program, but nearly all of its support comes from males who consider it to be their favorite program type. The vast majority of sports programming is of male sports, which surely contributes to the unbalanced rating. Women speak highly only of female volleyball matches.

TABLE 2 Male family members' favorite program types*

Program type	No. of mentions	% of mentions
Drama	73	31
Drama series specials	32	14
Chinese opera	18	8
Foreign drama	10	4
Movies	5	2
War dramas	6	3
Foreign movies	1	0
Historical drama	1	0
Sports	81	35
Sports (all)	63	27
Kung-fu	18	8
Information	58	25
News	38	16
Educational/TVU	7	3
Travel	7	3
Documentaries	3	1
Language	2	1
Political	1	0
Light entertainment	21	9
Variety	11	5
Children/cartoon	2	1
Animal shows	2	1
Crosstalk	2	1
Game shows	1	0
Music shows	2	1
Comedy	1	0
TOTALS	233	100

* Excluding children 11 years old and younger
Slight discrepancies in column totals are due to rounding error.

TABLE 3 *Female family members' favorite program types**

Program type	No. of mentions	% of mentions
Drama	110	67
Drama series specials	52	32
Chinese opera	43	26
Foreign drama	4	2
Movies	5	3
War dramas	2	1
Foreign movies	2	1
Historical drama	2	1
Sports	6	4
Sports (all)	3	2
Kung-fu	3	2
Information	17	10
News	8	5
Educational/TVU	5	3
Travel	2	1
Documentaries	1	1
Language	1	1
Political	0	0
Light entertainment	31	19
Variety	18	11
Children/cartoon	4	2
Animal shows	3	2
Crosstalk	2	1
Game shows	2	1
Music shows	1	1
Comedy	1	1
TOTALS	164	100

* Excluding children 11 years old and younger
Slight discrepancies in column totals are due to rounding error.

Men are also more likely than women to like informational programs, especially news. One-fourth of the men prefer informational shows, while but 10 percent of the women do so, making it their least preferred type of show. Light entertainment is the men's least favorite programming, but a popular type for women. Many women speak nostalgically about their love for the artistic content of these shows, sometimes lamenting that they can now only vicariously experience music or dance through television. A number of other less frequently mentioned light entertainment favorites have no gender-based pattern.

Children's favorite shows

Cartoons and children's programming (often the same thing) are heavy favorites for boys and girls aged 11 and under (boys: 53 percent; girls: 68 percent). There is no discernible pattern of second favorites for boys; for girls, dramas are popular. Many teenaged boys like sports and kung-fu programs and girls favor the dramas, but adolescents commonly complain that very little programming suits their interests.

VIEWERS CRITICIZE CHINESE TELEVISION

'When the climax of a television drama is not obvious, it has good flavor. You watch, think, and watch some more. But Chinese programs are very plain . . . our Chinese life is very simple and so is our television.' (21-year-old male artist, Beijing)

The quality of TV sets, number of television channels, and amount and diversity of programming have all increased or improved since television first became part of family life. But at the same time, viewers have become more sophisticated and demanding in their expectations. So, while they recognize the improvements, they also strongly criticize the forms and conventions of the programs and commercials. In one sense, the relatively rapid availability of television in China has ultimately undermined the medium's appeal, especially as the recent economic and political crisis sharpened popular criticism about everything. China does not yet produce many attractive or technically-sophisticated programs.

Program quality

Many viewers believe that Chinese programs are extremely boring and predictable. Except for their favorite shows, the people think that the Chinese dramas are especially deadly. In their words:

'Chinese dramas are so simple you only have to watch the head, not the tail.'

'Our dramas are so predictable. The stories always fit the same pattern and aren't any fun to watch.'

'Domestic series are tasteless . . . same story.'

'Chinese drama is too simple, easy, and predictable in the old style.'

'We always know where the dramas are headed.'

'Our country has a low quality TV system . . . only three channels . . . boring . . . good shows are not on enough. There is nothing to attract me.'

'There are twin problems with Chinese television now . . . it is too boring to begin with and it is becoming too commercial.'

'We need new programs . . . more variety.'

'Chinese shows tend to be the same all the time, especially kung-fu . . . always the same themes.'

'The programs are not very good. After you watch them you have no special feeling . . . no impression . . . you just forget it, it's finished. Some parts should be exciting but they are not. We must improve the quality of TV content.'

Repetition

Television stations often repeat programs and different stations in the same area sometimes carry the same show at different times. Programs are sometimes repeated by the province stations in order to present a popular show in the local dialect. The ability of the Chinese television system to produce a large number of programs is limited by the country's economic and political condition, so many programs are shown more than once simply to fill airtime. This fact doesn't console viewers much. They are annoyed by the repetition.

Production quality

Viewers often criticize domestic TV programs for what they term 'amateurish' production techniques. Chinese people say that foreign countries generally are better at the artistic and technical aspects of television production. A couple of anecdotes illustrate the problem. An American professor friend told me that what he remembered best about Chinese television was a public service program where a close-up shot of a Bunsen burner emanated from the screen. My friend left the room where the TV was located and returned ten minutes later only to find the exact same inanimate image showing on the screen with little or no narration. One young Guangzhou viewer held a still photograph in front of us as he explained that in Chinese shows 'nothing moves . . . nothing happens . . . the shows are flat. If they don't improve TV they will never be able to attract young people.' A young Beijing viewer called Chinese production techniques 'rough,' and said that even less-developed countries have greater production skill.

Timing

Some viewers believe that the good TV shows are scheduled too late (after 9 or 10 p.m.), creating problems for older people, students, and workers.

The more interesting common complaint, however, is that certain program elements – especially commercials and late night news inserts – interrupt dramatic presentations. When commercials or news follow an episode of a popular dramatic series, for instance, viewers are annoyed by the sudden introduction of unrelated and usually unannounced program material. Commercials appear in clusters that sometimes last ten minutes or more and are not listed in the TV program guides.

Alterations in TV program schedules are also common. Programs do not always begin at the publicized times. Substitutions are sometimes made without notice. Programs are added that are not in the listings, thereby throwing off the entire schedule. Shows run longer than scheduled. These adjustments negatively affect millions of people. A Beijing meatcutter describes the inconvenience: 'We work hard, catch the bus, push, push, push to see the TV shows we want . . . but then they just run commercials or other useless shows.' The parents of a Xian girl said that she is 'nervous and out of breath' when her favorite shows don't appear on time.

Popular serials are generally scheduled for one or two episodes per week, a rate of presentation that many viewers think is too slow. Some viewers complain that the stories themselves don't develop fast enough while others say they lose track of the plot because there is so much time between episodes, causing them to become apprehensive about the stories.

THE PROBLEM OF COMMERCIALS

'The people told us, "Don't put commercials inside the programs. Put them all together or we will turn off our TVs." So we did. We try to follow the audience's suggestions. But we cannot follow their biggest suggestion: "Take the commercials off the air!" ' (Chen Ro Rou, Director of Audience Research, CCTV)

Some viewers consider commercials to be necessary, but most people hate them. Criticisms are made of both their form and content. People feel first of all that there are simply too many commercials and that they interrupt viewing even though they generally do not appear during the programs.[1] Viewers complain that the same commercials are presented over and over, appearing unchanged on some stations for a year or more. The low production quality of domestic commercials compared to foreign spots is even more apparent than are differences in full-length programs. Because of their crucial importance in marketing products in capitalist countries, commercials are among the most technically and aesthetically advanced forms of television production. Compared to the fast and flashy American and Japanese commercials, Chinese television ads are 'tiresome,' in the words of a Shanghai viewer. Visual transitions are rough, directors tend to be zoom crazy, and audio tracks are muffled and inconsistent from spot

27 The new domestic necessities in China: refrigerator, washer, color TV, audio cassette/dubbing machine.

to spot. China has recently imported various special effects equipment in order to improve the production quality of domestic commercials. A broadcast official in Shanghai said he hopes this will encourage the audience to 'tolerate the commercials better.'

Because China's economy is based in part on planning and market demand that is not directed solely toward individual consumers and families, many commercials on Chinese television are designed to reach buyers for factories and other work units. So, it is not unusual to see commercials for enormous power generators, hydraulic cranes, and two-ton trucks on prime-time TV. The frequency of these commercials increases to intolerable proportions when the big industrial items are overstocked. Imagine how viewers feel when these commercials appear. The people cannot understand why they have to sit through announcements for something 'that we don't even know what it's for!' according to one man. In recent years with the growth of the private sector economy, viewers now also speculate that the advertised industrial products may be within financial grasp of some of China's rich entrepreneurs, a suspicion that further intensifies viewers' great distaste for these odd commercials.

Viewers also believe that much of the information contained in commercials is untrue. One person remarked, 'they say things like "we're number one in the whole world" . . . "we're internationally famous," and so on.

28 One of the industrial commercials to which viewers are routinely subjected.

It's not true.' Another person said that sponsors 'say their product is better and cheaper but they never tell us the price.' The vast difference between the reality that is presented in commercials and what citizens encounter in their everyday lives is perhaps most clearly dramatized in how service is portrayed on TV. Commercials routinely show caring store clerks cheerfully helping customers when in reality it is nearly impossible to get good service in stores anywhere in China. Furthermore, these overblown commercials are, indeed, a curiosity in a system, and a culture, that generally does not condone overstatement. In that sense, TV commercials may be the most capitalistic feature of modern China. Advertising's rhetorical excesses irritate even those who favor more private enterprise.

The people are even more cynical about the relationship between advertising messages, the availability of advertised products, and product performance. Many products that are advertised on television are not available in the stores and as a result viewers feel misled and they are angry about it. They interpret the problem as either inefficiency in the economic system or a blatant disregard for the truth on the part of the television stations. Either way, viewers are mightily irritated. Let me provide some examples.

A Beijing viewer blames Chinese television stations for indulging in unethical behavior: 'Some commercials even cheat people . . . the television stations just accept money for commercials. They don't care about the

quality of the product or its availability . . . they just play the commercials.'
Many people say that constant discrepancies between advertising claims,
product availability, and product performance has led to serious credibility
problems.

Irresponsible advertising has become commonplace in China as stations
have grown more and more dependent on commercial revenues and have
become willing to accept the short-term profits that can be turned by
overlooking unethical advertising claims. China's lack of an effective legal
system in general, and its inability to regulate communications activity in
particular, further contribute to the problem. As the people started to
suffer greatly from inflation in the late 1980s, they became far less tolerant
of these ever-increasing abuses. Viewers do not consider these problems to
be isolated difficulties. Misleading advertising messages have dramatically
helped spread the belief in China that the entire system is not working well
and that television stations, like virtually everything else in the country, are
corrupt. The commercials advertise the corruption as much as they do the
products.

A perspective on these problems, with special reference to the advertising
of imported products, is provided by a young, highly-educated couple in
Xian (he is a college instructor; she is a public relations consultant):

Husband: 'I teach economics but I don't like commercials. Some of
them are not responsible. We cannot buy many of the
products shown.'

Wife: 'They show the Japanese trademark of an automatic
clothes washer . . . but we can't buy one in the store
[because of import limitations]. Sometimes they advertise
even without having the product just to build up a reputation. The government limits how many of these products
can come to China, but the audience dreams about these
products.'

Husband: 'China doesn't know how to make commercials. You have
to tell the truth to people. They are tired of exaggerations.'

Fighting the transportation system to go to a store where the product is
supposed to be, then not being able to buy it, infuriates people. The whole
situation is a test of the economic system. When difficulties are encountered
following the suggestions of advertising, people become angry at television,
commercials, the stores, and the entire Chinese manufacturing and marketing system.

IMITATION, LEARNING, AND SOCIAL BEHAVIOR

'I know that the amount of TV viewing that people do in the West
is like a disease. We will probably have the same problem in China,

but so far we don't have very many channels so the problem isn't serious yet.' (37-year-old male teacher in an industrial economics college, Communist Party member, Xian)

'My daughter is only 7 years old but she is already learning how to wear makeup and jewelry. She even learned to jump up and kiss daddy and mommy when they come home from work – that's a completely Western custom.' (43-year-old male television producer, Shanghai)

'In China we don't have much violence like they have in America. We don't want to pass the idea of violence along to people. We prefer to use television for positive propaganda . . . TV should not emphasize the cruel parts of the world. If kids are home and watch TV, they should get positive information.' (81-year-old male retired geologist, Beijing)

'We encourage students to watch certain programs because young people really like to imitate television. We encourage them to imitate the good characters on TV.' (39-year-old secondary-level teacher, Shanghai)

A story is told in China about a young girl who killed herself after watching a television program that reminded her of her own situation. The girl had viewed a Japanese drama in which the lead character suffered from a rare disease. The story ends when the girl in the drama loses her will to live and takes a small boat out into the ocean where she commits suicide. The girl who watched this program had a similar disease and identified with the actress's circumstances. Depressed from her illness and fearing that her parents did not love her, the girl sailed a small boat into the sea where she killed herself.

This story got a lot of play in the Chinese press and became the ultimate example of television's potential negative influence. Although this case is recognized as extreme, people generally think that television stimulates young people to imitate the images and actions it presents. Indeed, a major objective of television programmers is to provide positive role models that audience members *will* imitate. Parents realize that even very young children imitate what they see on television, particularly physical action:

– A 2-year-old child watches a marathon race on TV and imitates the cheerleaders.
– The same child learns to recognize foreigners from TV.
– A 16-month-old child knows her favorite television characters by sight.
– A 3-year-old child imitates perfectly the actions of characters on the Japanese cartoon shows.

166

29 The American TV program *Hunter*. Children playing on the streets of Shanghai.

– Grade school children routinely sing and play out the cartoon dramas at school.

– A 3-year-old moves his arms in 'show dance style' to television disco dancing.

– Another 3-year-old memorizes and sings back the theme songs to commercials.

One character that young chlidren love to imitate is *Chi-kung* (or *Chi-tien*), the 'drunken Buddha' or 'crazy monk.' He is a famous literary figure from centuries ago known for his quirky personality and individualism. *Chi-kung* has become a famous cartoon character on TV. His unique clothes, speech pattern, and funny behavior all attract children. Virtually every youngster in China knows *Chi-kung* – but this is the first generation to know him from television. For adolescents, it is television and film stars, pop singers, and sports heroes who are the popular role models today.

Kung-fu: Chinese violence

For boys especially, role models who really stand out on television now are the kung-fu heroes, China's action–adventure stars. A Shanghai man said: 'A lot of kids like to learn kung-fu. A few months ago the newspaper reported that a young boy learned kung-fu from TV and hurt somebody.' A 14-year-old Xian boy said that his teacher tells the students not to use kung-fu techniques to beat the younger children. This boy says that 'without kung-fu life would be boring . . . but too much kung-fu isn't good either because I can't concentrate on my schoolwork. I always want to watch it.' A mother from Beijing agreed that kung-fu has the most influence: 'The children are curious about it. After they watch they either physically imitate it, or talk about the story and how the actors did the kung-fu. Kids imitate the exciting parts.'

Parents do not seem greatly concerned about the impact of kung-fu, despite the news reports and even the observed behavior of their own children. The father of a 5-year-old Shanghai boy, for instance, says that his son likes to 'fight with me, kung-fu style.' He said that he isn't worried about the future effect of this, since 'he is very obedient in nursery school.' A Beijing mother noticed that her male children like kung-fu and war movies: 'These programs interest children very fast and the kids imitate the shows quickly too. They just play with each other, though. They usually don't hurt each other.' Still, kung-fu is China's most popular form of televised violence. A Guangzhou father lamented, 'Kids don't think about kung-fu, they just imitate it. This kind of violence is human nature. It's the common sickness of the whole world.'

The Chinese audience: a cultural perspective

In what ways are viewer preferences, criticisms, and the social effects of television in China unique to the culture? This is an important question to ask about the implications of television as cultural contexts invariably help shape viewing experiences. Certain features of television seem to inspire near universal responses, while other aspects differ greatly from culture to culture (Lull, 1988).

In China we find that the program preferences of viewers are extremely similar to those of television audiences in other countries. The gender-differentiated patterns resemble the program preferences of men and women from countries with very different levels of economic development, government systems, and television systems. Men's interest in sports, information, and action-based drama and women's preferences for drama and performance art seem to be universal phenomena. The generational differences in China also mirror other societies.

The basic processes of social learning from television in the People's Republic also do not differ from other countries, except that China makes a concerted effort to provide positive role models which they hope the people will imitate. This strategy doesn't work very well in today's political environment. Furthermore, China's young 'television generation' finds other representations more alluring. Especially for boys, the exciting images of action and sport are far more tempting to imitate. Though China does not telecast the endless highly-violent action adventure serials that have become so familiar to viewers in the West, the amount of violent imagery is steadily creeping upward. China's original violent programming, kung-fu dramas and war movies, are supplemented now by an increasing number of imported foreign action serials, movies, and cartoon programs. Consequently, Chinese children increasingly imitate violent acts that involve fighting and weapons. Toy guns are readily available in the stores.

Criticisms that Chinese viewers have of television are more culturally specific. As the novelty of television has worn off and viewers have become more sophisticated and demanding of television, certain criticisms are frequently voiced. Although the government has made a major commitment to develop and use television to propagandize, provide entertainment, and stimulate the economy, the people are not content with what television has to offer them. They readily attribute their dissatisfaction with the dramatic and technical quality of domestic programs, the high amount of repetition, and the difficulties with timing to what they consider to be a philosophy of television programming, and of life in general, that is predictable and unexciting. Television is there for all to see; it identifies, emphasizes, and symbolizes certain fundamental contradictions and shortcomings of Chinese socialist society in a way that is most persuasive to its audience.

169

These tendencies are then strengthened by viewers' exposure to foreign television programs, a theme which I will now develop more.

THE CULTURAL REFERENCE POINT

A key argument I will now make is that television has become the main reference point which Chinese people use to compare and evaluate their own national status, a development that has inspired viewers to dream of a better future while at the same time they have become frustrated and angered by the barriers that stand in the way. Television has irreversibly altered the consciousness of the Chinese public. It has introduced, reinforced, and popularized ideas and images that have fueled the imagination of the people in ways that far exceed what government planners had in mind when they first promoted the medium's widespread adoption.

The mind opener

China is not the only communist government that has been radically undermined by television in recent years. The shocking dissolution of communism in eastern and central European countries, particularly East Germany, is directly traceable to a cultural upheaval that resulted in part from the intrusion of foreign television signals and their interaction with other forms of resistant local 'popular' culture (Wicke, 1991). In contrast, however, the television images that threaten the political status quo in China are all transmitted by the government's own telecommunications apparatus.

Though the people don't care much for the majority of the programs that are fed to them, television is nonetheless appreciated for its general ability to 'open the minds' of viewers, providing not just new ideas to consider, but a whole new way to think. Our narrators explain how television has expanded their consciousness:

> 'You don't learn very fast from books . . . but with TV, in one or two hours you can really understand something. Having a TV is a big step for the human being.'

> 'It makes my sight broader.'

> 'It opens my mind, gives me new thinking, makes me happier.'

> 'helps my mental development.'

> 'can activate my child's brain.'

> 'helps children develop their thinking.'

> 'TV brings a new lifestyle and improves our life greatly.'

170

'stimulates children . . . now our child asks questions like, "how can an airplane fly?" '

'we use our brains to figure out the mystery shows.'

'has made my mind and brain more clear. For example, I can understand what they report on the news.'

'Now we cannot be without TV. If it is broken, we have to repair it as soon as possible. I would try to repair it myself because if we had to send it out for repair we would feel very uncomfortable.'

Vicarious travel

Except for a few lucky students and professionals, very, very few Chinese people ever leave the country. Fewer still expect to get out now with the tightening that has followed the Tiananmen Square turmoil. Viewers commonly say that television is the only way they can visit foreign lands. Using television for vicarious travel is common in cultures everywhere. But the use of the medium is more meaningful for Chinese viewers since they realize that they are unlikely to ever leave the country:

'We aren't like foreigners who can come to see us . . . we can't get out to see them.'

'We stay at home but we learn about the whole world.'

'When we first got color TV it was just like going to a foreign country.'

'With TV we can know everything. We can watch people who are far, far away.'

'You can travel . . . right in front of your eyes . . . it's not just a screen.'

Comparing China to the rest of the world

'In our daily lives we just go to work and come home, so we want to see something that is different from our own life. TV gives us a model of the rest of the world.' (58-year-old male accountant, Shanghai)

'Television encourages us to ask more of ourselves than ever before.' (42-year-old male manager in electric company, Communist Party member, Guangzhou)

'Television helps us understand the condition of other countries. Now

171

we realize that China is very different from the advanced countries.'
(22-year-old male clerk in hospital, Beijing)

'I want to know why foreign countries are more advanced than
China. I do think socialism is better than capitalism, but foreigners
seem to have a much higher standard of living and better technology.
Why?' (29-year-old male textile factory worker, Xian)

'Now, with TV, we can understand the feelings of human beings
everywhere.' (51-year-old male vehicle dispatcher for construction
company, Beijing)

Before television and the advent of the Open Door policy, Chinese people
had precious little information about life outside their country, and the
impressions they did receive were highly propagandistic. Now, nearly
everyone in China not only gets information about the outside world, they
develop critical perspectives on it. Television is the main source. Chinese
viewers readily compare their lives to the images of foreign countries that
they see on TV. In recent years especially they've had many opportunities
to do so. Among the TV programs featured in just one week in fall 1989,
in Beijing, for instance, were: *Oh, My Child*, a drama serial from Japan,
The Detective, a serial from Germany, *The Red Sun Sets Again*, a soap opera
from Taiwan, *The Municipal Functionaries*, a film from Czechoslovakia, *Man
of Steel*, a CBS feature film from the United States, *Hunter*, an action–adventure serial, and *Our House*, another serial, both also from the United States,
Around the World: Iraq, a travel documentary, *Ciranda de Pedra*, a soap opera
from Brazil, *Looking at the World: Kyoto*, a travel documentary about Japan,
Clever Ikkyu, a Japanese cartoon, as well as language lessons in French,
English, and Japanese.

Viewers are drawn to the screen for more than the entertainment value
of foreign programs. More than anything they simply want to see what is
going on in the rest of the world – not just the political issues and events
of foreign places, but simply what other countries look like. This collective
curiosity inspires selectively attentive viewing styles. Some people told us,
for instance, that when they watch international news, they pay far more
attention to street scenes from foreign cities than to the political reporting
that accompanies the pictures. Other genres and forms of television provoke
similar involvements. Commercials stimulate viewers to think about their
material standard in relation to other countries. The United States and
Japan are most often compared to China. What the Chinese viewers see
in the foreign programs and commercials are extremely glamorous,
idealized images of life outside their country, making the cultural contrasts
extraordinarily sharp. Television has influenced the audience's thinking on
topics that range from sports and consumer activity to the most profound

30 Television presents a provocative clash of values.

political, economic, and cultural issues. Our narrators further illustrate
how they make these comparisons:

> 'From television we can see that China needs to work hard in order
> to compete in world football.' (41-year-old male maintenance worker,
> Shanghai)

The passion that men have for televised sports is dampened sometimes by
the failure of Chinese football teams to compete well with teams from
other countries. Viewers compare how teams from different countries play
football by watching games on television. A Beijing man who loves to
watch Chinese teams play said, 'Foreign teams play like their lives depend
on it. They run to the ball. Chinese players just stand there and wait for
the ball to come to them.' His teenage son added, 'We are too slow, too
soft.' And, again, the father: 'There is big wind, small rain in China. We
say something but we can't do it.' This brief snippet of conversation reveals
how deep the comparisons go. Viewers begin by comparing one aspect of
their society (football-playing skill) to another society, an evaluation that
is made possible by television. But they soon generalize beyond the boundaries of the original comparison. China suffers in the process. Viewers are
discouraged.

173

We asked a Shanghai family if they thought it is possible to be influenced by the images of Western countries that now appear on Chinese television. Would they want to adopt a Western lifestyle? A woman answered:

'Look at the Western people's kitchen. Western people come home from work, go into the kitchen, open this and that, and cook dinner. In my family we have to put the refrigerator in the bedroom! Western people take a shower and go to bed. We don't have a shower in the house. Western people go to the supermarket to pick up food, pay for it, and go home . . . it's so easy. We still have to wait in lines to get food sometimes. We cannot compare China with the West.' (42-year-old female worker in a watch factory, Shanghai)

But of course viewers *do* make the comparisons. The simplistic and condemning impression of the West that China's government has promoted for so many years backfires now that everyone watches television and makes their own interpretations of life outside the country. The restrictive Chinese television system still leaks powerful images that fuel alternative visions of the West. The influence does not always come from American programs. A 32-year-old female hotel service worker in Beijing, for instance, says that the Mexican drama series, *Slanders*, gave her a new perspective on people in the West:

'Through gossip we have always known something about the West. But TV shows us that the West is not as terrible as what we have heard from government information and from our relatives. *Slanders* shows that the West is not so bad. For example, the Mexican family in the program is very close, just like a lot of Chinese families . . . and Western people work hard to improve themselves.'

Chinese viewers are fascinated by the similarities and dissimilarities between their country and the rest of the world. Analyzing the differences gives them new perspectives not only on the outside world, but on their own government and system too. One university student in Beijing, for instance, told me that the main impression of the United States she has gotten from television is that of workplace efficiency: 'You have assembly lines in America. In China we just waste our time.' Another narrator comments:

'We watch foreign shows to see the customs, lifestyles, and industrial development of foreign nations. I want to know how far we are behind foreign societies. If our propaganda doesn't represent the truth, the people will make their own analyses and comparisons. Before the Cultural Revolution the government exaggerated the domestic and foreign situations. They said nothing is valuable outside China. But when we look at the TV programs we can see that the

West is not bad. So, when the government makes propaganda now it should not be so dramatic – the people can immediately see if it is true. We need to *say* what is true and *do* what is true in order to develop now . . . We can learn good things from foreign countries, not just close our eyes and say we are the best. We can make up our shortcomings by learning from other countries. The government is looking for ways to solve our problems, but so far it hasn't found them.' (57-year-old male foreign investment manager, Beijing)

Some foreign television programs are confusing culturally. Long hair on male football players was noticed by one viewer, for instance, who said he thought this fashion was 'strange . . . but interesting.' He also realized that the long-haired players were far better than the short-haired Chinese squad. Another person said that from TV she noticed that 'in the West, even terrible people have cars!' The imported television movie, *Man of Steel*, which was playing on the national network during my return visit in 1989, has a scene where a terrifyingly emotional man throws his wife against a wall as he screams at her – quite a contrast to family values promoted in China.

Imagine what Chinese children must think of the world that is constructed in the weekly cartoon program, *Mickey Mouse and Donald Duck*. Consider the contents of one half-hour show. The first segment is 'Mickey Mouse Disco.' All the Disney characters are playing in a disco band, singing English lyrics to an infectious, heavy, dance beat. Donald is called 'Macho Duck' as he dances wildly and kisses several other ducks. Suddenly the scene changes to Rio de Janeiro where Mickey Mouse also dances out of control at the beach to the Supremes' song, 'You Keep Me Hanging On.' In the next segment, flaxen-haired, blue-eyed Cinderella is kidnapped by the devil and taken to Hell where she is held hostage. At the end, Donald speaks perfect Mandarin as he plays with dozens of little animals who bounce around the screen singing. This is an especially touching scene in a society where families don't have pets and rarely have contact with animals except at the zoo or on television.

OSHIN – THE JAPANESE SOAP OPERA INVADES CHINA

A case study of how the most powerful foreign television imagery does not always come from the west

By analyzing a foreign program that became extremely popular in the People's Republic of China, I want to explore other dimensions of the idea that television has introduced provocative imagery to the Chinese public that has confused, frustrated, and inspired them all at the same time. The famous Japanese television soap opera *Oshin* gave Chinese people a first-

175

hand look at the successful development of their longstanding Asian competitor through the touching life story of an exceptional woman. The program was presented on CCTV two nights each week during the summer of 1986. *Oshin* was dubbed into Mandarin for airing in the People's Republic, but it has also been translated into several other foreign languages for showing in Hong Kong, Singapore, Seoul, Brussels, New York, and Tehran (where it also had a profound, though very different, cultural impact), among other places.

The story centers around constant hardships and tragedies which the lead character, Oshin, encounters but somehow always manages to overcome. The story is set during and after World War Two. Oshin's oldest son dies during the fighting. Her husband commits suicide when Japan loses the war. She adopts the son of a close friend. She loses her house to an unscrupulous competitor. She takes her daughter-in-law away from a life of prostitution which the girl had undertaken to pay Oshin back materially for her kindness. She fights to re-establish a profitable family business. She holds the family together during the toughest of times in Japan. *Oshin* is well-cast and acted, and is of superb technical quality.

More than anything, the program is powerful ideologically. Oshin is a hard-driving family manager with a capitalist vision – her steadfast refusal to let her adopted son follow his heart into the world of art, encouraging him instead to become a businessman, reveals her priorities. She is a tragic heroine. Her ability to transcend a sequence of seemingly endless crises comes from personal strength, intelligence, cunning, and aggressiveness in looking out for the well being of her family and in doing business. Despite the frequency and severity of misfortunes that confront her, Oshin never despairs.

Walking through China's neighborhoods during the steamy summer, one could not miss hearing the sounds of *Oshin* filtering out of the houses onto the street. Entire families watched together. People who worked outside the home while *Oshin* was on the air sometimes took FM radios that receive television audio signals with them so they could follow the story. Children who fell asleep during the show asked their parents the next morning to fill them in on what they had missed. *Oshin* was a true television phenomenon in China.[2]

The series was popular for many reasons. Some of the reasons can be guessed from what I have already said about television in the People's Republic – few serials (even fewer of high dramatic and technical quality), a limited number of channels to choose from, and few other leisure activities. But above all else, *Oshin* resonated culturally with the Chinese audience, striking at least four responsive chords. First, as we shall see in the next few paragraphs, people thought that the values portrayed in the show are similar to China's dominant cultural values. Second, Oshin was greatly admired as a person – an individual who not only exhibits acceptable cultural values, but possesses great personal qualities. Third, Oshin's personal struggles symbolize what Japan has endured and accomplished since its defeat in World War Two. Chinese citizens are well aware of the technological progress and economic power that Japan has amassed since 1945. They reluctantly admire Japan's success. So, Oshin's ability to maintain a family and develop a profitable business against all odds is considered to be symbolic of Japan's success and a model for contemporary China. Finally, *Oshin* was often thought to be a 'woman's show.' Though it was viewed by many men, it appealed more to women who readily identified with Oshin and regarded the program as something of their own. Because of the great importance of this program in China, I will now elaborate on the first three of these analytical issues.

Cultural values

Chinese viewers certainly saw something of the customs and traditions of their own society represented in the most basic assumptions and social practices of scenes from *Oshin*. This is especially true of human relationships. Many viewers spoke of the perceived sameness between China and Japan. A mother from Beijing, for instance, observed: 'Love relationships between Japanese people are similar to Chinese. We can understand the way the characters act in *Oshin*. We can't accept some other foreign programs so easily, especially their attitudes about love and man–woman relationships.' Another woman said that she sometimes cried when she watched the show, particularly when someone is treated unfairly. According to her: 'Traditionally the daughter-in-law is mistreated by the mother-in-law in our societies. The parents eat first, then the daughter-in-law can eat.'

Many people identified with and became very emotionally involved in the misery and near hopelessness of Oshin's situation. Consistent with the Confucian notion that an individual must tolerate hardships and strive for harmony and virtue despite the surroundings, Oshin was an archetypal role model for Chinese people. Oshin had to endure the most miserable life imaginable. Viewers said that this tolerance for suffering was something that they understood culturally.

The overall cultural similarity between Japan and China, even the fact that the people resemble each other physically, means that imagery from Japanese television programs is interpreted very differently by the Chinese from that of Western countries. The cultural resonance encourages Chinese viewers to earnestly compare their way of life to the Japanese. In *Oshin*, for example, the heavy emphasis that is placed on maintaining the cohesiveness and integrity of the family and on working hard as a group in order to overcome adversity are cultural values that Chinese embrace. More subtle verbal and nonverbal messages such as the ways that decisions are made, how men, women, and children talk to each other, and how emotions are shown, to name but a few considerations, also promote a perception of cultural compatibility. *Oshin* may be the most striking illustration of how Japanese programs are more influential in many respects in China than American and other Western programs ever could be. Because Chinese people watch Japanese programs with a common cultural frame of reference, the judgments they render when comparing the two nations have a much different weight and significance.

Oshin – the woman

Oshin was called 'superwoman' (*nu qiang ren*) by several viewers, a Chinese term that acknowledges someone's true genius and talent. People were amazed that Oshin could continue to focus on the tasks she faced and do so well. In the words of a female Shanghai viewer, 'Oshin can eat the bitter,' a traditional Chinese expression of respect. Her ability to persist is a supreme personal quality. According to a Beijing man, 'The program shows people how to live without fear of what's in their way.' A Shanghai woman added: 'When people have this kind of tolerance they can achieve anything they want.' Another viewer: 'No one can compete with her.' A Beijing man said: 'The woman has a certain goal in life that she wants to come true . . . no matter how bad life is, she just keeps going. Yesterday, finally, she moved into her new house!'

Other viewers describe Oshin thus: strong-willed, brave, capable, smart, independent, peaceful (in the program she disagreed with Japan's military involvements), industrious, kind, patient, and optimistic. Moreover, she is praised for her constant desire to improve herself. One female narrator said that 'Oshin is a good role model for our children. Kids can learn from this program not to ignore or discriminate against old people.' Other viewers admire her because she continued to respect her husband despite the hard times they had and the differences that existed between them.

Japan's economic power

Another common theme that emerged in our discussions with viewers about the program was admiration for Japan's recent success as a world economic power and the hope that China can do the same thing. Of course Chinese people knew about Japan's economic prosperity years before *Oshin* was telecast. They had seen revealing pictures on television before, including news coverage of Deng Xiaoping's first visit to Japan (Perkins, 1986: 58). But *Oshin* personalized the process of economic success. Many viewers believe that Oshin's story reflects what is needed at the individual level for an entire society to prosper. In fact, this general theme coincides perfectly with ideological lessons that Chinese citizens regularly receive.

Oshin's story begins at a time when Japan was demoralized and impoverished economically. The country developed anew from bankruptcy and was saddled with the human devastation of Hiroshima and the immeasurable sadness and embarrassment of having lost the war. Chinese citizens fully realize how far Japan has progressed economically since the late 1940s – the very point in political history when their own nation was established. They suffer from knowing of the great disparity in living standards between the two countries, knowledge that comes from television and by observing the many Japanese tourists who visit China. Nonetheless, many Chinese people feel that if the Japanese can do it, so can they.

Oshin helped Chinese people understand *how* Japan succeeded. A nuclear scientist who lives in a housing complex in Beijing where many of the country's most respected technical experts reside has an especially insightful description of *Oshin*:

'Right now we are in a period of super development in economics and technology. From TV we need programs to stimulate people's attitudes and spirit to work for economic development and technological improvement in order to make China strong. We can look to the Japanese for an example. They had such a hard time in World War Two, but now they are strong. They learned about modern technology from the West. Take automobiles, for example. Now the Japanese occupy a strong position in the American car market. They make money from the West. Japan focuses on practical science. From *Oshin* we learn that in hard times you must work hard and develop your career. Only if people adopt this attitude can we realize the four modernizations.'

But viewers also know that the context for Oshin's success in Japan differs in some important ways from China. Her material success was made possible because of the freedom she had to choose her own profession – a theme that contrasts with career realities in China – and because she was able to work within Japan's essentially capitalist economic system. The program makes it clear that Japanese workers are rewarded for taking initiative, even within the boundaries of the collective work ethic that exists there. So, for the millions of Chinese who followed this series – and it was a program that nearly everyone saw – *Oshin* helped inspire visions of personal freedom that most of them cannot realize, despite the cultural and personal encouragement that the program gave.[3]

THE UNMANAGEABLE CULTURE

The development of friendly relations with Japan, the United States, and other countries has led to the importation of television programs from all over the world. The imported images have become resources in the ongoing construction of distinct, powerful, and irreversible cultural influences – an audience-constructed initiative that draws from highly disparate sources while it also reflects the influence of China's economic and political crisis. The new understandings and perspectives have developed gradually within the past decade. Beverly Hooper saw the wave swelling even before television signals blanketed the cities:

> Economic affluence is probably the major image that most young people have of the West. After years of official rhetoric about the dramatic progress made in China since liberation, they have become only too aware of their country's relative backwardness. Despite the increasing availability of consumer goods, there is an immense contrast between China's overcrowded living conditions and almost subsistence-level living standards, and the idea they have of everyday life in the West . . . No longer can the Chinese government convince young people that China has a satisfactory standard of living compared with other countries or that their restrictive way of life is the only possible lifestyle.
>
> (Hooper, 1985: 139, 148)

Culture cannot be managed by government decree. The government may be able to fix prices of commodities, but it cannot fix the people's thinking. The stream of cultural imagery that has cut paths through China since 1979 has produced a formidable corpus of alternative visions that has encouraged Chinese people to imagine radical new ways of living. Television is the foremost instrument in the evolution of the new consciousness, not least of all because of the 'leaky' nature of programming policy in an expanding system, the whirlwind pace of life embraced within the telecommunications age, and the indeterminate nature of ideological and cultural hegemony. Television guarantees that a uniform ideology cannot be maintained. The resulting contradictory impulses demand a confused, then frustrated, then angry response from at least some of the audience. Ideological disjunctures are particularly striking in China as the shining, singleminded, idealistic visions promoted within the official rhetoric of communism have clouded. The strongest reactions have come from urban residents who have the greatest access to information, including the mass media, a wider variety of human contacts in the course of everyday living, greater education, and less temporally and physically demanding work that permits more time to reflect on the issues.

The closed, smug attitude of the Chinese government has left many people feeling betrayed as they have begun to zealously exercise the greatest human resource – the imagination. And while most people may not wholeheartedly embrace Western ideas, they have a sense now of the complexity of the West – and that, in and of itself, intrigues them. China's staid and stoic society stands in stark contrast to a more diverse and exciting life represented in television's portrayal of foreign lands. This does not mean that the Chinese people are ready to throw away the essential principles or practices of socialism completely, only that they now demand to face reality. The way viewers compare their own television programs to the imported shows symbolizes the story of the society: Chinese programs are boring and they are not getting better.

9

TIANANMEN SQUARE AND BEYOND

China's insurmountable image problem

'The recent student unrest is not going to lead to any major disturbances. But because of its nature it must be taken very seriously. Firm measures must be taken against any student who creates trouble at Tiananmen Square . . . No concessions should be made · in this matter . . . If any of them disturb public order or violate the law, they must be dealt with unhesitatingly . . . This is not a problem that has arisen in just one or two places or in just the last couple of years; it is the result of the failure over the past several years to take a firm, clear-cut stand against bourgeois liberalization.' (Deng Xiaoping, from remarks made to members of the Central Committee of the Chinese Communist Party, December 30, 1986; published in Deng, 1987)

'Students and workers have different reasons for protesting, but we travel our roads together in the same direction.' (22-year-old female university student, Beijing, 1989)

This is one chapter that I would have preferred not to have written. At least it is possible to imagine scenarios far more agreeable than what finally happened in Beijing in the early summer of 1989. But as Deng intimated more than three years before the eventual crackdown, some kind of confrontation between government hardliners and the country's progressive forces was inevitable. In a period of less than two months, from April 18th to June 4th, the Tiananmen Square drama unfolded in Beijing and on television screens worldwide. The military repression that was finally ordered by Deng against an unarmed public was not only morally reprehensible, it was an enormous political mistake for which China is now paying and will continue to pay for a long time.

If there ever was a news story where the heroes and villains were more clearly identifiable, I have yet to hear about it. Media representations highlighted the contrast: idealistic students suffer from a hunger strike imposed to create dialogue with the very government that was readying its army; a single man stands courageously in front of a line of menacing

tanks; the homemade Goddess of Democracy statue is erected during the
waning days of the protest and is later knocked down by People's Liberation Army soldiers, and so on. This is not only the stuff of news; it was
a poignant drama especially fitting for quick and certain interpretations
by broadcast journalists and by an international television-viewing public.

The story is more complex than what television revealed. Covering
the story during its climactic moments was very difficult for journalists,
particularly the television crews who had to avoid detection of their bulky
equipment by the martial law soldiers. Consequently, video images of what
is widely termed the 'Tiananmen Square Massacre' are unclear about the
details of what happened the night of June 3rd and early morning of June
4th, a confusion that has been exploited by the Chinese in their post-
Tiananmen Square propaganda. As it turns out – a fact that is now
admitted even by several Western journalists – perhaps no one, or just a
very few people, died *at* Tiananmen Square, and the body count reported
by the media at the time is probably far greater than the actual number
of deaths.[1]

Chinese media accounts of the turmoil that appeared after martial law
was declared were grossly distorted to fit the propagandist intentions of
the government. Even so, Chinese television has presented some extremely
provocative images of the turmoil that have not been seen by the world
television-viewing public. Incredibly gruesome pictures of violent activity
enacted by the people during the days leading up to the military crackdown, and the day after, are shown in the propaganda programs. I analyze
the propaganda and describe the role of television throughout the period
leading up to June 3rd and 4th later.

CHINA'S REVOLUTIONARY MOMENT

An extraordinary combination of events contributed to the revolutionary
spirit that spread throughout China in the spring of 1989: the death of
ousted Communist Party chief Hu Yaobang; Mikhail Gorbachev's visit to
China a month later; stirring, uncompromising speeches given by Fang
Lizhi advocating democracy, freedom, and science; the rise of a handful
of bright and charismatic student leaders; the generally favorable coverage
of the movement given by many broadcast and print journalists in China;
the unforgettable television debate between Li Peng and student leaders;
the hope that Zhao Ziyang, who had assumed Hu's position as top party
official, would ultimately find a way to enact political reform within the
top echelons of government; and agreeable early summer weather all played
important roles.

These conditions and developments were fused onto circumstances that
had already agitated the people – corruption and profiteering, bureaucratic
inefficiency and unfairness, an unstable and unequal economy, political

repression, lack of free speech and a free press – all those issues that I have already discussed at length. The student movement, including a boycott of classes, hunger strike, constant pressure on government and presence on television, and the defiance of martial law, became the catalyst for Chinese people from all walks of life – including many Communist Party members – to rally together and speak out in a kind of national catharsis not unlike the emotional charge we saw a few months later in Eastern Europe. And, in a manner that is also similar to what happened in East Germany in particular, Chinese political protestors did not advocate overthrow of the Communist Party or the dismantling of socialism. The ultimate consequences of the protestors' modest demands, however, could not be predicted. As eventually happened in Germany, it is likely that thoroughgoing political change would have resulted once the movement achieved sufficient momentum – a scenario that in fact seemed to be unfolding during the struggle in China. Regardless, in the midst of all the turmoil, a positive emotional climate emerged in China in the spring of 1989. Orville Schell observed that 'people seemed suddenly possessed by a sense of optimism, hope, and generosity . . . there was . . . a new feeling of fraternity, openness, and goodwill the likes of which I had never experienced during fifteen years of visiting China' (Schell, 1989: 36).

The massive demonstration at Tiananmen Square was the culmination of nearly three years of episodic protests led by students in 20 major cities located mainly in the north. The wave of student demonstrations began in Hefei and Wuhan in early December 1986. Later that month, tens of thousands of students in Shanghai, and a smaller number in Beijing, took to the streets to demand political reform in what was becoming the largest show of force for democracy since 1978–9 (Nathan, 1985). Students were already being branded 'counterrevolutionaries' and were accused by the government of beating police. A fight between students and police broke out in Tiananmen Square on January 1st, 1987. Students in the square burned copies of the *Beijing Daily*, which had editorialized the pro-democracy movement as 'poisoned by capitalist ideas.'

These disturbances had repercussions. Although Deng blamed himself for the student uprisings in 1986 and 1987, he criticized the then CCP chief Hu Yaobang for protecting the students. Hu and a top national security official were subsequently dismissed by the politburo for being too lenient in their treatment of the student protestors. Party officials ultimately blamed creeping 'bourgeois liberalization' for the trouble and demanded that students be given new ideological training. They were required to demonstrate 'five loves': for socialism, the Communist Party, labor, science and technology, and the motherland. Already Deng, in his role as chief of military affairs, was coordinating forces in case the lessons were not well learned.

The protests didn't stop. Large demonstrations over the same issues resumed late in 1987 and took place episodically throughout 1988. A new wrinkle appeared: in Nanjing, riots broke out when some Chinese college students claimed that African students studying in China are given special and unwarranted privileges. The reasons for the Chinese students lashing out against the Africans are as much cultural as they are political. Nonetheless, the unsettled situation contributed to the unrest that was spreading in China; it further convinced the people that there are indeed different social classes in their supposedly classless society. Furthermore, the overly-reactive handling of the situation by police in Nanjing, as well as the constant military repression in Tibet, signalled what could happen elsewhere.

Through all this, Zhao Ziyang, who had assumed party leadership in late 1987, tried desperately to find a compromise solution that would permit economic and political development while appeasing both ends of the ideological spectrum – students and government hardliners – at the same time. In truth, Zhao was never on firm ground. His demise was rumored from the start of his tenure and his true position on many issues was never known. He praised Deng lavishly at the Thirteenth Congress in 1987, for instance, while he strongly criticized Chinese leadership, bureaucracy, and corruption. He advocated 'socialist democracy' and 'townhall politics' while also claiming that opposition parties are not needed in China. He continued to promise a bright economic future if market forces are allowed to function while at the same time claiming that gaps between rich and poor should not develop in the country. He embraced the students for their ideals but said that political turmoil cannot be tolerated.

The single event that lifted the revolutionary moment to epic proportions was the death of Hu Yaobang on April 15th, 1989. From the students' perspective, Hu was much more a hero than was his successor, the man who became their only sympathizer among top government leaders, Zhao. Distraught and sickly after an inglorious removal from his post in January 1987, the sincere and kindly Hu became a martyr for the students. His death spurred the biggest protest in Beijing in more than two years. About 10,000 students assembled in Tiananmen Square on April 18th to mourn him and to demand that the government reevaluate his contribution to the country. Besides praising Hu, the students again voiced their complaints about the array of enduring problems in China. It is extremely important to emphasize the importance of this gathering taking place in Tiananmen Square. For the Chinese there is no place to match the symbolic meaning of the square. The socialist nation was born there when Mao Zedong stood at Tiananmen Gate on October 1st, 1949, to proclaim the founding of the People's Republic. Furthermore, the square is huge: more than a million people can mill around Tiananmen Square at any one time.

A hardcore group of young people refused to leave Tiananmen Square after April 18th. Three days later, the government took to television to warn the demonstrators to go home or face grave consequences. The very next day more than 150,000 citizens defied the government order by marching from Beijing University in the city's western suburbs to Tiananmen Square, a journey of more than 11 miles. Workers joined up with students and people all along the route cheered the youthful protestors, many of whom sang the socialist anthem, 'Internationale,' as they walked. The movement was not only gaining great momentum, it was becoming far better organized. Two days later, April 24th, students at the major universities in Beijing, all of which are located in the same part of town, escalated the confrontation by boycotting classes. Many of them joined the protest activities full-time. Sympathetic to the cause, their professors did not stand in the way. Informed and inspired by television reports of the activity in Beijing, political demonstrating also heated up in many other cities in China by early May. At the same time, anti-riot military forces were being mobilized in various parts of the country. The government continued to insist that Communist youth organizations, not the *ad hoc* student groups, were the proper channels for voicing opinions and settling differences. The ultimate rationale given by the government for its stern insistence on 'stability' was the future of the Chinese reformation itself. Deng insisted that 'ulterior motives' underlay the resistance; that a 'counterrevolutionary' rebellion was a threat to revolutionary progress, which, after 1979, meant the national reformation. Propaganda focused on one fundamental theme: reform requires unity among the Chinese people.

The Soviet Union designed and helped construct some of the buildings that surround Tiananmen Square in the 1950s. But during his visit to the People's Republic a month after the demonstrations in Beijing had begun, Mikhail Gorbachev was unable to visit the heart of the country because of its occupation by the students and their now-growing ranks of supporters. Gorbachev's visit, like the Hu memorial, further inspired the demonstrators who by now had become quite confident that their tactics were working. The Chinese government, of course, was deeply embarrassed about the situation when Gorbachev arrived. The Soviet leader used the occasion to call for world detente, suggested that domestic political turmoil is sometimes necessary, cautiously praised the students, and negotiated political issues with Deng, including demilitarization of the long-contested border between the two huge nations. But their meetings were greatly overshadowed by what was going on downtown. Furthermore, the enormous corps of international journalists who had descended on Beijing to cover the historic Sino–Soviet meetings became far more caught up in the protests which by now had hundreds of thousands of people congregating in the square.

Immediately after Gorbachev's departure, the mood in the capital city became extremely tense and explosive. Zhao tried to find a compromise by guaranteeing the students that steps toward reform would be taken if they would leave the square. He promised them on TV that the government will 'never stop listening to you . . . never!' The students didn't buy it. Momentum increased as more and more people found the courage to stand up and join what looked like a successful, peaceful revolution – a real chance for social change. A contingent of well-known journalists, including some from Xinhua and the *People's Daily*, joined forces with the demonstrators. Li Peng and Zhao met with the hunger strikers. But then, right when it appeared that the Communist Party could very well lose its tight grasp on the country, the threats Deng had issued nearly three years before were acted upon. Martial law was declared in Beijing on May 20th in order to 'maintain social stability and the normal life of the people,' according to a Xinhua editorial. Li Peng appeared on television where he angrily rationalized the government action – a performance that may have reassured or persuaded some, but also alienated many Beijing citizens who previously had not openly taken sides. As significant as Li's televised speech was the absence of Zhao Ziyang from the media. Clearly, a shift in power from Zhao to Li was in the works.

Most of the students, as well as the foreign journalists, defied the dictates of martial law at first. Protestors stayed at the square and video coverage of the confrontation continued to pour out of China through satellite hookups, many of which had been arranged for coverage of Gorbachev's visit. Students formed motorcycle and bicycle troupes to speed around the city with the latest rumors and news. In a politically unfortunate act that was denounced by student leaders, a portrait of Mao Zedong that hangs on Tiananmen Gate was vandalized May 23rd. Sensing that the patience of the Chinese government was being pushed to the extreme, world leaders urged the Chinese government not to use violence to quell what so far had been a largely peaceful uprising.

Though the number of protestors in Tiananmen Square fluctuated during the last days of May, it was the students, not the government, who seemed to control the city. Li Peng appeared on television again on May 26th to announce that the People's Liberation Army, which was now mustering throughout Beijing, would soon have to intervene, 'with restraint.' He said the protests must stop and that the 'law' would be enforced. Zhao Ziyang had become even more conspicuous by his absence from public view, but students continued to hope that he was still somehow representing their interests behind the closed doors of the mysterious Chinese government. On May 29th, the Supreme People's Court also threatened 'severe punishment' for those 'causing disorder.' Despite the increasing presence of martial law troops in Beijing, and all the official threats, the protest spirit only heightened. The next day the students erected the the most inspiring and widely-recognized icon of the movement – the plaster and foam 'Goddess of Democracy' statue.

THE MASS MEDIA BATTLEGROUND

Political posters, which are specifically banned by the Chinese constitution, began to appear again during the protests in 1986, signaling the beginning of the recent era of popular resistance. At the same time, the major mass media, especially television, were being used by the government to advocate its positions and to threaten punishment of 'wrongdoers.' Communications media of all types were the weapons of the intense ideological battle that led up to June 4th.

As we have already seen, the government does not completely control even the most mainstream media. Oppositional voices had seeped into China's mass media before the 1986 demonstrations, but especially during the months before martial law was declared many media outlets were busy developing their own agendas, influenced by thousands of young journalists, producers, and directors who refused to mindlessly articulate the party line. Though the government's voice has always ultimately ruled China's 'news' coverage, oppositional breakthroughs haven't been limited strictly to clever wording in an article here and there.

The most dramatic break from China's generally restrictive journalistic tradition, however, was the coverage that the student protestors got from the mass media in the spring of 1989. For several weeks leading up to the declaration of martial law, a previously unheard chorus of voices rang out on television news and in other media. Journalists continued to pay requisite attention to the official warnings and directives of government, but they also sought out and featured opposing accounts and opinions, despite a stern warning from conservative politburo members in late April that they should not recognize the students. Chinese journalists were enjoying their greatest freedom ever. Shocking images from Tiananmen Square suddenly appeared on national and regional television. Mark Hopkins describes what the people saw on CCTV:

> The audience, accustomed to unimaginative footage of factory workers turning out machine tools and peasants harvesting grain, tuned in to something startlingly different in May; moving scenes of young students on a hunger strike in Tiananmen Square. There they lay in make-shift tents, ministered to by fellow students, taken away in ambulances through crowds when their condition weakened to the point of death – their only demand being a hearing from their leaders. It would have been television at its most powerful anywhere; in China the impact was unimaginable.

(Hopkins, 1989: 35–6)

188

31 CCTV coverage of the student hunger strike and occupation of Tiananmen Square.

The coverage increased sympathy and support for the movement. Students and other demonstrators learned how to play the domestic media, especially television, to their advantage. People began to realize that the encampment at Tiananmen Square was not just the annual plea for freedom and democracy that before had somehow always fizzled out. This was an ideological bombshell and a media event the likes of which had never been seen in China.

Discussions between students, Li Peng, and Zhao Ziyang (explored below) were telecast. State radio praised the students. Newspaper editorials questioned official positions. Military officers wrote a letter published by the *People's Daily* in mid May asking that martial law not be enacted. Support for the student movement within the ranks of working journalists crystallized when the Communist Party banned an issue of the *World Economic Herald*, a progressive newspaper in Shanghai, and fired its popular editor, Qin Benli, on April 25th. Within two weeks, more than 1,000 journalists petitioned the government to give the Chinese press more autonomy, to permit coverage of a wider range of stories, including the student demonstrations, and to reinstate Qin.

Despite the advances they realized, the students never let up on the press freedom issue. Groups of protestors marched to the new CCTV building, the Central People's (radio) Broadcasting Station, Xinhua,

Guangming Daily, and the *People's Daily*. To the tune 'Frère Jacques' they sang, 'Lying to the people, lying to the people, very strange, very strange.' A favorite rhyme emerged: *'People's Daily* deceives the people; *Guangming* ("brightness") *Daily* is not bright; *Beijing Daily* talks nonsense; CCTV turns black into white!'

Channels of communication

Despite the increasing openness of Chinese mainstream media during the weeks that preceded martial law, the students had to develop forms of communication that they could control themselves. Posters began to appear at Beijing University in the middle of April and on the other campuses shortly thereafter. Political cartoons and graffiti were scrawled on every surface. Meetings were called. People spread information privately by word of mouth, a tradition Chinese call 'alley talk' (*xiaodao xiaxi*). A makeshift radio station, the 'Voice of Beijing University,' was set up in a dormitory room to broadcast political commentary, news, even revolutionary music at high volume on speakers set up across campus. Loudspeakers were placed at the front gate of the nearby People's University where political information was announced to students and passersby. Thousands of citizens, even entire families, gathered at night on the lawn in the front of the campus to listen to the broadcasts. Such a public address system became the major medium for the students at Tiananmen Square too. They set up microphones, amplifiers, and mixer boards, mounted loudspeakers on poles throughout the square, and turned up the volume to drown out the government's messages which also bellowed from loudspeakers scattered throughout public spaces in China, including the square. Old mimeograph machines and a Chinese character typewriter became the hardware for publication of the students' daily newsletters at Tiananmen Square. Public mail and telephones were used to coordinate activities from one city to another.

The government regularly used television, radio, newspapers, and loudspeakers to tell the demonstrators to quit and to ask the people not to support them. New big character posters (*tatzepao*) appeared throughout Beijing, imploring everyone to 'Maintain Order in the Capital,' 'Maintain Unity and Stability,' and 'Oppose Bourgeois Liberalization.' Helicopters flew over Tiananmen Square dropping leaflets which condemned disorder. In the last week of May, an additional propaganda committee was established to assert official positions even more vigorously.

The foreign alternative: Voice of America

The Voice of America says it is the 'number one' source of information for Chinese people from outside China, and my interviews in 1986 and

1989 confirm the claim. The VOA transmits nine hours of Chinese language news alone into China on shortwave radio channels per day. The BBC foreign service, which is also appreciated by the Chinese, broadcasts about three hours of news per day. VOA Director Richard Carlson told the Cable News Network (CNN) that between 60 and 100 million Chinese people listened to VOA every day during the crisis in 1989. Five Mandarin-language channels still beam into China 24 hours a day along with other channels in Cantonese and English. During martial law, when the Chinese government jammed several of the channels, the VOA responded by adding others. Foreign wire services are the main sources of VOA news, but during the turmoil in Beijing it added its own local reports. Carlson claims that the agency's intention is to provide 'fair, balanced, and honest' news coverage, though the organization has also been accused even by Americans of being mainly a propaganda organ for the United States.

Regardless of its image, intention, or actual performance, the VOA played an important role in the unrest in China especially after martial law reversed the trend toward a freer domestic press. VOA stories were recorded by Chinese listeners on their radio/audiotape recorders, then printed onto paper and tacked up on bulletin boards or retransmitted via the loudspeaker systems in an intertextual, mediated 'multi-step flow' fashion. VOA news was crucial to the students and other protestors in Beijing and helped spread information to the other cities who were following the lead from the capital city. Editorials appeared in Chinese newspapers and on CCTV to denounce the foreign 'intervention' of the VOA for 'spreading rumors that have fueled the counterrevolutionary movement.' The VOA, according to the Chinese government, was 'confusing the citizens.' The government's criticism of the VOA and the BBC only led many people to believe the reports even more confidently.

The premier meets the people

'We call on Li Peng to come here! Why can't the people's premier come out and meet the people?' (remark by a student during discussion between protestors and government officials on CCTV, April 25th, 1989)

For the first time in the history of Chinese television, fiery debates between protestors and political officials took place in a special three-hour program aired during prime time on CCTV on April 29th. Government officials were grilled by students for failing to comply with their request to enter into real dialogue over the issues. Li Peng was chastized for not joining the discussions. As students and government representatives argued in front of the cameras, people all over China gathered around TV sets to watch this completely uncharacteristic media moment: a live, spontaneous, confrontative discussion between demanding, youthful students and a handful of apprehensive, noncommittal political officials. Despite the breakthrough onto CCTV's golden time, student activists weren't satisfied. They said the government representatives were not sufficiently responsive to them and that the program was 'meaningless.' They demanded a reprise, again on CCTV, live, and this time they wanted Li Peng.

It happened. After arriving late and being scolded in front of the cameras for his tardiness by Wuer Kaixi, president of the Beijing Autonomous Student Union, Li did indeed square off with the students on national television. Again, however, no tangible concessions were made though the students had the upper hand in the discussions. The participants ended up lecturing each other more than negotiating possible solutions. Li was not about to make any compromises. This incredible event in the history of Chinese politics – the premier of the country being talked down on national television by a group of unrelenting and insufficiently deferential students, innocent and charming as they were – would not be repeated. Deng and Li had seen enough. Martial law was declared the next day and Li appeared on television that very day – this time without his young sparring partners – to announce in no uncertain terms that 'resolute and powerful measures [will be used] to curb the turmoil,' an appearance that personalized the growing desperate authority of the Communist Party. The speech was repeated by CCTV and regional stations throughout the day. The 'freedom and democracy' movement abruptly had been rendered much less free and democratic.

The media under martial law

China's domestic media immediately suffered the effects of martial law. Opinions that had been expressed the weeks and months before were reduced to one. To insure compliance, the facilities of CCTV, Beijing Broadcasting, *People's Daily*, and Xinhua were occupied by soldiers. Journalists were assailed for having made 'serious mistakes' during the previous weeks in their news coverage. Students and other protestors, who had depended on domestic media for coverage before May 20th, now turned to the foreign press who had been less immediately affected by the ideological retrenchment. More and more protest signs and banners began to appear in English.

Officially, foreign journalists and broadcasters were restricted too. They were not to interview Chinese citizens and were prohibited from gathering news in Tiananmen Square and other sensitive areas. Until about June 1st, however, many foreign correspondents ignored the rules. Chinese citizens even intervened to protect American and Japanese journalists when they were harassed by police.

A major form of control that the Chinese government had over the foreign electronic news gathering services, however, was access to satellite channels which are used to beam television signals out of the country. After much confusion at first, the Chinese-leased INTELSAT channel, which had been subleased to the foreign news services, was taken away from the foreigners. Other transmission facilities were made available, subject to constant review. Later, no pictures were sent out. Pulling the plug on the satellite channels was itself a journalistic drama. Television viewers of Cable News Network (CNN) in many parts of the world watched live coverage of Chinese telecommunications authorities negotiate with the cable channel's Beijing producer over the legal right to withdraw access to the satellite. The Americans claimed that their contract to cover Gorbachev's visit to Beijing extended into June. The Chinese said Gorbachev was gone: 'Your work here is finished.' CBS News also lost its satellite channel despite the on-air legalistic pleadings of Dan Rather. The Chinese overruled all objections saying that the requirements of martial law, and the return to order that it presupposes, supersede all other arrangements.

TAKING TIANANMEN SQUARE: THE TELEVISION PROGRAM

In the face of the savage rioters, officers and soldiers, burning with rage, driven beyond forbearance, and unable to move forward, were compelled to shoot into the sky to open the way after giving repeated warnings, and to counterattack, killing some of the vicious rioters. As there were numerous onlookers, some were unavoidably hit by stray bullets.

(*A Record of the June Turbulence in Beijing*, CCTV)

The one question that I was asked repeatedly when I returned to China in fall 1989 was, 'Did you see any television coverage of PLA troops killing people at Tiananmen Square?' Students in particular wanted to know if I had information that they did not have. When I was first asked this question, my response was, 'Well, yes . . . yes, certainly.' Upon reflection, however, I realized that I hadn't seen any actual footage of killing in the square. I remember a shot of the Goddess of Democracy being toppled by soldiers, but the most compelling evidence from the media that people had died *in the square* was mainly eyewitness accounts that were reported in publications such as *Time* and *Newsweek*. Still, my general impression was that hundreds, perhaps thousands of Chinese people, most of them students, were slaughtered by the military in Beijing. It was not clear in my mind exactly where it happened. Like everyone else, I had just assumed that most of the killing was in the square itself.

By the students' own count, I quickly learned that the number of deaths within their ranks is lower than is popularly believed outside China.

According to them – and they are fiercely opposed to the government, they are *not* trying to belittle the tragedy – somewhere between 20 and 40 students died in the bloody confrontation the night of June 3rd and early morning, June 4th. The vast majority of people who died were civilians, estimated by Nicholas Kristof of the *New York Times* to be between 400 and 800, a number the students say is probably correct. Kristof and the Chinese authorities place the number of soldiers dead at between 12 and 16. In the final analysis, no reliable sources have indicated that the numbers are much greater than this.

But as one student insisted, 'It doesn't matter where people died or if the total number killed was one or ten thousand. The point is that our government turned its guns on its own people!' He's right. The government, nonetheless, has waged an intensive propaganda campaign that is based on two fundamental themes that arise from the chaos of the first few days in June in order to justify the military action. It has tried to show that, beyond doubt, there was an uprising bordering on fullscale anarchy that was underway for many days in Beijing and that whatever violence the army had to use to restore order is understandable given the terrifying, out-of-control status of the protestors. Second, a version of the details of *how* Tiananmen Square itself was cleared by the military is featured. The basic theme of this second campaign is to convince the people that no one died within the square itself. The programs insist that the disturbances were caused by civilians, forcing the hand of the military, and that the taking of Tiananmen Square was done peacefully despite violent attacks that were made by some of the protestors.

The symbolic importance of Tiananmen Square is a paramount assumption maintained throughout the programs. The thought that students were slaughtered in their frail formations and encampments at Tiananmen Square is indeed repulsive to all Chinese and is an image that the government could not permit to go unchallenged. Occupation of the square by the students symbolized two related, but fundamentally contradictory, themes from the government's perspective. It was, first of all, the site of a counterrevolutionary movement that seriously threatened national stability. But it was also the place where thousands of China's children were camped. The counterrevolutionary ideology had to be extinguished, but the children had to be spared. The Chinese television audience, which had been exposed for weeks to deeply sentimental images of youthful protestors transforming Tiananmen Square into makeshift homes, could not easily accept the most horrific scenario: that troops and tanks crushed defenseless children at the square. For the government, it is certainly better to admit that some killing took place on the streets as the military moved toward the square than to permit the alternative vision to fester in the public mind.

I have acquired videotape copies from CCTV of all propaganda programs produced since June 4th about the 'turmoil' (the government's preferred descriptor) in Beijing. These programs have all been shown many times on Chinese television. The programs are produced in Mandarin for the domestic audience of course, but some programs narrated in English have also been shown on Chinese television mainly as part of the government's attempt to keep foreign investors from fleeing the country. The programs are propaganda in raw form.[2] While they pretend to be journalistic, documentary-style reports of the turmoil, they do nothing but show the most selective video footage of confrontations between demonstrators and soldiers. With one exception, which I will take up at length below, they give no voice to the students or to others involved in the resistance movement. Using a detached, authoritative voice-over technique, the narration is a simplistic, completely one-sided story of what happened.

They are powerful. Even the most skeptical viewer of these programs would have to concede one fundamental point to the Chinese government: before unleashing its terrible violence, the military suffered loss of life in grotesque ways, endured tremendous material destruction, and tolerated great humiliation. Please don't misread my understandings or intentions here. Had I been a Chinese in Beijing, I would have been in the front ranks with the demonstrators. But what these television programs reveal in graphic form is that the government's official line – that the military at first acted with restraint and suffered great losses – is not a completely false claim.

The videos make it clear that there was in fact a serious rebellion underway in Beijing. With pictures of demonstrators flailing away at soldiers, the narrator claims that police and martial law troops simply tried to quell an uprising that was, at root, inspired by subversive elements inside and outside the country. What is not said, of course, is that the rebellion was greatly intensified by the very presence of the military. The editing and narration is framed in such a way as to completely hide the fact that it was a protest by unarmed people who were prompted to action by cumulative, intolerable economic and political circumstances. Furthermore, the story of the violence in the capital is reconstructed to appear as a chronological unfolding of events, but the editing clearly reveals that scenes are taken completely out of context, then spliced together in order to create an impression of continuity. And, of course, no alternative courses of action to the eventual violent solution were discussed.

Most of CCTV's propaganda programs contain footage of the physical conflict in Beijing city. They don't blame the students directly for what happened. Instead, the programs claim that military action had to be taken against 'ruffians, thugs, and hooligans' who had 'hoodwinked' innocent students. The narrator claims that Taiwanese spies and 'paramilitary terrorist organizations' infiltrated China, turning 'simple-minded, young students' into counterrevolutionaries who were then responsible for this

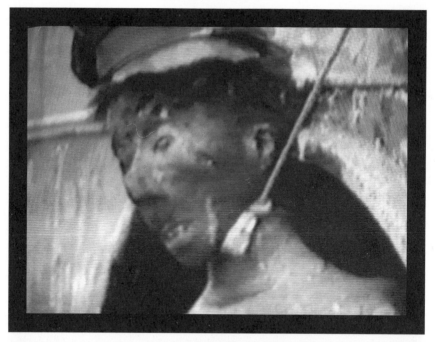

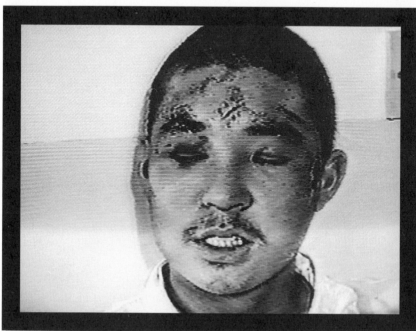

32 Gruesome images of military casualties from the CCTV production, *A Record of the June Turbulence in Beijing*, fall 1989.

33 The apparent stoning to death of a People's Liberation Army vehicle driver taken from a government propaganda program.

'sudden' turmoil. The counterrevolutionaries then further spread the poison: 'They have taken advantage of the grievances of the broad masses of people to disrupt social order in Beijing and cause confusion throughout China so as to overthrow the present government.'

Video footage that is shown to support the government's position is, indeed, impressive. We see shots of demonstrators throwing rocks at soldiers and vehicles, joyriding in a commandeered armored personnel carrier, pushing and shoving passive, scared soldiers, setting fire to literally hundreds of vehicles (one shot reveals a line of at least 30 or 40 abandoned vehicles all burning out of control along a city street), turning over other vehicles, impeding emergency vehicles, blocking traffic. Horrifying images are shown of the charred bodies of soldiers who had been trapped inside vehicles set ablaze by demonstrators. A dozen men jump up and down on top of a tank. Others wave weapons. A military vehicle that is moving rapidly in a convoy suddenly stalls and comes to a halt along the side of the road where dozens of protestors, who had been throwing rocks at the passing convoy, stood. The civilians run to the stalled military truck and smash the windows with stones. Although it is not completely clear in the televised pictures, the narrator claims that the driver was stoned to death by the crowd. In fact, it does look like that's what happened.

197

In all, the invisible but mightily present narrator lists the government's statistics of casualties and damage. He then explains, 'Among the non-military casualties were rioters who deserved the punishment, people who were injured by stray bullets, and people who were wounded by ruffians who had seized rifles.' He calmly adds, 'Is there any country in the world whose laws can bear this kind of freedom and democracy?'

Preserving the sanctity of the square

Without suffering any clashes or one single death, the illegal, long-time occupation of Tiananmen Square was finally brought to a peaceful end.

(A Record of the June Turbulence in Beijing, CCTV)

Another episode of the propaganda series is meant to do nothing more than assure the people that no one died in Tiananmen Square and that the clearing of the square was done humanely. This program features no gory graphics. It presents interviews with protestors who discuss at length what they say happened at Tiananmen Square the night of June 3rd and 4th. The primary interviewees are Hou Dejian, a famous singer in his mid thirties and a real Chinese patriot who defected to the mainland from Taiwan many years ago and was part of the student movement all along, including the hunger strike, and three others, all of whom are teachers in Beijing. These men say they were the main negotiators acting on behalf of the demonstrators who occupied Tiananmen Square to the very last minute, a claim that coincides with several journalistic accounts. Brief comments are also made during this program by a Chinese doctor who was at the square the last night and by three students from Qinghua University. Before I summarize what they say in the program, I will describe my understanding of the events that led up to the military's sweeping of the square as dawn broke on June 4th.[3]

Briefly, the story unfolds this way: military units moved toward Tiananmen Square both from the northeast along Jianguomenwai Avenue and from the northwest along Changan Avenue on June 3rd under orders to get everyone out of the square by dawn the next day. These two wide avenues meet at the northern entrance to Tiananmen Square, the very place that separates the square from Tiananmen Gate and the entrance to the Forbidden City. The people had erected barriers of destroyed vehicles and formed human chains to prevent the soldiers from breaking through to the square. It was along these two streets, and the side streets that branch off from them, that most of the violent confrontations took place. On my trip to Beijing in 1989 I saw homes tucked away in the alleys along these streets that are riddled with bullet holes. As the military grew more and more aggressive in its effort to get to the top of the square,

198

34 Hou Dejian (above) explains his role in the students' retreat from Tiananmen Square (below) in a CCTV propaganda program.

the people became equally determined to prevent that from happening. Now no longer willing to hold back, soldiers on both streets opened fire, sometimes randomly, sometimes not, into crowds, at buildings, into the air – everywhere. The worst story is of soldiers repeatedly cutting down scores of people as they stood in rows along Changan Avenue near the entrance to the square. It was a gruesome nightmare. In all, hundreds of people fell dead or injured. Hospitals were overrun with casualties. Fires broke out. The air was filled with the stench of smoke and teargas. Beijing – the heart and soul of the People's Republic of China – was under siege by the People's Liberation Army who were not to be denied their mission. The sounds and smells wafted into Tiananmen Square where a few thousand students and supporters held firm despite reports that hundreds of people were being killed on the streets nearby. A few minutes after midnight a military armed personnel carrier broke through the blockade at the top of the square and was poised to move toward the student encampment. It was clear that the military would attack anyone who refused to leave Tiananmen Square.

This is where the four interviewees come in. They claim that hasty negotiations took place between two of them and two others (doctors from the Chinese Red Cross who also represented the protestors), and a man identified as Lieutenant Ji from the People's Liberation Army whose unit had just broken through the barriers at the northern end of the square. The lead spokesman for the protestors was Hou Dejian. After pleading twice with Ji for more time to allow the remaining thousands in the square to leave peacefully, Hou and the three others returned to the students to explain that the military had promised not to fire on them if they would retreat from the square using the southeast corner – away from the military's position – as an exit. There were a hundred different opinions among the students about what to do. Wuer Kaixi, weakened to the point of exhaustion from the hunger strike, gave a speech saying 'I'm going to die in Tiananmen Square!' But he fainted before he could finish and was taken into a tent, and later away from the square. The interviewees claim that Wuer does not know what finally happened because he was not there at the end. Chai Ling, the tiny young woman who became so familiar to TV viewers in China and abroad because of her fiery presence during the protests, took the microphone and said, 'Students and civilians, if you want to retreat . . . feel free to do so. If you want to stay, we welcome you.' Others argued for the importance of maintaining a peaceful protest and for not engaging the soldiers in combat under any circumstances. In the midst of the chaos – with tanks roaring into position, the sound of gunfire on the nearby streets, and government loudspeakers blaring away – in a fashion true to their cause, the students took a voice vote to determine if they should leave. Majority sentiment was to go. Two of the protest leaders retreated with the students out of the southeast corner.

Two others stayed back to insure that everyone got out safely. Moving into the square to chase the students out, soldiers shot the protestors' loudspeakers off the sound posts and fired bullets randomly into the air as they chided the less willing, 'Do you want to leave or not?' Hou said he begged the soldiers to shoot even higher so as not to endanger lives. All four of the protest leaders claim that none of the retreating students was killed as they sadly filed out of Tiananmen Square, giving up their dream for the time being at least, in the face of certain death if they did not leave. Tearfully, some of them sang 'Internationale' as they walked. The protestors were gone from the square by 6.30 a.m.

This ending to the story differs sharply from many accounts we have read in the West where witnesses claim to have seen many deaths take place in the square itself – even claims that the army fired machine guns into the retreating line of students as they left the square. But the story told by the four men, corroborated by supplementary televised interviews with many others, is a reasonable and consistent one that has surely convinced many citizens that while something horrible happened in Beijing in June, apparently Tiananmen Square itself was not stained by Chinese blood.

THE AFTERMATH

The government's version of the prelude and finale in Beijing was just part of the television coverup. Several themes emerged: the capture and punishment of 'guilty' parties; an assault on remnants of 'divisive' ideology; an attempt to unite the people behind the reconstructive work of the military; and the reemergence of China's political leaders, including the appointment of yet another chief of the Communist Party, Jiang Zemin.

All of China watched videoclips on CCTV's news of the arrests and sentencing of those who were blamed for the 'counterrevolutionary' activity. Two guilty types were shown: grim, disheveled, shameful men who are described as 'thugs' or 'hooligans,' and key figures from the Beijing Autonomous Student Union and other student groups. Within just two weeks after June 4th, more than 1,500 arrests were announced in what may be the biggest human purge ever presented on any nation's television. Peasant-class men with their heads bowed, placards dangling around their necks, were humiliatingly led into courts where most of them 'admitted' their 'crimes' and were sentenced to death as television news cameras captured their pathetic presence. Pictures of 21 student leaders were repeatedly shown on television; a telephone 'hotline' was set up to turn in the youthful demonstrators (prompting one young woman to turn in her brother, according to reports); the government kept the public informed of the running tally of student 'most wanteds' who had been apprehended. Ignoring world political opinion and the criticism of human rights agencies,

35 'Socialism is Good!' Government banner that was put up near Tiananmen Square after the violence in Beijing in 1989.

government authorities continued to publicly arrest and punish dissidents for nearly two years after the Beijing uprising.

A 'party purification' campaign was undertaken. All those suspected of sympathizing with the student movement were required to provide detailed explanations of their actions, day by day, for unaccountable time during the disruptive weeks. Cadre in workplaces throughout Beijing called meetings of their workers to discuss the lingering implications of the turmoil. Workers were required to give their opinions of the resistance movement. To endorse the ideology or actions of the protestors was tantamount to self-incrimination. Workers were informally required to support the government's perspective. To say nothing in these meetings was implicit criticism of the government and that also was not acceptable. As one bright young female media specialist told me in 1989, 'We not only don't have freedom of speech in China, we don't have freedom of silence either.' Interpersonal relationships suffered. The crackdown in Beijing had brought back the horror of the Cultural Revolution when people simply didn't know who they could trust to reveal their true feelings about anything political.

A crackdown on foreign media was made as copies of newspapers and magazines were removed even from hotels catering almost exclusively to foreigners. Several foreign reporters, including one from the VOA, were expelled from China for 'spreading rumors and distorting facts.' Fang

Lizhi, who had escaped into the United States embassy during the fighting, was attacked by CCTV. The network read letters from the audience denouncing him as a traitor. And, in order to convince the people that the government will wage a battle against corruption despite the recent havoc, many cases of officials being tried and sentenced for various crimes were shown on television.

The post-June 4th propaganda sweep did not dwell solely on the negative, punitive side of things. Soldiers were shown on the news, and in the documentary programs, cleaning the square, distributing food, meeting with schoolchildren and workers, and generally restoring life in Beijing to normal. Families of slain soldiers were honored by the government. Military officers applauded each other during evaluation sessions. Citizens were shown giving presents (including flowers, bicycles, TV sets, and pigs) to the soldiers as thanks for ending the turmoil. A bank officer went on CCTV to try to dispell rampant financial fears. Classrooms were shown filled once again with eager students. Workers thanked the military for keeping their factories open. New political education programs were established for college students, especially those at Beijing University where a new president was also named. The People's Republic of China's 40th Anniversary celebration – live on television from Tiananmen Square – went off as scheduled.

Re-establishing an image of political stability was very important. During the height of the protest, political control of China had seemed to be slipping away from the communists. The Chinese media equivocated about who was in power. First Li was in, then Zhao was making a comeback, then Li supposedly was back in control though Zhao, with the title of general secretary, was still technically in charge. Li had not been seen by the people since May 24th and Deng a week before that. Their disappearance from public view signalled to many people that the old guard had lost control of China. But when the smoke cleared at Tiananmen Square, which is located just a few blocks from China's government headquarters, the familiar array of leaders, minus Zhao Ziyang, was in public view again. But they didn't show up straightaway. Despite rumors that Deng had suffered a heart attack, that Li Peng had been shot in the thigh, that Zhao Ziyang could still be wielding some power, and that military units were set to battle with each other in a full-scale revolutionary war, none of China's leaders was seen or heard from until June 8th, when Li Peng, together with aged military officer Wang Zhen, appeared on CCTV. Deng returned to CCTV's airwaves the next day.

Their appearance on television absolutely marked the return to power of the hardline communist leaders. Both Li and Deng appeared in Mao jackets, rather than Western suits. Li had obviously not been shot and Deng was smiling. They each praised the military, reaffirmed the ideological inclinations of Chinese communism, called for security and stability,

36 Schoolchildren sing patriotic songs in Tiananmen Square.

encouraged prosecution of troublemakers, and promised that the reformation was still on track with 'openness and economic reform.' By June
14th, all but three of the 16 politburo members had appeared on television.
Zhao was one of the missing. Three days later he was fired as chairman
of the party and from all senior posts, a dismissal that was made into a
news special from the Great Hall of the People just before the 7 o'clock
news that night. Within a week Jiang Zemin, a politburo member from
Shanghai who had been faithful to Deng during the ordeal (he was responsible for firing *World Economic Herald* editor Qin Benli and was extremely
intolerant of the student activists), was given the job. Compatible in their
perspectives, Jiang and Li stabilized prices of key commodities and were
able to slow down the runaway inflation.[4] Just as important was the
subtextual message sent by reinstituting central economic planning – the
re-establishment of the pervasive authority of the Communist Party and
the forced dependency that it requires of the people.

The flow of information after June 4th

The crisis spawned and prompted the adaptation of a variety of communication channels from outside China that were intended specifically to
spread the word inside the country of what had happened during the

military crackdown. The VOA, of course, continued to broadcast news into China. Some VOA transmissions were even sent specifically to nearly 2,000 military satellite receiver installations in China, a strategy that was designed to reach potentially resistant military forces. The BBC continued to send reports into the country, as did Hong Kong radio and television stations.

For those who tried to inform Chinese people of the details of the military assault, the hope was that mediated accounts of the crackdown would be spread interpersonally through routine contact between and among family members, friends, co-workers, and classmates. Copies of foreign newspapers smuggled into China were posted in public places; others were copied and handed from person to person. Overseas Chinese phoned families and friends back home to tell them what they had seen on television. The telephone was used for another purpose: to jam hotlines established by the government for turning in protestors – a tactic that also benefitted from the low quality of the Chinese telephone system.

High technology came into play. Fax machines were used by Chinese outside China to electronically transmit written and photographic accounts of the Beijing violence into the country, a practice that continued for several months after June 4th. International computer networks that link universities and other research institutions, including some inside China, were full of messages that described the crackdown. The Silicon Valley in California, near my home, was a center for much of this high-tech activity as more than 20,000 Asian engineers and professionals, many of them Chinese, live in the area. Weather balloons loaded with propaganda from Taiwan were sent across the Formosa Strait.

Chinese students and their supporters throughout the world staged massive demonstrations to emphatically register their shock and contempt. International news agencies ate up the story. The Goddess of Democracy was symbolically resurrected in several places. Rock concerts and rallies were held from Hong Kong to Paris to New York. Foreigners who came to China after June 4th, including many businessmen, told their stories.

Television in international political communication

World response to what happened in Beijing has been a continuing controversy. As was later learned, American President George Bush had dispatched secret political envoys to China several times after June 4th. But during and in the immediate aftermath of the crisis, Bush said he had no direct communication with his old friend, Deng Xiaoping, or other government officials in Beijing. According to Bush, he couldn't get through to Deng by telephone! Instead, he relied on the reports coming from television, especially CNN, whose very content and tone seem to have provided

205

at least one fundamental basis from which the United States formulated its political response.

Chinese TV was seen outside its borders too. For weeks following the crackdown, foreign television newscasts regularly featured video segments from CCTV that showed the trials and sentencing of dissidents. CCTV's images were intercepted from its satellite television transmissions. Not to be outdone, CCTV managed to borrow pictures from American and Hong Kong TV and used them in the production of its own propaganda programs. The famous picture of the lone man standing in front of the row of tanks, which appears prominently in the CCTV programs (for reasons I explain in the next chapter), is one of the captured images. To forestall this activity, American networks now transmit signals from China in a way that makes it difficult to steal their pictures. And, in order to protect Chinese students and other sympathizers of the resistance movement, the faces and voices of Chinese who are interviewed on television in the United States are distorted because American television programs are also being videotaped and analyzed by Chinese authorities.

VISIONS OF CHINA

As the 'counterrevolutionary' activity increased, China's elder leaders finally retreated from any participation in the democratic ideological forum that was evolving in their country and called upon the last bastion of influence – the military. With economic, political, and cultural practices and policies running out of control, it was decided that military and ideological force must be strongly imposed. In the wake of the violent crackdown, the Chinese television audience, already weary of uninteresting domestic programs and the paternalistic, pedagogical tone of the government's news and information, was now a target to be intimidated by the medium. Deng Xiaoping and Li Peng, on TV scolding and threatening the 'bad elements' in China while at the same time promising a bright and prosperous future for the country, became mediated caricatures of themselves who would never have the confidence of many people again.

Television had made transparent to alert viewers how unstable the government really is. Before martial law, indelible images of a democratic alternative were transmitted to the massive audience in the journalistic coverage that was blossoming. Television viewers throughout the country could also see that while popular support for the resistance movement was increasing, the government's ability to control or settle the situation peacefully was decreasing. Until the post-mortem propaganda programs appeared, TV had made it clear that in a system based on absolute political control, no one seemed to be in control.

China's leaders must have believed after June 4th that at least the nation's peasants and ordinary workers would respond correctly to the

206

propaganda and support the party. The main propaganda themes – that the government was forced to act militarily and that no one died at Tiananmen Square – were repeated endlessly. It is very difficult for anyone to determine the effect of the propaganda. In fact, there is something to be said about the power of the repeated message. One 21-year-old university student who had taken part in the Tiananmen Square protest told me that his parents, peasants from a province near Beijing, basically believed the government's story and that he too began to question his feelings about what he *knew* had happened in June after watching the propaganda programs several times in his parents' home during the summer. But the propaganda certainly has also had the opposite effect, serving to further unify and reinforce rather than reduce the commitment held by many people to democratic change. Television also made it inevitable that world public opinion about China would be set back beyond the dark days of the Cultural Revolution. Through it all, mistreating his people like an old father who had failed to realize that his children have already grown up, Deng seemed completely out of touch with where China was going without him, and what long-term effects his military and ideological strikes would bring.

10

TELEVISION, CULTURE, AND POLITICS

The electronic amplification of contradiction

China's motherland stretches from the vast Manchurian plains to the steep mountains of Tibet, from the foreboding Mongolian desert to tropical Hainan Island. The land itself has changed very little through the ages. Her political authority has likewise persisted. Beginning with the absolutist dictates of Qin Shi Huang, China's first feudal emperor, the idea of a supreme authority – one who stands above the people and guides them to their destiny – has been a fundamental trait of Chinese society. While forms of government ranging from the extreme right to the extreme left have ruled the country, Chinese people have always placed their trust in this notion of a central authority, personified by a national leader, to whom they are fiercely loyal. Cast in terms of unity of purpose and of total devotion to ideological principles, one need not go back further in history than the Cultural Revolution to see clearly the lengths to which this passionate faith can be taken and the consequences it can bring. But today history may be catching up with itself. Perhaps more than anything else, the resistance movement in China, with its twin emphases of freedom and democracy, has strongly challenged the tradition of autocratic rule. It could not have happened without television.

Television, of course, is itself an authoritarian institution of sorts, one that articulates confidently and widely. Critics in societies all over the world complain that the medium has the power to serve the political and economic interests of its owners and managers by creating a narrow agenda and monopolizing public opinion, that it debases culture, and that it nearly mesmerizes viewers psychologically. Precisely because it is so influential, television seems to be the perfect communications medium for the perpetuation of autocratic rule in a restrictive environment such as China. Certainly the perceived potential for doing so encouraged officials in Beijing to develop the television system as a mechanism to promote national modernization. But despite their intentions, a 'single leader, single voice' complementarity of communist politics and modern communications technology, wherein official mandates are diffused efficiently and unproblematically through the electronic wizardry of television, has not taken place.

Lightning-fast and ultimately uncontrollable, television has instead given rise to a diversity of cultural and political sentiments in China at a speed that disrupts stability and control. Furthermore, the often conflicting perspectives that television articulates do not simply stand alongside one another in the popular consciousness, unanalyzed and uncriticized by viewers. Television exaggerates and intensifies each stream of information in the ideological flood that it cumulatively delivers to its audiences, producing an electronic amplification of contradiction that has dramatically altered the nation's cultural and political contours.

Since 1979 China has desperately tried to develop its economy while at the same time promising to repair its internal political difficulties, especially the widespread corruption, and to modernize technologically while judiciously expanding its cultural horizons. The immense magnitude and ill-defined nature of such an undertaking has led to the formulation of policies and practices that are often in conflict with one another, creating a kind of national schizophrenia. As Orville Schell noted two years before the blowup in Beijing in 1989, 'On the one hand [China] continues to protest against despoilers of its socialist revolution, while on the other hand it promotes crypto-capitalism. The country often appears to be going in opposite directions at the same time' (Schell, 1987: 13–14). It is exactly contradictions such as this, manifest not only in economic policy but in virtually all aspects of life – highlighted, legitimated, and popularized by television – that have stimulated alternative, competing visions of China's collective future and the personal dreams of millions of Chinese citizens.

This is not what Deng Xiaoping had in mind in 1979. Above all else, the Chinese government has tried to act as a unified body. According to the principle of democratic centralism, Deng (the *de facto* supreme leader until death), as well as the general secretary of the Communist Party, the premier, and the politburo are supposed to demonstrate unity and solidarity by acting in full agreement. National objectives, as decided by the top leadership, are to be carried out at all levels within the society – a charge that is to be facilitated in part by television. There is, therefore, a chain of agents of authority designed to promote unity: the nation (including especially its history and many cultural traditions), the supreme ruler, the Communist Party, the current government, and, with its own type of influence owing mainly to technological capabilities, television. Through the years the people have deeply respected their own history and culture, have supported the Communist Party as their liberator from the wretched realities of feudalism and the social divisiveness of nationalism, have put their faith in charismatic political leaders, and have accepted the government as administrator of the socialist agenda. At first, television was an impressive addition to the history and character of Chinese political authority, its very presence testifying to the improved standard of living of the early 1980s, its attractiveness making it a domestic necessity, its efficiency promoting it as an unsurpassed instrument for the dissemination of information.

The unity ground to a halt late in the last decade. When the economy took a dramatic downward turn, the people strongly criticized the government's utopian visions as unrealistic while they still clung to their own dreams:

> 'At whatever cost necessary, [the people] must have that large color television set, refrigerator, washing machine, and tape recorder. Their material expectations are expanding far too fast, and right now our moral and institutional structure cannot cope with them.' (Shen Biezhong, Chairman, Shanghai Municipal Economic Relations and Trade Commission, quoted in the *San Francisco Chronicle*, May 26th, 1989)

> 'Our living standard is not good no matter what TV says all the time. We have more money now, but we are not rich like TV says.' (27-year-old male food products manager, Beijing)

> 'We have nothing but money.' (contemporary Chinese expression attributed to newly-rich private unit merchants)

> 'We have nothing.' (famous Chinese pop song in 1989 by Cui Jan)

The fundamental economic contradiction – a fast-developing class difference in a society that promises and promotes equality, but does not provide equal opportunity for financial success, produced extreme negative reactions from those who felt they were losing ground. Many of the brightest and most ambitious young men and women realized that the promise of the clay rice bowl was an apparition. Economic restructuring had come to a standstill. The old system would continue to prevent them from ever utilizing their potential, while other people – private unit merchants often engaged in less demanding work – would still benefit from the partial, undemocratic restructuring. The dilemma was magnified by television. Commercials and imported films and dramas celebrated the individualism and materialism of a consumer society at the very time the people could not break out of their monotonous routines or prosper from their own initiative. Industrial news and commercials expressed and intensified the economic class differences. Even the rich were not satisfied with the range of consumer choices available to them in China or with their lockout from participation in political life.

The people began to realize that other political and economic systems function far better than their own and that their personal freedoms are few. The moralizing and sacrificing lifestyle that is demanded of the citizenry was widely known not to be practiced even by high-ranking communist officials. The economic crisis of the late 1980s served to increase reliance on *guanxi wang*, leading to even more corruption, years after the government promised to reduce or eliminate the problem. In the name of solving the financial crisis, the Communist Party strongly reasserted its political authority. In fall 1989, Jiang Zemin promised 'no total Westerniz-ation' of China and Li Peng called for greater political control of ideology and the economy. Yet, at the same time, many television programs and commercials kept serving up concrete alternatives to the tiresome political rhetoric and the hard reality of everyday life.

The most fundamental contradictions in China, then, are glaring dispari-ties within the idealized, unified voice of the Communist Party that was first raised by Mao Zedong as he shouted into the public address micro-phone at Tiananmen Gate in 1949, alternative realities that are made known primarily by television, and the worsening state of everyday life. Coming to realize the discrepancies, contradictions, and broken promises, the people not only feel frustrated; they feel betrayed. The shift in their thinking has been fundamentally influenced by television which has acted like a two-edged sword piercing the armor of the Communist Party. Some television programming has sparked deep criticism and the imagination of a better life, while the doctrinaire and strident propaganda that appears on the very same channels has, for many viewers in the cities especially, crystallized resistance and undercut cultural and political hegemony in the process.

POLITICAL TELEVISION, POLYSEMY, AND THE DEMISE OF THE MASS AUDIENCE

In order to further understand how television has decisively stimulated the revolutionary change of consciousness taking place in China, we must consider specific institutional practices of the medium, the programming that is transmitted by the television system, and the particular ways that Chinese TV viewers interpret and use this symbolic material. To begin with, it is a mistake to try to determine what '*the* government' or '*the* system' is doing in China. Doing so presumes a singularity of purpose and an administrative efficiency that simply does not exist. Although in prin-ciple television should reflect and advocate a coherent political philosophy and suggest conforming social practices, what we find instead at all three analytical domains mentioned above – the institution of television, the programs it transmits, and audience activity – is diversity and contradic-tion. What I will now argue is that, first of all, the Chinese television system articulates a multiplicity of competing cultural and political visions that is the product of the carrying out of workplace routines by media professionals. Second, television programs, even when they are produced and selected under tightly-controlled circumstances, are not semantically homogenous. Finally, viewers frequently interpret and use television

211

symbolism in a manner that is not intended by the government. What makes these variations and divergences so significant in China is that they occur in circumstances where ideological unity and social conformity are promoted as keys to national stability, and where they are essential to the maintenance of political power by the Communist Party. Television makes it impossible for the government successfully to promote but one cultural or political system. The Chinese people no longer know or care what is *ru* (the official culture: see p. 153). The unchallengeable authority of the Communist Party has been strongly challenged.

Television as a cultural and political forum

> In its role of central cultural medium [television] presents a multiplicity of meanings rather than a monolithic dominant view. It often focuses on our most prevalent concerns, our deepest dilemmas. Our most traditional views, those that are repressive and reactionary, as well as those that are subversive and emancipatory, are upheld, examined, maintained, and transformed. The emphasis is on process rather than product, on discussion rather than indoctrination, on contradiction and confusion rather than coherence.
>
> (Newcomb and Hirsch, 1987: 62)

The diversity that inheres in the program content of American television has prompted the authors cited above, Horace Newcomb and Paul Hirsch, to regard television as a 'cultural forum.' The 'multiplicity of meanings' that are enabled within the electronic encoding does not result from design or from regulation. Nor do all ideas and visions have an equal chance to be represented on the system. Sponsors, station owners, and program managers all wield disproportionate influence in the selection of imagery that appears on television in capitalist countries. Still, even within a structure of economic and ideological supervision, diversity in the overall content of what television presents as a system is inescapable. It results from the cumulative work produced by media professionals who each have their own values, experiences, perspectives, and ways of expressing ideas. Inevitably, in one way or other, the multiple views and visions of people who comprise the television workforce become incorporated into the programs that are generated within the television system.

Naturally, we must be careful when we draw parallels in the practices of television professionals who labor under circumstances where the television systems, political systems, and cultures differ as much as they do between the United States and China. But the principle of television as a cultural forum certainly applies in China. Just as the institutional organizations and production processes of the television industry in the United States act to prevent the medium from serving only its controllers, the men and women who occupy the offices, studios, newsrooms, editing booths, and every other quarter of the Chinese television industry represent a hetero-geneity that has led to a diversity in what that system transmits too. These media specialists make the day-to-day decisions that introduce, emphasize, interpret, shade, and downplay the content of television. Their decisions are often self-consciously political and reflect the oppositional sentiment that has grown so precipitously in the cities since the mid 1980s. Artistic and journalistic freedoms in China are subtly and cumulatively won and originate within the ranks of the nation's media specialists. In fact, many ideological twists and turns that have come from the national government itself for the past several years in China have been influenced by nuances originating with workers in television and the other mass media who have dared to author unofficial ideas, accounts, and explanations. By invoking the government's own rhetoric and rationale of openness and reform, China's change agents in the media often have actually been able to do their oppositional work in the guise of sanctioned national interest.

The likelihood that diverse views, some of them quite subversive, can find their way onto the airwaves in China is further increased by the inability of the bureaucracy to manage state ideology well. This was the case most remarkably in the controversial airing of *New Star* and *River Elegy* – cultural and political events in China that further reveal the unique and compelling role of television as a communications medium, and the television series as a storytelling format, as interacting ideological fields of force. These television series articulated the Chinese 'subject in crisis,' stimulating all kinds of people throughout the broad and diverse nation to commune emotionally in repeated, ritualistic experiences of political resistance. Ideological contrasts are also reflected in the incredible contra-dictions that exist between the blatant materialism and individualism that are allowed to be promoted on television and the content of other program-ming that advocates traditional socialist values. Also, the desire of TV station officials to attract large audiences has encouraged them to take the interests and desires of their viewers more into account in recent years, creating another institutional shift of emphasis away from the sanctity and uniformity of official positions. Furthermore, the rapidly-expanding size of the television system in China, wherein more and more channels are added, each of which requires programs to fill airtime, likewise contributes to the diversity.

These specific conditions – multiple visions and intentions held by employees at every level within the TV industry, an inefficient and con-fused bureaucracy that cannot manage or control, contradictory values expressed in programs and commercials, a trend toward trying to attract and please larger audiences, and the appetite of a growing television system, have all made the medium a potent 'cultural *and political* forum' in China. In fact, the government finally admitted during the stressful summer in 1989 that it had lost control of its own media, that the plethora of perspectives had assumed a dangerous life of its own.

Some steps have been taken to exercise greater control over television content since the period of martial law in 1989. Two of CCTV's most popular personalities – prime-time news anchorwoman Du Xian and anchorman Xue Fei – have been reassigned to non on-air positions after they dressed in black and tearfully read the news on the night of June 4th. By late 1990, the term 'comrade' (*tongzhimen*) was once again being used by the newscasters to address their audiences. The government also tried to use television to directly counteract the influence of the TV program that is commonly thought to have contributed greatly to the unrest – *River Elegy*. In the wake of the 1989 military crackdown, CCTV produced a series of short programs titled *One Hundred Mistakes of River Elegy*. Each installment was designed to refute one major historical claim or cultural criticism that had been made in the original production. *River Elegy* was popular and controversial precisely because it dared to dishonor Chinese culture. Like *New Star*, it stood out conspicuously on the TV system, influencing viewers in ways that thousands of hours of propagandistic television programs could never do. The remedial program, *One Hundred Mistakes of River Elegy*, may have actually extended the influence of the original by calling attention to *River Elegy* once again. It also confused viewers. The perplexity was perhaps best articulated by the young daughter of one of my narrators in 1989, when she said: 'Daddy, how come *River Elegy* was 100 percent right before June 4th, and 100 percent wrong after?' The bewilderment was exacerbated by the spate of commercials which often appeared immediately after an episode of the corrective program, advocating behavior that directly conflicts with the moral lessons that had just been given. Contradictory juxtapositions of imagery such as this are commonplace on Chinese television contributing to its role as a cultural and political forum.

Television's messages and meanings

Even in the most controlled television systems, programs can never foster a single understanding or response on the part of the audience. How viewers interpret television's messages do not simply reflect the aims of the producers, and the apparent implications of programs do not necessarily reveal the meanings that audiences take away from viewing. Television programs do not have a single meaning, connotation, or objectively definable significance. Television's images are, instead, polysemic (Fiske, 1987). They are pregnant with meanings. More specifically, programs are repositories of potential interpretations that are actualized in viewers' varying involvements with them. This is not to say that TV programs are completely open texts that encourage limitless or wholly unguided

214

interpretations. We must be careful not to overstate or romanticize the role of the viewer in the reception and use of television content. The specific images, framing, format, the internal structure of any specific program, and the program's relation to other symbolic material on the medium, all help establish cues for preferred 'readings' by audiences (Hall, 1980). And, of course, the assumptive worlds that television programs present – the implicit, subtextual content, not just the obvious messages – also, even subconsciously, suggest and prefer certain audience responses.

Certainly television does have its intended effects, in some ways, for some of the audience, some of the time. Nonetheless, even in cases where program producers are clear in their own minds about what a program should say, they cannot, ultimately, control the way audiences will respond to their creations. Even the most seemingly uncomplicated attempts to 'transfer meaning' greatly oversimplify the nature of viewers' negotiations with television. This has certainly been the case in China. Recall my earlier example, for instance, of news viewers who pay more attention to the street scenes from foreign cities than to the political messages which accompany the visuals. The main message that many viewers got from *Follow Me*, the English language lesson TV program, was not improved language skills, but instead a deep appreciation, even love, for the Westerner who hosted the program, Britain's Kathy Flowers. Or, consider once again how viewers came away from watching *Oshin* with the strong feeling that the lead character's success was made possible not only because she worked hard, but because of the freedom she enjoyed in the conduct of her private business. Television's messages, then, can never impose a single meaning, or produce only the intended effects, no matter how carefully constructed or seemingly one-sided they are. The polysemy of television imagery over-rules any possibility that the interpretation of programming can be managed by authority.

Polysemy does not simply open up the possibility of subversive, alternative readings, however. One of the most memorable images to ever appear on Chinese television, and on TV all over the world, is the famous video footage of the lone man standing in front of a line of tanks moving along Jianguomenwai Avenue near the Beijing Hotel. This image has been widely celebrated outside China as the definitive representation of defiance and courage – the personification of resistance to political and military repression. George Bush praised the man in one of his speeches. It appeared on the cover of magazines and on the front page of newspapers everywhere. In the West, the video footage was played again and again as we marvelled at the courage of the man – so vulnerable and gallant – standing before the intimidating tanks just hours after the massacre on the streets near Tiananmen Square.

The very same video footage was played many times in propaganda programs on Chinese television too. But the propagandists framed the famous incident quite differently, as the narration reveals: 'If the soldiers had not exercised restraint, how could this man, hailed as a hero by some Western media, have been able to show off in front of these tanks?' For advocates of the military measures that were taken to 'restore order to the capital' in China, the exact same image that to some viewers symbolized bravery in the face of violent military repression, was used as evidence to argue that the military 'acted with full restraint.'

Chinese television viewers saw this footage in programs that featured other forms of disobedience such as the images I discussed in the last chapter. Viewers saw hundreds of young Chinese men and women throwing rocks and sticks at military vehicles, apparently attacking and beating the drivers, torching some of the vehicles with the men still inside, and so on. Despite the gravity of their surfaces, all these images are richly polysemic. Television does many things at the same time; propaganda and resistance can spring simultaneously from precisely the same source. It is not predetermined, for instance, how protestors throwing rocks at passing military vehicles will be interpreted: heroic or irresponsible, though the narrator tries to frame the response according to the latter. Furthermore, how viewers come to interpret messages such as these are influenced greatly by the economic, political, and cultural conditions that impinge upon their lifeworlds – the macrosocial factors – which by spring of 1989 had become intolerable. But semiotic negotiations that take place between viewers and programs must also be considered in relation to the interpretive work of audience members who occupy individualized contexts – their microsocial worlds.

The Chinese TV audience at work

While the government tries to use television to unify China, in the cities, at least, just the opposite has happened. The Chinese audience is not a mass. It does not respond to television in a uniform way. Viewers interact with television's symbols and semiotic structures to create their own meanings, promote their own understandings, and develop their own ideological coalitions. Though television surely has the ability to influence viewers in ways that benefit its controllers, the role of the viewer as an agent in the construction of his or her own experience with the medium should not be underestimated.

The political contexts of many communist countries (past and present) throughout the world have stimulated television viewers in those nations to become masters of interpretation, reading between the lines in order to pick up the less obvious messages. This was common in Eastern Europe, for instance, and it has certainly been the case in China. Many of my narrators describe not only what they watch, but how they watch television. Because viewers know that the government often bends and exaggerates

216

37 The famous polysemic image, featured in *Newsweek* magazine and on CCTV.

its reports, they become skilled at imagining the true situation. What is presented, what is left out, what is given priority, how things are said – all these modes are noticed and interpreted sensitively. Changes in consciousness brought on by television in China, therefore, are stimulated not just by exposure to new information and ideas, but by the inventive ways that viewers critically interpret and use TV's symbolic content. The often taken-for-granted activity, 'watching television,' signifies something in China that is very different from that to which most of us are accustomed.

Certain basic characteristics of Chinese culture and communication invite distinctive interpretive practices. It begins with language. The people must listen very attentively in spoken interaction and read print messages carefully and creatively in order to decode messages. In spoken Chinese, for instance, each sound can be expressed in four tones: flat, ascending, descending, and a combination of ascending and descending. The meaning of the utterance depends greatly on the inflection, so listeners become very good at carefully picking up the most subtle shifts of emphasis. Written Chinese characters likewise require skill in interpretation as they are individually far less denotative than are the basic symbols of other language groups. The characters are uniquely meaningful in relation to the linguistic structure in which they are embedded, a circumstance that requires the reader 'correctly' to infer the meaning from the *associations* of the characters, a challenging and imprecise activity. Hence, Chinese language is more 'aesthetic' – metaphorical and poetic – than it is 'efficient,' in the purely functional sense of the word. Because the language is so inexact in this way, it encourages playful articulations and interpretations, which, in a repressive political environment, enhances the opportunity for communicating subversive messages. Nonverbal forms of communication – gestures, body movement, facial expressions, paralanguage – are also extremely subtle and sensitively read in Chinese culture. These intricate communications are not limited to unmediated interpersonal exchanges. An unacknowledged, strategic coordination between sources of public messages in China – the journalists, TV producers, and filmmakers, for instance – and the audience, makes it possible to represent unofficial commentaries and views in the Chinese media. In this way, the television system has been appropriated by the people for purposes of resistance to the very authority which, theoretically, controls them.

Chinese people also readily deconstruct institutional pronouncements by means of their alert and ambitious involvement with television. The country's depressed economic status, its broadening culture, and the stinging political turmoil all encourage critical interpretations of the public face and voice of government. I have identified several domains of these interpretations already – disbelief of news items, hatred of the government's constant self-promotion, mocking of the 'model worker' programs, disgust with misleading commercials, and so on. The turmoil in 1989 has sharpened critical viewing even more. A Beijing viewer, for instance, points out that propagandists have routinely used television to claim that the People's Congress, China's quasi-democratic body of national lawmakers, has real authority to represent the people. This was one of the most debated issues during the turmoil in 1989 when it became painfully clear to nearly everyone that the People's Congress in fact does not adequately represent the people. The propaganda nonetheless kept flowing, becoming a highly salient and thoroughly rejected message for many viewers who may not have thought much about the issue before. This is but one example of how television can undermine rather than sustain the government's objectives when the people know that the information contained in an official message is false.

Audiences for television are not constituted solely in acts of watching programs. 'The audience' is also formed at times when television's symbolic agenda is recognized, reconstructed, and transformed in the routine discourses of viewers' everyday lives. Political sentiments often develop more clearly and firmly in these moments of social interpretation – ideological editing that takes place in the minds of viewers as they talk about and reflect further upon what they see on TV. The power of *New Star* and *River Elegy*, for example, derived not just from their presence on television or from the immediate impressions and interpretations of viewers, but also from how the programs stimulated political discussion and provided a common referent for the construction of everyday social interaction. In an environment like China, this type of public dialogue confirms individual viewers' political sentiments and socially validates their feelings through the formation of constituencies of resistance. But television's agenda is reproduced, reconstructed, and transformed even in the most routine talk about programs in any political environment. The medium is a resource that, because of its sweeping presence, appeal, and social utility, expands an ideological agenda in a way that no other form of communication can, sometimes in accord with the intentions of its controllers, sometimes not. As we have seen, this is by no means an entirely imposed or predictable process. The ideological consequences of television rest as much with the audience as they do with the producers and presenters of programs.

CHINA TURNED ON

When students and workers took to the streets of Beijing in 1989, the government self-righteously disparaged them as 'counterrevolutionaries' – enemies of the people. This loaded term is habitually invoked to promote the idea that the government still spearheads a heroic communist revolution against the evils that confronted China before 1949 and continue to threaten her stability and progress today. In truth, of course, the real revolution in China now is a struggle against the 'revolutionary' government that 40 years after its founding has become far more a force of repression than of liberation. Resistance to totalitarian rule in China is not simply a cry for change in the political structure or a desperate reaction to a faltering economy. More than anything else, what the people want is freedom – of the press, of personal expression, to choose and change jobs, to travel, to chart one's own destiny. While these issues have political and economic origins and consequences, they are profoundly cultural matters. Modifications in the cultural identities and visions of China's urban population have interacted with economic realities and perceived political possibilities to provoke widespread discontent. Television is the eye of the cultural storm, its presence influencing the future of China in ways that no other technology or human agency can.

NOTES

1 MODERNIZING CHINA

1 This problem is of such importance that it was the main focus of a highly popular and controversial television series in China. The program, *New Star*, is the subject of Chapter 6.

2 IN THE NAME OF CIVILIZATION

1 It must be kept in mind that the meaning of a person's wages in China differs greatly from many other countries because many of the most expensive necessities, including housing, are paid for or cost very little for state employees.
2 Thanks to Wang Jiangang of the People's University of China and CCTV for providing the latest statistics.

3 KNOWING CHINA

1 See Guldin (1987) and Thurston and Pasternak (1983) for thoughtful discussions of these developments.
2 As very little social research has been conducted in China, scholars there must depend on foreign-language materials. Unfortunately, very little work published outside China has been translated into Chinese or made available to the scholarly community there.
3 Even before the Tiananmen Square crackdown there had been a reduction in the number of students permitted to study abroad, although about 40,000 Chinese students were enrolled in American universities alone in 1990. Statistics are not available, but estimates of the number of students who fail to return to China after studying overseas are high and even those who have gone back to China have sometimes suffered for becoming too 'Westernized.'
4 But like so many social scientists, they nonetheless drew inferences based on statistical tests that assume random sampling and a normal distribution of cases.
5 Other difficulties with the Hong Kong research include memory loss, limitations on interviewing imposed by Chinese and British authorities in Hong Kong, and 'demand characteristics' – immigrants trying to please the researchers by answering the 'right' way, whatever it may have been perceived to be. Whyte also admits that their accounts lack color. He suggests that this indirect and scientifically problematic method fails to get at the real 'feeling of China,' including especially the 'attitudes, values, and emotions' of the people there (Whyte, 1983: 71).
6 A small grant was given by San Jose State University in California.

4 TELEVISION IN URBAN CHINA

1 Going to the park, however, continues to be a favorite activity as parks are good places to escape the congested living conditions.
2 Neena Behl (1988) reports a similar influence of television on the families of Indian villagers, though the cultural circumstances are much different from China.

5 CROSSING THE ELECTRONIC BRIDGE

1 One of the most stunning contradictions in Chinese socialist society is the difference between the prescribed egalitarianism of gender relations and the reality. Virtually all government officials are males. The evening CCTV newscast brings this distortion home to viewers every night, especially in the seemingly endless coverage of government meetings where virtually all the people shown in the large halls are men.

6 CHINA'S *NEW STAR*

1 Kuo reportedly fled China during the turmoil in 1989.
2 I have developed this summary of *New Star* only after repeatedly viewing scene by scene a videotape of the entire series with scholars from the People's Republic. We spent days doing this – playing and stopping the videotape to make exact translations and to discuss the political and cultural significance of the images.
3 In the novel, however, this optimistic feeling sours when it is revealed that praise for Li given by the Province Secretary is the result of the prodding of his daughter, Xiaoli. This detail is not made clear in the television series, but for readers of the novel this was a disturbing and disappointing development. It further indicated the *guanxi* problem. Xiaoli's influence is not a good reason to praise Li or to support the concept of the reformation.
4 Most of the remainder of the sample also was not negative about *New Star*. Seven percent had no opinion while but two percent said they didn't like it.

7 THE FREEDOM TO HAVE FUN

1 Much of the information presented in the following discussion is taken from these articles which appeared in American newspapers: Edward Gargan, 'China's cultural crackdown,' *New York Times Magazine*, July 12th, 1987; Edward Gargan, 'Revolution in China for movie makers,' *San Francisco Chronicle*, December 30th, 1987; Judy Stone, 'Chinese film maker leaving key post,' *San Francisco Chronicle*, September 9th, 1988; Judy Stone, 'Chinese film maker battles military protests,' *San Francisco Chronicle*, March 20th, 1988; David Armstrong, 'Director's first film a big hit,' *San Francisco Examiner*, November 6th, 1988; Judy Stone, 'Controversial *Red Sorghum* is Chinese director's celebration of life,' *San Francisco Chronicle*, October 30th, 1988.
2 Su reportedly left China in the midst of the crackdown in 1989.

8 LOOKING IN AND LOOKING OUT

1 The official policy against inserting commercials inside programs is wavering. Commercials are now routinely placed inside films which are shown on television.
2 While *Oshin* was extremely popular in China as high-quality entertainment with an inspirational message, the show had its critics, though they are few in number

and are usually reluctant to offer a truly condemning analysis. Generally, men are more likely than women to criticize the show, partly because they feel it doesn't appeal to them thematically. Some younger viewers, especially males, feel that the ponderous pace of the show is simply too dragged out. Young viewers also were often less interested than their parents in the program's content as it deals with a history that is distant from them. Some viewers complain that all the tragedies that befell Oshin were simply unrealistic. A clothing factory worker from Shanghai, for instance, said: 'Lots of guys at the factory think that the show is bad because it is impossible to have so much tragedy going on at the same time!' A 28-year-old Beijing mother also questions the realism saying that women today cannot do what Oshin did decades earlier.

3 Another important television program, *Four Generations in One House*, was presented in China about the same time that *Oshin* was on the air. The show stimulated considerable interest among viewers, particularly in the Beijing area where this historical drama was set. It is the story of a Chinese family of four generations that lived in a simple, groundfloor housing complex during the occupation of China by Japan prior to their defeat at the end of World War Two. The lives of ordinary Chinese were shown, with three sons in the family each taking a different path (resister; traitor; pacifist) in the face of Japanese oppression.

The great majority of viewers said that they watched the program primarily for cultural reasons, particularly older viewers who had experienced what the program depicts. One old grandfather in Beijing broke into tears as he described his feelings about the program to us. The program was a damning portrayal of the Japanese occupation of China that fueled strong patriotic feelings and anti-Japanese sentiments among some viewers. People said the program stimulated feelings of self-respect and love of country while other viewers expressed rage about the Japanese occupation. The story is indeed about a dark moment in Chinese history, a time when life was truly miserable for many innocent people. Some viewers were emotionally distraught, calling the Japanese 'imperialists,' 'criminals,' and 'cheaters.' An old grandmother couldn't watch because, 'I experienced that myself in reality . . . I don't like to watch Chinese suffer at the hands of the Japanese.' And the most eloquent, lengthy commentary about the program came from a young (32) female party member in Beijing:

> 'This program helps young people understand that the Japanese perpetrated criminal behavior – they were guilty. Today, young people don't like to look back. Of course, we should look to the future, but we can't forget that we have been treated cruelly by foreign interventionists from the past. We should remember this. *Four Generations in One House* made many young people go back to the past. It helps stimulate people to build up the four modernizations and to realize the country's dream about becoming healthy, plentiful, rich, and strong. Only when we are strong will no one dare invade us again.'

9 TIANANMEN SQUARE AND BEYOND

1 As a resident of San Francisco, I was reminded again just a few months after the Beijing hostilities of the tendency of the mass media to exaggerate the body count of disasters. The *San Francisco Chronicle*, for instance, ran the headline: 'Hundreds dead in freeway collapse' following the earthquake in the city when the actual number of persons who died in the structure was about 60. In Beijing, where reporters were denied access to official sources, to Tiananmen Square itself, and to the ordinary citizens who cannot speak English and were afraid to

interact with foreigners anyway, the problems of reporting the details of such a terrifying event were compounded greatly.

2 I have viewed the programs several times and have had each Mandarin-language program translated into English. Special thanks to my colleague and friend, Wen-shu Lee, for her extremely helpful translations and insights.

3 A very incisive and brilliantly photographed account of what happened is Turnley *et al.* (1989).

4 In the process, however, many factories and businesses were forced to close, raising grave concerns about long-term prospects of the economy.

REFERENCES

Behl, N. (1988) 'Equalizing Status: Television and Tradition in an Indian Village', in J. Lull (ed.) *World Families Watch Television*, Newbury Park, CA: Sage.

Bishop, R. L. (1989) *Qi Lai: Mobilizing One Billion Chinese: The Chinese Communication System*, Iowa City: Iowa State University Press.

Butterfield, F. (1982) *China Alive in the Bitter Sea*, New York: Bantam Books.

Chu, C-n. (1988) *The Chinese Mind Game: The Best Kept Trade Secrets of the East*, Beaverton, OR: AMC Publishing.

Deng, X-p. (1987) *Fundamental Issues in Present-day China*, Beijing: Foreign Languages Press.

Dietrich, C. (1986) *People's China*, New York: Oxford University Press.

Fiske, J. (1987) *Television Culture*, London: Methuen.

Gargan, E. (1987) 'China's Cultural Crackdown', *New York Times Magazine*, July 12th: 26.

Gold, T. B. (1985) 'Personal Relations in China since the Cultural Revolution', *The China Quarterly* 104: 657–75.

Goodman, D., Lockett, M., and Segal, G. (1986) *The China Challenge: Adjustment and Reform*, London: Routledge.

Guldin, G. E. (1987) 'Anthropology in the People's Republic of China', *Social Research* 54: 757–78.

Guo, Z. (1986) 'A Chronicle of Private Radio in Shanghai', *Journal of Broadcasting and Electronic Media* 30: 379–92.

Hall, S. (1980) 'Encoding/Decoding', in S. Hall, D. Hobson, A. Lowe, and P. Willis (eds) *Culture, Media, Language*, London: Hutchinson.

Harding, H. (1986) 'Political Development in Post-Mao China', in A. D. Barnett and R. N. Clough (eds) *Modernizing China: Post-Mao Reform and Development*, Boulder, CO: Westview Press.

Hareven, T. K. (1987) 'Reflections on Family Research in the People's Republic of China', *Social Research* 54: 663–89.

Hooper, B. (1985) *Youth in China*, Victoria, Australia: Penguin Books.

Hopkins, M. (1989) 'Watching China Change', *Columbia Journalism Review*, Sept./Oct.: 35–40.

Howkins, J. (1982) *Mass Communication in China*, New York: Longman.

Jia, P-a. (1989) *Anxious*, Beijing: China Books.

Ju, Y. and Chu, G. C. (1989) 'Changing Family Relations in China: Some Preliminary Findings in a 1987 Survey of Cultural Change in Shanghai', paper presented at the annual convention of the International Communication Association, San Francisco, May.

Lau, T-y. and Lo, Y-k. (1990) '*Heshang* (River Elegy): A Television Orchestration of a New Ideology in China', paper presented to the International Communication Association, Dublin, Ireland, June.

Li, J. (1989) 'Controversial TV Series, "River Elegy" ', *China Reconstructs*, January: 47–9.

Lu, W-p. (1987) Department of Sociology, Beijing University. Personal correspondence.

Lull, J. (1982) 'How Families Select Television Programs: A Mass Observational Study', *Journal of Broadcasting and Electronic Media* 26: 801–11.

—— (1988) *World Families Watch Television*, Newbury Park, CA: Sage.

McCormick, R. (1986) 'The Radio and Television Universities and the Development of Higher Education in China', *The China Quarterly*, 105, March.

Ming, A-x. (1987) *China's Mass Communication for the Two Civilizations: Some Aspects of the Transformation of the Mass Communication System in China*, Matrainvest, Hungary: Mass Communication Center of Budapest.

Mishler, E. G. (1986) *Research Interviewing: Context and Narrative*, Cambridge, Mass.: Harvard University Press.

Morley, D. (1986) *Family Television: Cultural Power and Domestic Leisure*, London: Comedia.

Nathan, A. J. (1985) *Chinese Democracy*, New York: Alfred A. Knopf.

Newcomb, H. and Hirsch, P. (1987) 'Television as Culture Forum', in H. Newcomb (ed.) *Television: The Critical View*, New York: Oxford University Press.

Pan, L. (1987) *The New Chinese Revolution*, London: Penguin.

Parish, W. L. and Whyte, M. K. (1978) *Village and Family in Contemporary China*, Chicago: University of Chicago Press.

Pasternak, B. (1983) 'Sociology and Anthropology in China: Revitalization and its Constraints', in A. F. Thurston and B. Pasternak (eds) *The Social Sciences and Fieldwork in China: Views from the Field*, Boulder, CO: Westview Press.

Perkins, D. H. (1986) 'The Prospects for China's Economic Reform', in A. D. Barnett and R. N. Clough (eds) *Modernizing China: Post-Mao Reform and Development*, Boulder, CO: Westview Press.

Pye, L. W. (1985) *Asian Power and Politics: Cultural Dimensions of Authority*, Cambridge, MA: Harvard University Press.

Reynolds, E. (1989) *China Briefing, 1989*, Boulder, CO: Westview Press.

Rogers, E., Zhao, X., Pan, Z., and Chen, M. (1985) 'The Beijing Audience Study', *Communication Research* 12: 179–208.

Schell, O. (1984) *To Get Rich Is Glorious: China in the 1980's*, New York: Pantheon.

—— (1987) 'Serving the People with Advertising: From Propaganda to PR in the New China', *This World*, June 7th: 13–14.

—— (1988) *Discos and Democracy*, New York: Pantheon.

—— (1989) 'Lost Chance: How Bush Failed the Heroes of Tiananmen Square', *Mother Jones*, Sept.: 36–9.

Sobel, R. (1987) 'Chinese Television Getting Oriented to U.S. Programs', *Television/Radio Age*, April 13th: 38–9, 71–3.

Sun, L. (1987) 'China Television: An Update on its Development and Related Systems', *PTC Quarterly* 8: 20–2.

Thurston, A. F. and Pasternak, B. (1983) *The Social Sciences and Fieldwork in China: Views From the Field*, Boulder, CO: Westview Press.

Turnley, D., Turnley, P., and Liu, M. (1989) *Beijing Spring*, New York: Stewart, Tabori, & Chang.

Wang, Z. (1988a) 'The Chinese Mass Media: Environmental Coverage (A Case Study)', paper presented to the International Association for Mass Communication Research, Barcelona, July.

REFERENCES

—— (1988b) 'Changing Practice in Changing Politics: New Developments of the Chinese Mass Media', paper presented to the International Association for Mass Communication Research, Barcelona, July.

Whyte, M. K. (1983) 'On Studying China from a Distance', in A. F. Thurston and B. Pasternak (eds) *The Social Sciences and Fieldwork in China: Views From the Field*, Boulder, CO: Westview Press.

Whyte, M. K. and Parish, W. L. (1984) *Urban Life in Contemporary China*, Chicago: University of Chicago Press.

Wicke, P. (1991) 'The Role of Rock Music in the Political Disintegration of East Germany', in J. Lull (ed.) *Popular Music and Communication* (revised edition), Newbury Park, CA: Sage Publications.

Womack, B. (1986) 'Editor's Introduction: Media and the Chinese Public', *Chinese Sociology and Anthropology* 18: 6–53.

Wu, V-c. (1986) 'Some Stories Before and After "New Star" was Produced: A Chat with the "New Star" Producer', *Shanghai TV Monthly* 49, July: 9–11.

Zhou, Y-p. (1986) 'The Early Morning "New Star" – Audience Response Investigation Report About the Television Drama, "New Star",' in *Contemporary Literature and Art Thought*, Beijing: Government Printing Office.

INDEX

228

229